Essential Mathematics

Book 7

David Rayner

Elmwood Press

First published 2001 by
Elmwood Press
80 Attimore Road
Welwyn Garden City
Herts. AL8 6LP
Tel. 01707 333232

Reprinted 2001, 2002, 2003, 2004, 2005

British Library Cataloguing in Publication Data

Rayner, David

© David Rayner
The moral rights of the author have been asserted.
Database right Elmwood Press (maker)

ISBN 1 902 214 129

Numerical answers are published in a separate book

Artwork by Stephen Hill

Typeset and illustrated by Tech-Set, Gateshead, Tyne and Wear
Printed and bound by WS Bookwell

PREFACE

Essential Mathematics Books 7, 8 and 9 are written for more able pupils in years 7, 8 and 9. Most classrooms contain children with a range of abilities in mathematics. These books are written to cater for this situation.

The author is an enthusiastic supporter of the National Numeracy Strategy. The books have been prepared with the cooperation of teachers and pupils in NNS pilot schools. It is encouraging that most teachers are confident that this more structured approach will help to raise standards of understanding and attainment. There is a comprehensive NNS guide at start of the book with references to all topics.

There is no set path through the books but topics appear in the order suggested in the NNS planning charts. Broadly speaking, parts 1 and 2 can be studied in the Autumn Term, parts 3 and 4 in the Spring Term and parts 5 and 6 in the Summer Term.

The author believes that children learn mathematics most effectively by *doing* mathematics. Many youngsters who find mathematics difficult derive much more pleasure and enjoyment from the subject when they are doing questions which help them build up their confidence. Pupils feel a greater sense of satisfaction when they work in a systematic way and when they can appreciate the purpose and the power of the mathematics they are studying.

No text book will have the 'right' amount of material for every class and the author believes that it is better to have too much material rather than too little. Consequently teachers should judge for themselves which sections or exercises can be studied later. On a practical note, the author recommends the use of exercise books consisting of 7 mm squares.

Opportunities for work towards the 'Using and Applying Mathematics' strand appears throughout the book. Many activities, investigations, games and puzzles are included to provide a healthy variety of learning experiences. The author is aware of the difficulties of teaching on 'Friday afternoons' or on the last few days of term, when both pupils and teachers are tired, and suitable activities are included.

David Rayner

CONTENTS

		Page
Part 1		
1.1	Sequences	1
1.2	Number machines	6
1.3	Arithmetic (written)	12
1.4	3D objects, nets	21
1.5	Decimals 1	27
1.6	Rounding numbers	32
1.7	Area and perimeter	36
Part 2		
2.1	Fractions	46
2.2	Coordinates	51
2.3	Rules of algebra	58
2.4	Percentages	67
2.5	Mental methods	72
2.6	Mathematical puzzles	78
Part 3		
3.1	Properties of numbers	83
3.2	Order of operations	92
3.3	Using a calculator	96
3.4	Metric and imperial units	101
3.5	Handling data	107
3.6	Mid-book review	120
Part 4		
4.1	Calculating angles	128
4.2	Ratio and proportion	135
4.3	Construction	139
4.4	Decimals 2	146
4.5	Solving equations	152
4.6	Straight line graphs	158
4.7	Solving problems (no calculators)	163
Part 5		
5.1	Rotation	168
5.2	Reflection	175
5.3	Translation	181
5.4	Long multiplication and division	182
5.5	Averages and range	185
5.6	Negative numbers	189
5.7	Mathematical reasoning	195
Part 6		
6.1	Probability	199
6.2	Fractions, decimals, percentages	208
6.3	Formulas	212
6.4	Interpreting graphs	221
6.5	Mixed problems	230
6.6	Mathematical games and crossnumbers	238
Part 7		
7.1	Multiple choice papers	241
7.2	Mixed exercises	246

Using and applying mathematics to solve problems

Applying mathematics and solving problems

2.6 • **Solve word problems and investigate in a**
   range of contexts:
4.7   number, algebra, shape, space and measures,
     and handling data; compare and evaluate
     solutions.
6.5 • Identify the necessary information to solve a
     problem; represent problems mathematically,
     making correct use of symbols, words,
     diagrams, tables and graphs.
4.7 • **Break a complex calculation into simpler**
     steps, choosing and using appropriate and
     efficient operations, methods and resources,
     including ICT.
   • Present and interpret solutions in the context of
     the original problem; **explain and justify**
     methods and conclusions, orally and in writing.
5.7 • Suggest extensions to problems by asking 'What
     if … ?'; begin to generalise and to understand
     the significance of a counter-example.

Numbers and the number system

Place value, ordering and rounding

1.3 • Understand and use decimal notation and place
     value; multiply and divide integers and decimals
     by 10, 100, 1000, and explain the effect.
1.5 • Compare and order decimals in different
     contexts; know that when comparing
     measurements they must be in the same units.
1.6 • Round positive whole numbers to the nearest
     10, 100 or 1000 and decimals to the nearest
     whole number or one decimal place.

Integers, powers and roots

5.6 • Understand negative numbers as positions on
     a number line; order, add and subtract positive
     and negative integers in context.
3.1 • Recognise and use multiples, factors (divisors),
     common factor, highest common factor and
     lowest common multiple in simple cases, and
     primes (less than 100); use simple tests of
     divisibility.
3.1 • Recognise the first few triangular numbers,
     squares of numbers to at least 12×12 and the
     corresponding roots.

Fractions, decimals, percentages, ratio and proportion

2.1 • Use fraction notation to describe parts of
     shapes and to express a smaller whole number
     as a fraction of a larger one; **simplify fractions**
     by cancelling all common factors and identify
     equivalent fractions; convert terminating
     decimals to fractions, e.g. $0.23 = \frac{23}{100}$; use a
     diagram to compare two or more simple
     fractions.

2.1 • Begin to add and subtract simple fractions and
     those with common denominators; calculate
     simple fractions of quantities and
     measurements (whole-number answers);
     multiply a fraction by an integer.
6.2 • Understand percentage as the 'number of parts
2.4   per 100'; **recognise the equivalence of**
     percentages, fractions and decimals; calculate
     simple percentages and use percentages to
     compare simple proportions.
4.2 • Understand the relationship between ratio and
     proportion; use direct proportion in simple
     contexts; use ratio notation, reduce a ratio to
     its simplest form and divide a quantity into two
     parts in a given ratio; solve simple problems
     about ratio and proportion using informal
     strategies.

Calculations

Number operations and the relationships between them

1.2 • Understand addition, subtraction,
     multiplication and division as they apply to
1.3   whole numbers and decimals; know how to
     use the laws of arithmetic and inverse
     operations.
3.2 • **Know and use the order of operations,**
     including brackets.

Mental methods and rapid recall of number facts

2.5 • Consolidate the rapid recall of number facts,
     including positive integer complements to 100
     and multiplication facts to 10×10, and quickly
     derive associated division facts.
6.2 • Consolidate and **extend mental methods of**
     calculation to include decimals, fractions and
     percentages, accompanied where appropriate
     by suitable jottings; solve simple word
     problems mentally.
1.6 • Make and justify estimates and approximations
     of calculations.

Written methods

1.3 • Use standard column procedures to add and
     subtract whole numbers and decimals with up
     to two places.
5.4 • **Multiply and divide three-digit by two-digit**
     whole numbers; extend to multiplying and
     dividing decimals with one or two places by
     single-digit whole numbers.
     For calculations with fractions and
     percentages, see above.

Calculator methods

3.3 • Carry out calculations with more than one step
     using brackets and the memory; use the
     square root and sign change keys.

3.3 • Enter numbers and interpret the display in different contexts (decimals, percentages, money, metric measures).

Checking results

1.6 • **Check a result by considering whether it is of the right order of magnitude** and by working the problem backwards.

Algebra

Equations, formulae and identities

2.3 • **Use letter symbols to represent unknown numbers or variables;** know the meanings of the words *term*, *expression* and *equation*.

2.3 • **Understand that algebraic operations follow the same conventions and order as arithmetic operations**

2.3 • Simplify linear algebraic expressions by collecting like terms; begin to multiply a single term over a bracket (integer coefficients).

4.5 • Construct and solve simple linear equations with integer coefficients (unknown on one side only) using an appropriate method (e.g. inverse operations).

6.3 • Use simple formulae from mathematics and other subjects; substitute positive integers into simple linear expressions and formulae and, in simple cases, derive a formula.

Sequences, functions and graphs

1.1 • Generate and describe simple integer sequences.

1.1 • Generate terms of a simple sequence, given a rule (e.g. finding a term from the previous term, finding a term given its position in the sequence).

6.3 • Generate sequences from practical contexts and describe the general term in simple cases.

6.3 • Express simple functions in words, then using symbols; represent them in mappings.

4.6 • Generate coordinate pairs that satisfy a simple linear rule; **plot the graphs of simple linear functions,** where y is given explicitly in terms of x, on paper and using ICT; recognise straight-line graphs parallel to the x-axis or y-axis.

6.4 • Begin to plot and interpret the graphs of simple linear functions arising from real-life situations.

Shape, space and measures

Geometrical reasoning: lines, angles and shapes

4.3 • Use correctly the vocabulary, notation and labelling conventions for lines, angles and shapes.

4.1 • **Identify parallel and perpendicular lines: know the sum of angles at a point, on a straight line and in a triangle,** and recognise vertically opposite angles.

4.1 • Begin to identify and use angle, side and symmetry properties of triangles and quadrilaterals; solve geometrical problems involving these properties, using step-by-step deduction and explaining reasoning with diagrams and text.

1.4 • Use 2-D representations to visualise 3-D shapes and deduce some of their properties.

Transformations

5.1 • Understand and use the language and notation
5.3   associated with reflections, translations and rotations.

• Recognise and visualise the transformation and symmetry of a 2-D shape:

5.2 – reflection in given mirror lines, and line symmetry;

5.1 – rotation about a given point, and rotation symmetry;

5.3 – translation;
explore these transformations and symmetries using ICT.

Coordinates

2.2 • Use conventions and notation for 2-D coordinates in all four quadrants; find coordinates of points determined by geometric information.

Construction

4.3 • Use a ruler and protractor to:
 – measure and draw lines to the nearest millimetre and angles, including reflex angles, to the nearest degree;
 – construct a triangle given two sides and the included angle (SAS) or two angles and the included side (ASA);
explore these constructions using ICT.

1.4 • Use ruler and protractor to construct simple nets of 3-D shapes, e.g. cuboid, regular tetrahedron, square-based pyramid, triangular prism.

Measures and mensuration

3.4 • Use names and abbreviations of units of measurement to measure, estimate, calculate and solve problems in everyday contexts involving length, area, mass, capacity, time and angle;
convert one metric unit to another (e.g. grams to kilograms); read and interpret scales on a range of measuring instruments.

4.3 • Use angle measure; distinguish between and estimate the size of acute, obtuse and reflex angles.

1.7 • Know and use the formula for the area of a rectangle; calculate the perimeter and area of shapes made from rectangles.

1.7 • Calculate the surface area of cubes and cuboids.

Handling data

Specifying a problem, planning and collecting data

3.5 • Given a problem that can be addressed by statistical methods, suggest possible answers.
  • Decide which data would be relevant to an enquiry and possible sources.

3.5 • Plan how to collect and organise small sets of data; design a data collection sheet or questionnaire to use in a simple survey; construct frequency tables for discrete data, grouped where appropriate in equal class intervals.

3.5 • Collect small sets of data from surveys and experiments, as planned.

Processing and representing data, using ICT as appropriate

5.5 • Calculate statistics for small sets of discrete data:
  – find the mode, median and range, and the modal class for grouped data;
  – calculate the mean, including from a simple frequency table, using a calculator for a larger number of items.

3.5 • Construct, on paper and using ICT, graphs and diagrams to represent data, including:
  – bar-line graphs;
  – frequency diagrams for grouped discrete data;
  use ICT to generate pie charts.

Interpreting and discussing results

3.5 • Interpret diagrams and graphs (including pie charts), and draw simple conclusions based on the shape of graphs and simple statistics for a single distribution.

5.5 • **Compare two simple distributions using the range and one of the mode, median or mean.**

3.5 • Write a short report of a statistical enquiry and illustrate with appropriate diagrams, graphs and charts, using ICT as appropriate; justify the choice of what is presented.

Probability

6.1 • Use vocabulary and ideas of probability, drawing on experience.

6.1 • **Understand and use the probability scale from 0 to 1; find and justify probabilities based on equally likely outcomes in simple contexts;** identify all the possible mutually exclusive outcomes of a single event.

6.1 • Collect data from a simple experiment and record in a frequency table; estimate probabilities based on this data.

6.1 • Compare experimental and theoretical probabilities in simple contexts.

Part 1

1.1 Sequences

Sequences are very important in mathematics. Scientists carrying out research will often try to find patterns or rules to describe the results they obtain from experiments.

- A number sequence is a set of numbers in a given order

- Each number in a sequence is called a *term*.

- Here are three sequences. Try to find the next term.

  a   5, 8, 12, 17, ?

  b $\frac{1}{2}$, 1, 2, 4, ?

  c   15, 14, 16, 13, 17, ?

Exercise 1

1. The numbers in boxes make a sequence. Find the next term.

(a) | 9 | 7 | 5 | 3 | |

(b) | 4 | 9 | 14 | 19 | |

(c) | 2 | 9 | 16 | 23 | |

(d) | 2 | 3 | 5 | 8 | 12 | |

In Questions **2** to **17** write down the sequence and find the next term.

2. 21, 17, 13, 9,

3. 60, 54, 48, 42,

4. 1, 2, 4, 8, 16,

5. $\frac{1}{2}$, 1, $1\frac{1}{2}$, 2,

6. 3, $4\frac{1}{2}$, 6, $7\frac{1}{2}$

7. 60, 59, 57, 54, 50,

8. 5, 7, 10, 14,

9. 3, 30, 300, 3000,

10. 1·7, 1·9, 2·1, 2·3,

11. 1, 3, 9, 27,

12. 8, 4, 0, −4, −8,

13. 7, 5, 3, 1, −1,

14. 1, 2, 4, 7, 11

15. −2, −1, 0, 1,

16. 200, 100, 50, 25,

17. 11, 10, 8, 5, 1,

18. Write down the sequence and find the missing number.

(a) | 3 | 6 | 12 | 24 | ☐ |

(b) | 4 | ☐ | 10 | 13 | 16 |

(c) | 32 | 16 | 8 | 4 | ☐ |

(d) | ☐ | 6 | 3 | 0 | −3 |

The next four questions are more difficult. Find the next term.

19. 1, 2, 6, 24, 120,   **20.** 2×4^2, 3×5^2, 4×6^2,

21. $\frac{1}{3}$, $\frac{2}{5}$, $\frac{3}{7}$, $\frac{4}{9}$,   **22.** 2, 2, 4, 12, 48, 240,

Sequence rules

- For the sequence 10, 13, 16, 19, 22, ... the first term is 10 and the term-to-term *rule* is 'add 3'.

  For the sequence 3, 6, 12, 24, 48, ... the term-to-term rule is 'double'.

Exercise 2

1. The first term of a sequence is 20 and the term-to-term rule is 'add 5'. Write down the first five terms of the sequence.

2. You are given the first term and the rule of several sequences. Write down the first five terms of each sequence.

	First term	Rule
(a)	8	add 2
(b)	100	subtract 4
(c)	10	double
(d)	64	divide by 2

3. The rule for the number sequences below is

> *'double and add 1'*

Find the missing numbers

(a) 2 → 5 → 11 → 23 → ☐

(b) ☐ → 7 → 15 → 31

(c) ☐ → 51 → ☐ → ☐

4. The rule for the number sequences below is

'multiply by 3 and take away 2'

Find the missing numbers

(a) $2 \rightarrow 4 \rightarrow 10 \rightarrow \boxed{}$

(b) $\boxed{} \rightarrow 7 \rightarrow 19 \rightarrow 55$

(c) $1 \rightarrow \boxed{} \rightarrow \boxed{} \rightarrow \boxed{}$

5. Write down the rule for each of these sequences.

(a) $2, 2\frac{1}{2}, 3, 3\frac{1}{2}, 4, \ldots$

(b) $5, 10, 20, 40, 80, \ldots$

(c) $1 \cdot 5, 1 \cdot 6, 1 \cdot 7, 1 \cdot 8, \ldots$

(d) $81, 27, 9, 3, 1, \ldots$

6. Here is the start of a sequence of rectangles

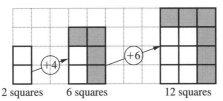

2 squares   6 squares   12 squares

(a) Draw the next rectangle in the sequence and count the squares.

(b) The number of squares in the rectangles makes a number pattern. Copy and complete the boxes and circles below.

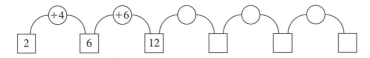

7. Here is the start of a sequence of shapes. Each new diagram is made by adding squares around the outside of the last shape.

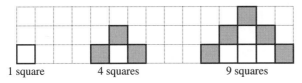

1 square   4 squares   9 squares

(a) Draw and shade in the next shape in the sequence and count the squares in the shape.

(b) The total number of squares in the shapes makes a number pattern. Copy and complete the boxes and circles below.

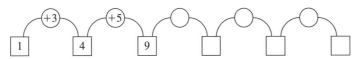

8. In the sequence of squares the number of matches is shown.

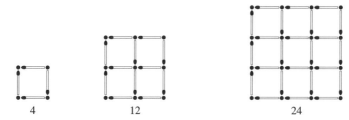

4   12   24

    (a) Draw the next square in the sequence and write down the number of matches in the square.

    (b) Copy and complete the number pattern below.

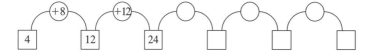

9. In this question the rule for several *different* sequences is 'add 5'.

    (a) Find a sequence for which all the terms are divisible by 5.

    (b) Find a sequence for which none of the terms is a whole number.

    (c) Can you find a sequence with the 'add 5' rule in which all the terms are odd numbers?

10. Copy this pattern and write down the next three lines. Do not use a calculator!

$1 \times 999 = \ \ \ 999$
$2 \times 999 = 1998$
$3 \times 999 = 2997$
$4 \times 999 = 3996$

11. (a) Copy this pattern and write down the next two lines

$$3 \times 5 = \ \ \ \ \ 15$$
$$33 \times 5 = \ \ \ \ 165$$
$$333 \times 5 = \ \ \ 1665$$
$$3333 \times 5 = 16\,665$$

    (b) Copy and complete $333\,333\,333 \times 5 =$

12. (a) Look at the pattern below and then continue it for a further three rows.

$$2^2 + 2 + 3 = \ 9$$
$$3^2 + 3 + 4 = 16$$
$$4^2 + 4 + 5 = 25$$
$$\vdots \quad \vdots \quad \vdots \quad \vdots$$

    (b) Write down the line which starts
$12^2 + \ldots$

13. (a) Copy this pattern and write down the next line.

$$1 \times 9 = \qquad 9$$
$$21 \times 9 = \qquad 189$$
$$321 \times 9 = \qquad 2889$$
$$4321 \times 9 = \quad 38\,889$$
$$54\,321 \times 9 = 488\,889$$

(b) Complete this line $87\,654\,321 \times 9 =$

14. (a) Copy this pattern and write down the next line.

$$1 + 9 \times \quad 0 = \quad 1$$
$$2 + 9 \times \quad 1 = \quad 11$$
$$3 + 9 \times \quad 12 = \quad 111$$
$$4 + 9 \times 123 = 1111$$

(b) Find the missing numbers

$$\boxed{} + 9 \times \boxed{} = 1111111$$

15. (a) Copy this pattern and write down the next line

$$3 \times 4 = 3 + 3 \times 3$$
$$4 \times 5 = 4 + 4 \times 4$$
$$5 \times 6 = 5 + 5 \times 5$$

(b) Copy and complete

$$10 \times 11 =$$
$$11 \times 12 =$$

16.* The odd numbers can be added in groups to give an interesting sequence

$$1 \qquad\qquad\qquad = \quad 1 \quad = \quad 1^3 \qquad (1 \times 1 \times 1)$$
$$3 + 5 \qquad\qquad = \quad 8 \quad = \quad 2^3 \qquad (2 \times 2 \times 2)$$
$$7 + 9 + 11 \quad = \quad 27 \quad = \quad 3^3 \qquad (3 \times 3 \times 3)$$

The numbers 1, 8, 27 are called *cube* numbers. Another cube number is 5^3 (we say '5 cubed')

$$5^3 = 5 \times 5 \times 5 = 125$$

Write down the next three rows of the sequence to see if the sum of each row always gives a cube number.

17.* A famous sequence in mathematics is Pascal's triangle.

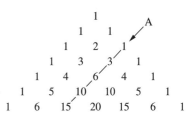

(a) Look carefully at how the triangle is made.
   Write down the next row. It starts: 1 7 ...
(b) Look at the diagonal marked A.
   Predict the next three numbers in the sequence
   1, 3, 6, 10, 15, ...
(c) Work out the *sum* of the numbers in each row
   of Pascal's triangle. What do you notice?
(d) Without writing down all the numbers, work out the sum
   of the numbers in the 10th row of the triangle.

1.2 Number machines

- A number machine performs an *operation* on numbers.
- A simple *operation* could be   add   (+)
                                      subtract   (−)
                                      multiply   (×)
                                  or divide   (÷)

- The *input* number goes into the machine.   input   output
- The *output* number comes out of the machine.

Examples

	input	machine	output	output solution	reason
1.	5 →	+ 7	→ ?	? = 12	(5 + 7 = 12)
2.	8 →	− 3	→ ◆	◆ = 5	(8 − 3 = 5)
3.	3 →	× 6	→ ■	■ = 18	(3 × 6 = 18)

Exercise 1

Find the outputs from these number machines.

1.   4 → + 5 → ☺   2.   7 → + 11 → ◤

3.   10 → − 3 → ■   4.   14 → − 9 → ▬

5.   6 → × 7 → ▨   6.   8 → × 2 → 🐟

7. 525 → ÷ 5 → ?   8.   24 → ÷ 4 → ☺

9.   39 → + 13 → ▮   10.   7 → × 9 → ◣

11. 64 → − 46 → ⚃   12. 660 → ÷ 6 → 👢

13.   8 → × 90 → 🐟   14. 73 → + 37 → ✠

15. 545 → ÷ 5 → ◆   16. 51 → − 15 → ■

17. 33 → × 3 → ◣   18. 80 → × 8 → 🎄

19. 120 → ÷ 20 → π   20. 52 → ÷ 4 → ∅

Exercise 2

Find the output.

1. $6 \rightarrow \boxed{+5} \rightarrow \boxed{+2} \rightarrow$?

2. $3 \rightarrow \boxed{+6} \rightarrow \boxed{+8} \rightarrow$ ●

3. $13 \rightarrow \boxed{-9} \rightarrow \boxed{-3} \rightarrow$ ▲

4. $17 \rightarrow \boxed{-8} \rightarrow \boxed{-5} \rightarrow$ ◆

5. $4 \rightarrow \boxed{\times 2} \rightarrow \boxed{\times 5} \rightarrow$ π

6. $3 \rightarrow \boxed{\times 3} \rightarrow \boxed{\times 3} \rightarrow$ ∅

7. $20 \rightarrow \boxed{\div 5} \rightarrow \boxed{\div 2} \rightarrow$ ◢

8. $48 \rightarrow \boxed{\div 4} \rightarrow \boxed{\div 6} \rightarrow$ ◣

9. $17 \rightarrow \boxed{+71} \rightarrow \boxed{-8} \rightarrow$ ▬

10. $34 \rightarrow \boxed{+43} \rightarrow \boxed{-70} \rightarrow$ 👢

11. $5 \rightarrow \boxed{+4} \rightarrow \boxed{\times 3} \rightarrow$ 🐟

12. $7 \rightarrow \boxed{+9} \rightarrow \boxed{\times 0} \rightarrow$ ☺

13. $12 \rightarrow \boxed{+6} \rightarrow \boxed{\div 6} \rightarrow$ ◆

14. $39 \rightarrow \boxed{+13} \rightarrow \boxed{\div 4} \rightarrow$ ▨

15. $89 \rightarrow \boxed{-15} \rightarrow \boxed{+4} \rightarrow$ ▨

16. $73 \rightarrow \boxed{-5} \rightarrow \boxed{+9} \rightarrow$ ▬

17. $42 \rightarrow \boxed{-38} \rightarrow \boxed{\times 7} \rightarrow$ 👢

18. $100 \rightarrow \boxed{-81} \rightarrow \boxed{\times 3} \rightarrow$ ▮

19. $85 \rightarrow \boxed{-58} \rightarrow \boxed{\div 9} \rightarrow$ 🌲

20. $76 \rightarrow \boxed{-67} \rightarrow \boxed{\div 9} \rightarrow$ ⚅

In Questions **21** to **25** there are several operations.

21. $5 \rightarrow \boxed{\times 3} \rightarrow \boxed{-10} \rightarrow \boxed{\times 2} \rightarrow \boxed{\div 10} \rightarrow$ ☂

22. $7 \rightarrow \boxed{\times 9} \rightarrow \boxed{\times 2} \rightarrow \boxed{-66} \rightarrow \boxed{\div 12} \rightarrow$ ⌢

23. $50 \rightarrow \boxed{\times 10} \rightarrow \boxed{-123} \rightarrow \boxed{+13} \rightarrow \boxed{\div 10} \rightarrow \boxed{\div 13} \rightarrow$ ↑

24. $17 \rightarrow \boxed{\times 5} \rightarrow \boxed{+25} \rightarrow \boxed{\div 11} \rightarrow \boxed{\times 13} \rightarrow \boxed{\div 2} \rightarrow \boxed{+7} \rightarrow$ ⚑

25. $13 \rightarrow \boxed{+84} \rightarrow \boxed{\times 0} \rightarrow \boxed{+14} \rightarrow \boxed{\times 5} \rightarrow \boxed{-15} \rightarrow \boxed{\div 11} \rightarrow$ **❗**

Inverse operations

- Using the *inverse* (or reverse) we can find the input for any machine, by using the output.

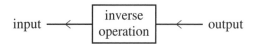

Operation	Inverse operation
+7	−7
−8	+8
×4	÷4
÷6	×6

- Example: Find the input.

$$? \rightarrow \boxed{+9} \rightarrow 20$$

Solution: Change arrows direction and use the inverse operation

$$? \leftarrow \boxed{-9} \leftarrow 20$$

$$? = 11 \text{ since } 20 - 9 = 11$$

Exercise 3

Find the input to these systems

1. ● → $\boxed{+6}$ → 11

2. ▲ → $\boxed{+4}$ → 13

3. ⚅ → $\boxed{-7}$ → 2

4. ◢ → $\boxed{-12}$ → 24

5. ▆ → $\boxed{\times 3}$ → 18

6. ☺ → $\boxed{\times 5}$ → 45

7. $ → $\boxed{\div 8}$ → 1

8. 👢 → $\boxed{\div 7}$ → 8

9. 🐟 → $\boxed{+14}$ → 72

10. 〰 → $\boxed{+11}$ → 29

11. ◢ → $\boxed{-13}$ → 31

12. ◆ → $\boxed{-72}$ → 27

13. ◆ → $\boxed{-72}$ → 27

14. π → $\boxed{\times 9}$ → 72

15. ? → $\boxed{\div 4}$ → 80

16. ◤ → $\boxed{\div 60}$ → 7

17. ▬ → $\boxed{\times 9}$ → 54

18. ? → $\boxed{\times 8}$ → 560

19. ☺ → $\boxed{\div 7}$ → 7

20. ◢ → $\boxed{\div 3}$ → 27

Exercise 4

Find the input to these machines

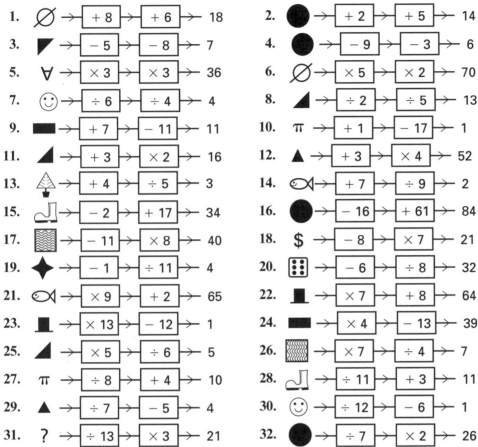

1. ∅ → +8 → +6 → 18
2. ● → +2 → +5 → 14
3. � → −5 → −8 → 7
4. ● → −9 → −3 → 6
5. ∀ → ×3 → ×3 → 36
6. ∅ → ×5 → ×2 → 70
7. ☺ → ÷6 → ÷4 → 4
8. ◢ → ÷2 → ÷5 → 13
9. ▬ → +7 → −11 → 11
10. π → +1 → −17 → 1
11. ◢ → +3 → ×2 → 16
12. ▲ → +3 → ×4 → 52
13. ▲ → +4 → ÷5 → 3
14. ◁ → +7 → ÷9 → 2
15. 👢 → −2 → +17 → 34
16. ● → −16 → +61 → 84
17. ▨ → −11 → ×8 → 40
18. $ → −8 → ×7 → 21
19. ◆ → −1 → ÷11 → 4
20. ⚁ → −6 → ÷8 → 32
21. ◁ → ×9 → +2 → 65
22. ▮ → ×7 → +8 → 64
23. ▮ → ×13 → −12 → 1
24. ▬ → ×4 → −13 → 39
25. ◢ → ×5 → ÷6 → 5
26. ▨ → ×7 → ÷4 → 7
27. π → ÷8 → +4 → 10
28. 👢 → ÷11 → +3 → 11
29. ▲ → ÷7 → −5 → 4
30. ☺ → ÷12 → −6 → 1
31. ? → ÷13 → ×3 → 21
32. ● → ÷7 → ×2 → 26

Mystery machines

The following inputs go into a mystery machine ...

　　　3, 6, 27 and 0.

The diagram shows the outputs produced ...

input	machine	output
3 →	?	→ 6
6 →	?	→ 9
27 →	?	→ 30
0 →	?	→ 3

The 'mystery' machine has added three to produce the outputs because it links *all* the inputs to the outputs in the same way.

The mystery machine was ...　　input → +3 → output

Exercise 5

What operation is taking place in each of these machines?

1.

input	output
1 →⟶ ? ⟶ 5	
2 →⟶ ? ⟶ 10	
3 →⟶ ? ⟶ 15	

2.

input	output
63 →⟶ ? ⟶ 7	
54 →⟶ ? ⟶ 6	
27 →⟶ ? ⟶ 3	

3.

input	output
10 →⟶ ? ⟶ 8	
9 →⟶ ? ⟶ 7	
8 →⟶ ? ⟶ 6	

4.

input	output
3 →⟶ ? ⟶ 6	
8 →⟶ ? ⟶ 11	
7 →⟶ ? ⟶ 10	

5.

input	output
12 →⟶ ? ⟶ 6	
2 →⟶ ? ⟶ 1	
50 →⟶ ? ⟶ 25	

6.

input	output
19 →⟶ ? ⟶ 57	
9 →⟶ ? ⟶ 27	
7 →⟶ ? ⟶ 21	

7.

input	output
26 →⟶ ? ⟶ 11	
40 →⟶ ? ⟶ 25	
91 →⟶ ? ⟶ 76	

8.

input	output
9 →⟶ ? ⟶ 63	
4 →⟶ ? ⟶ 28	
8 →⟶ ? ⟶ 56	

9.

input	output
8 →⟶ ? ⟶ 64	
1 →⟶ ? ⟶ 8	
3 →⟶ ? ⟶ 24	

For Questions **10** to **15** copy and complete the number machines after working out the operation for each.

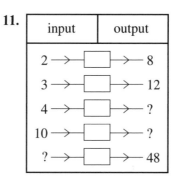

10.

input	output
1 →⟶ ☐ ⟶ 7	
7 →⟶ ☐ ⟶ 13	
13 →⟶ ☐ ⟶ ?	
? →⟶ ☐ ⟶ 26	
27 →⟶ ☐ ⟶ ?	

11.

input	output
2 →⟶ ☐ ⟶ 8	
3 →⟶ ☐ ⟶ 12	
4 →⟶ ☐ ⟶ ?	
10 →⟶ ☐ ⟶ ?	
? →⟶ ☐ ⟶ 48	

12.

input	output
12 →⟶ ☐ ⟶ 5	
7 →⟶ ☐ ⟶ 0	
18 →⟶ ☐ ⟶ ?	
? →⟶ ☐ ⟶ 13	
? →⟶ ☐ ⟶ 26	

13.

input	output
0 →☐→ 11	
3 →☐→ ?	
12 →☐→ 23	
? →☐→ 31	
39 →☐→ ?	

14.

input	output
3 →☐→ 1	
9 →☐→ 3	
? →☐→ 4	
15 →☐→ ?	
60 →☐→ ?	

15.

input	output
0 →☐→ ?	
5 →☐→ 50	
? →☐→ 40	
7 →☐→ 70	
? →☐→ 100	

Questions **16** to **20** are more difficult.

16. For each chart find the *single* operation which performs the same operation as the three operations shown.

(a) In →[+ 5]—[− 2]—[+ 10]→ Out

(b) →[− 4]—[+ 1]—[− 3]→

(c) →[+ 2]—[× 2]—[− 4]→

17. Find the two operations which give *both* the results shown.

4 →[?]→[?]→ 9

9 →[?]→[?]→ 19

18. Find the two operations which give *both* the results shown.

5 →[?]→[?]→ 14

8 →[?]→[?]→ 23

19. Find the input number which gives the same output number for both charts below.

In →[× 4]→[− 1]→ Out   In →[× 2]→[+ 3]→ Out

20. Find the input number which gives the same output number for both charts below.

In →[× 3]→[− 2]→ Out   In →[× 2]→[+ 1]→ Out

1.3 Arithmetic without a calculator

Place value

- Whole numbers are made up from units, tens, hundreds, thousands and so on.

thousands	hundreds	tens	units
6	3	2	5

- In the number 6325:

  the digit 6 means 6 thousands
  the digit 3 means 3 hundreds
  the digit 2 means 2 tens
  the digit 5 means 5 units (ones)

- In words we write 'six thousand, three hundred and twenty-five'.

Exercise 1

In Questions **1** to **8** state the value of the figure underlined.

1. 3̲7   **2.** 4̲85   **3.** 608̲   **4.** 627̲
5. 6̲140   **6.** 32̲104   **7.** 5̲180 000   **8.** 7̲30 111

In Questions **9** to **16** write down the number which goes in each box.

9. $393 = \boxed{} + 90 + 3$ **10.** $527 = 500 + \boxed{} + 7$

11. $834 = 800 + \boxed{} + 4$ **12.** $699 = \boxed{} + 90 + 9$

13. $7317 = \boxed{} + 300 + 10 + 7$ **14.** $5043 = 5000 + \boxed{} + 3$

15. $25\,410 = 20\,000 + 5000 + \boxed{} + 10$

16. $74\,612 = \boxed{} + 4000 + 600 + \boxed{} + 2$

17. Write these numbers in figures.
  (a) Four hundred and nine.
  (b) Six thousand, four hundred and one.
  (c) Sixteen thousand, two hundred and eleven.
  (d) Half a million.
  (e) Four hundred thousand and fifty.
  (f) Three and a half thousand.

18. Here are four number cards:

  (a) Use all the cards to make the largest possible number.
  (b) Use all the cards to make the smallest possible number.

19. Write these numbers in words.
   (a) 6200   (b) 90 000   (c) 25 010
   (d) 610 400   (e) 7010 000

20. Here are five number cards:

   (a) Use all the cards to make the largest possible *odd* number.
   (b) Use all the cards to make the smallest possible *even* number.

21. Write down the number that is ten more than:
   (a) 351   (b) 399   (c) 7025

22. Write down the number that is one thousand more than:
   (a) 425   (b) 6423   (c) 24100

23. (a) Lisa puts a 2 digit whole number into her calculator.
       She multiplies the number by 10.

       Fill in *one* other digit which you know must now be
       on the calculator.

   (b) Lisa starts again with the same 2 digit number and
       this time she multiplies it by 1000.
       Fill in all five digits on the calculator this time.

24. Write down the numbers in order, from the smallest to the
largest.
   (a)   2142   2290   2058   2136
   (b)   5329   5029   5299   5330
   (c) 25 117   25 200   25 171   25 000   25 500

25. Find a number n so that $5 \times n + 7 = 507$.

26. Find a number p so that $6 \times p + 8 = 68$.

27. Find a pair of numbers a and b for which $8 \times a + b = 807$.

28. Find a pair of numbers p and q for which $7 \times p + 5 \times q = 7050$.

Arithmetic

Here are examples to remind you of non-calculator methods.

(a)
$$\begin{array}{r} 4\ 2\ 7 \\ +5\ 1\ 8\ 6 \\ \hline 5\ 6\ 1\ 3 \\ \hline {\scriptstyle 1\ 1} \end{array}$$

(b)
$$\begin{array}{r} 2\ 7\ {}^{7}8\ {}^{1}4 \\ -\ \ 6\ 3\ 5 \\ \hline 2\ 1\ 4\ 9 \end{array}$$

(c) $57 \times 100 = 5700$

(d)
$$\begin{array}{r} 3\ 7\ 4 \\ \times\quad\ \ 6 \\ \hline 2\ 2\ 4\ 4 \\ \hline {\scriptstyle 4\ 2} \end{array}$$

(e)
$$7\overline{)3\ 7\ {}^{2}9\ {}^{1}4}\ \ {}^{\displaystyle 5\ 4\ 2}$$

(f)
$$5\overline{)6\ {}^{1}9\ {}^{4}4}\ \ {}^{\displaystyle 1\ 3\ 8\ \text{r}\ 4}\quad \text{or}\quad 138\tfrac{4}{5}$$

Exercise 2

Work out, without a calculator.

1. $317 + 228$	**2.** $2208 + 329$	**3.** $35 + 214 + 206$	**4.** $4186 + 25\,804$
5. $487 - 177$	**6.** $314 - 206$	**7.** $649 - 68$	**8.** $1024 - 837$
9. 85×10	**10.** 6×1000	**11.** 73×5	**12.** 314×4
13. 206×8	**14.** 1023×7	**15.** $340 \div 4$	**16.** $1944 \div 6$
17. $5295 \div 5$	**18.** $2600 \div 8$	**19.** $365 \div 7$	**20.** $920 \div 10$
21. $289 + 15 + 2009$	**22.** $9704 - 8816$	**23.** $6001 - 5994$	**24.** 54×20
25. $2906 - 1414$	**26.** $4716 \div 9$	**27.** 105×8	**28.** $1504 \div 8$
29. $6 + 1609 + 25$	**30.** $309 + 154 - 78$	**31.** $7 + 295 - 48$	**32.** 47×400

Remainders

- Suppose you need to share 267 cakes between 5 people.

  Work out $267 \div 5$:

$$\begin{array}{r} 5\,3 \quad \textit{remainder 2} \\ 5\,\overline{)\,2\,6\,{}^1 7} \end{array}$$

  Each person gets 53 cakes and there are 2 left over.

  Sometimes it is better to write the remainder as a fraction.
  In the calculation above the answer is $53\frac{2}{5}$.
  So each person could get $53\frac{2}{5}$ cakes.

- Work out $432 \div 7$:

$$\begin{array}{r} 6\,1 \quad \textit{remainder 5} \\ 7\,\overline{)\,4\,3\,{}^1 2} \end{array}$$

  The answer is '61 remainder 5' or $61\frac{5}{7}$.

Exercise 3

Write the answer: (a) with a remainder,   (b) as a mixed fraction.

1. $5\overline{)432}$	**2.** $4\overline{)715}$	**3.** $6\overline{)895}$	**4.** $3\overline{)164}$
5. $8\overline{)514}$	**6.** $9\overline{)375}$	**7.** $5\overline{)2642}$	**8.** $2\overline{)7141}$
9. $4079 \div 7$	**10.** $2132 \div 5$	**11.** $4013 \div 8$	**12.** $235 \div 6$
13. $657 \div 10$	**14.** $8327 \div 10$	**15.** $85\,714 \div 6$	**16.** $4826 \div 9$
17. $2007 \div 7$	**18.** $9998 \div 9$	**19.** $6732 \div 11$	**20.** $84\,563 \div 7$

Think about the remainder

- How many teams of 5 can you make from 113 people?

  Work out $113 \div 5$.

$$\begin{array}{r} 2\,2 \quad \textit{remainder 3} \\ 5\,\overline{)\,1\,1\,{}^1 3} \end{array}$$

  Here we round *down*. You can make 22 teams and there will be 3
  people left over.

- An egg box holds 6 eggs. How many boxes do you need for 231 eggs?

  Work out $231 \div 6$.

$$\begin{array}{r} 3\,8 \quad \textit{remainder 3} \\ 6\,\overline{)\,2\,3\,{}^5 1} \end{array}$$

  Here we round *up* because you must use complete boxes. You need 39
  boxes altogether.

Exercise 4

In these questions you will get a remainder. Decide whether it is more sensible to round *up* or to round *down*.

1. Tins of spaghetti are packed 8 to a box. How many boxes are needed for 913 tins?

2. A prize consists of 10 000 one pound coins. The prize is shared between 7 people. How many pound coins will each person receive?

3. There are 23 children in a class. How many teams of 4 can be made?

4. Eggs are packed six in a box. How many boxes do I need for 200 eggs?

5. Tickets cost £6 each and I have £80. How many tickets can I buy?

6. I have 204 plants and one tray takes 8 plants. How many trays do I need?

7. There are 51 children in the dining room and a table seats 6. How many tables are needed to seat all the children?

8. I have 100 cans of drink. One box holds 8 cans. How many boxes can I fill?

9. Five people can travel in one car and there are altogether 93 people to transport. How many cars are needed?

10. There are 332 children in a school. One coach holds 50 children. How many coaches are needed for a whole school trip?

11. I have 300 packets of crisps. One box holds 42 packets. How many boxes can I fill? (You can do this without 'long division'.)

12. How many 9 p stamps can I buy with a £5 note?

13. Find the missing numbers

(a) $\quad$ 7 1 4 r $\boxed{}$
$\quad$ 8) 5 7 1 4

(b) $\quad$ 5 6 r 4
$\quad$ 7) 3 9 $\boxed{}$

(c) $\quad$ 8 1 2 r 7
$\quad$ 9) 7 3 1 $\boxed{}$

Mixed problems

Exercise 5

1. How many 5p coins are worth the same as a hundred 2p coins?

2. A man has £1000. How much has he left after buying a television for £217 and a video recorder for £399?

3. How many spots are there on 20 ordinary dice?

4. Geoff grows peas with exactly eleven peas per pod. Geoff picks 77 pods. How many peas will Geoff have to eat?

5. Copy and complete this multiplication square.

×	3	7		
		35		45
8			32	
11	33			
				54

6. You are looking for a mystery number.
   Use the clues to find it.

   • the sum of the digits is 10
   • the number reads the same forwards as backwards
   • the number is less than 2000
   • the number has no zeros
   • the number has four digits

7. A man died in 1993 aged 58. In what year was he born?

8. A bird remains airborne for five days. How many hours is that?

9. How many £10 notes are in (a) £1000, (b) £2500, (c) £140 000?

10. How many £100 notes are in (a) £1800, (b) £200 000, (c) £5 million?

11. How many 1p coins are in (a) £10, (b) £500, (c) £2700?

12. Copy and complete these two sentences:
    (a) Multiplying by 100 is the same as multiplying by ⬚ and again by ⬚.

    (b) Multiplying by 1000 is the same as multiplying by ⬚, again by ⬚ and again by ⬚.

13. Cans of coke at 55p each are put in packs of 10.
Ten packs are put in a box.
One hundred boxes are put in a container.
Find the cost of:
(a) 1 pack
(b) 1 box
(c) 1 container
(d) 100 containers.

14. Magazines costing £2 each are wrapped in packs of 10.
Ten packs are put in a box.
Ten boxes are put in a van.
Find the cost of:
(a) 1 pack
(b) 1 box
(c) 1 van load
(d) 1000 van loads.

15. Write the numbers 1 to 9 in the circles so that each side of the square adds up to 12. [Hint: Put '7' in the middle.]

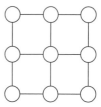

16. Here are three eggs. Arrange the numbers 1, 2, 3, ... 9 so that the numbers in each egg add up to 15. Put three numbers in each egg.
Try to find different ways of doing it.

17. Choose 3 digits from 2, 3, 5, 7.

  = 32

Put them in the boxes to make a true statement.

18. If you have 20 video tapes each of 360 minutes duration, how many minutes of taping can you do?

19.* Mike knows that $221 \times 31 = 6851$. Explain how he can use this information to work out 222×31.

20.* Given that $357 \times 101 = 36057$, work out 358×101 without multiplying.

Divisibility tests: an investigation

Whole numbers are divisible by:

2 if the number is even
3 if the sum of the digits is divisible by 3
4 if the last *two* digits are divisible by 4
5 if the last digit is 0 or 5
6 if the number is even and also divisible by 3
8 if half of it is divisible by 4
9 if the sum of the digits is divisible by 9
10 if _____ (fill in the space)

A Copy and complete the table below, using $\sqrt{\ }$'s and ×'s.

Number	Divisible by						
	2	3	4	5	6	8	9
363	×	$\sqrt{\ }$					
224							
459							
155							
168							
865							
360							
2601							

B You will notice that there is no test above for divisibility by 7. *Investigate* the following test for four-, five- or six-digit numbers:

Test 18 228

Find the difference between the last 3 digits and the digits at the front. $228 - 18 = 210$

If this difference is divisible by 7, then the original number is divisible by 7.

Try the test on these numbers:

37 177, 8498, 431 781, 42 329, 39 579, 910 987.

Now choose some numbers of your own.

C *Investigate* to find out whether or not a similar test works for divisibility by 11.

Inverse operations: find the missing digits

The word inverse means 'opposite'.

- The inverse of adding is subtracting $7 + 11 = 18,$ $7 = 18 - 11$
- The inverse of subtracting is adding $20 - 8 = 12,$ $20 = 12 + 8$
- The inverse of multiplying is dividing $8 \times 4 = 32,$ $8 = 32 \div 4$
- The inverse of dividing is multiplying $30 \div 5 = 6,$ $30 = 6 \times 5$

Find the missing digits.

(a) $\boxed{}2 \div 4 = 23$

Work out 23×4 because multiplying is the inverse of dividing.
Since $23 \times 4 = 92$, the missing digit is 9.

(b) $3\boxed{}7 \times 8 = 2616$

Work out $2616 \div 8$ because dividing is the inverse of multiplying.
Since $2616 \div 8 = 327$, the missing digit is 2.

(c)
```
    1 □ 6
  + 4 4 □
  ─────────
  □ 2   9
```

Start from the right. $6 + 3 = 9$
Middle column. $8 + 4 = 12$

Check
```
      1 8 6
    + 4 4 3
    ─────────
      6 2 9
        1
```

Exercise 6

Find the missing digits.

1. (a)
```
    3 1 4
  + □ 6 3
  ───────
    7 □ □
```
(b)
```
    3 5 □
  + □ 2 4
  ───────
    9 □ 8
```
(c)
```
    □ 5 8
  + 1 4 □
  ───────
    5 □ 2
```

2. (a)
```
    5 3 6
  + 2 □ 4
  ───────
  □   5 □
```
(b)
```
    2 □ 6
  + 3 5 7
  ───────
  □ 0 3
```
(c)
```
    6 3 4
  + □ 8 □
  ───────
    9 □ 8
```

3. (a)
```
        3 □
  ×       5
  ───────────
    1 8 5
```
(b)
```
        4 □
  ×       9
  ───────────
    4 2 3
```
(c)
```
      □ □ 4
  ×         8
  ───────────
    2 9 9 2
```

4. (a) ☐☐☐ ÷ 7 = 33   (b) ☐☐ × 11 = 143

(c) 12 × ☐ = 108   (d) ☐☐☐ ÷ 6 = 153

5. (a)
```
   8 ☐ 6
 − 3 2 ☐
 ────────
 ☐ 3 2
```
(b)
```
   8 ☐ 2
 − ☐ 1 ☐
 ────────
   4 1 7
```
(c)
```
   ☐ 4 ☐
 − 2 ☐ 8
 ────────
   3 5 7
```

6. (a) ☐☐ × 8 = 440   (b) ☐☐ × 11 = 231

(c) 400 ÷ ☐ = 50   (d) ☐☐☐ ÷ 6 = 163

7. (a) ☐☐ + 48 = 127   (b) ☐☐☐ − 49 = 463

(c)
```
   ☐ 5 3
 − 4 ☐ 7
 ────────
   1 6 ☐
```
(d)
```
   8 7 5
 − 5 7 ☐
 ────────
 ☐☐ 6
```

8. There is more than one correct answer for each of these questions. Ask a friend to check your solution.

(a) ⊡4⊡5 + ☐☐ − ☐☐ = 45

(b) ⊡7⊡2 − ☐☐ + ☐☐ = 71

(c) ⊡2⊡2 × ☐ ÷ ☐ = 11

(d) ⊡6⊡0 × ☐☐ ÷ ☐ = 600

9. Each of these calculations has the same number missing from all three boxes. Find the missing number in each calculation.

(a) ☐ × ☐ − ☐ = 12

(b) ☐ ÷ ☐ + ☐ = 9

(c) ☐ × ☐ + ☐ = 72

10. In the circle write +, −, × or ÷ to make the calculation correct.

(a) 9 × 5 ◯ 3 = 48   (b) 8 × 5 ◯ 2 = 20

(c) 8 ◯ 9 − 5 = 67   (d) 12 ◯ 2 + 4 = 10

(e) 60 ÷ 3 ◯ 5 = 15

11. Write the following with the correct signs.

(a) 5 × 4 × 3 ◯ 3 = 63

(b) 5 + 4 ◯ 3 ◯ 2 = 4

(c) 5 × 2 × 3 ◯ 1 = 31

1.4 Three dimensional objects

Three dimensional objects have three dimensions ... length, width and depth.
Three dimensional is abbreviated to '3D'.
3D objects are often referred to as 'solids' or 'solid objects'.

Special Names are given to certain 3D solid objects ...

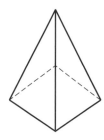

cube

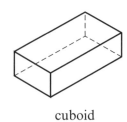

cuboid

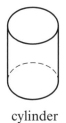

cylinder

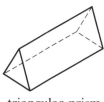

triangular prism
(see below)

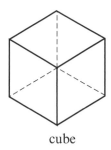

square based
pyramid

cone

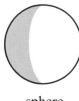

sphere

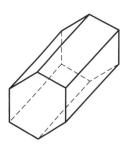

hexagonal prism
(see below)

- A *prism* has the same cross section throughout its length. Here is a triangular prism.

  If you cut through the prism parallel to its end, (the face marked A in the diagram) you produce a shape exactly the same as A (marked A′).

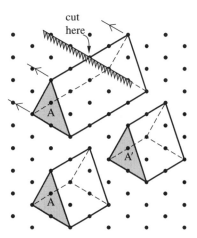

Exercise 1

Below are drawn ten 3D objects labelled A to J.

1. Write down the letters of all objects that are prisms and write next to the letter the name of the object.

2. Write down the letters of all the objects that are non-prisms and write next to the letter the name of the object.

3. For the 10 objects given, sort the objects into two groups (other than prisms and non-prisms). Write down your two groups and how you chose your groups.

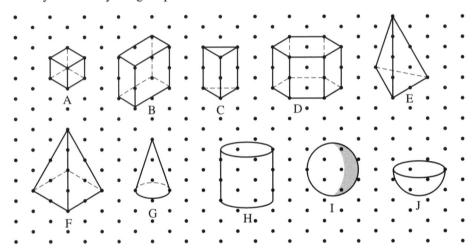

Faces, edges and vertices

Many three-dimensional shapes have *faces*, *edges* and *vertices* (plural of *vertex*). The diagram opposite shows a cuboid.

The *faces* of the cuboid are the flat surfaces on the shape.
There are 6 faces on a cuboid.
The *edges* of the cuboid are the lines that make up the shape.
There are 12 edges on a cuboid.
The vertices of the cuboid are where the edges meet at a point.
There are 8 vertices on a cuboid.

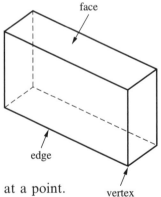

Visualising 3-D shapes

Exercise 2

1. For objects B and C in the last exercise state the number of faces, edges and vertices.

2. Imagine a large cube which is cut in half along the dotted lines. Describe the two new solids formed.
   How many faces, edges and vertices does each solid have?

3. 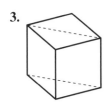 Suppose the same large cube is now cut in half along a different dotted line. Describe the two new solids formed.
   How many faces, edges and vertices does each solid have?

4. Suppose you cut off one corner from a cube. How many faces, edges and vertices has the remaining shape? How about the piece cut off?

5. These diagrams show different solids when viewed from directly above. Describe what each solid could be. [There may be more than one correct response but you only have to give one.]

   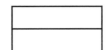

6. Describe two different ways in which you could cut a cylinder into two identical pieces. Describe and/or sketch the solids you would obtain in each case.

7. For objects A to F in Exercise 1, state the number of faces, edges and vertices. Make a table with columns: shape; faces; edges; vertices.

8. Try to find a connection between the number of faces, edges and vertices which applies to all the objects A to F.

9. Draw 3 pictures of a cube and label them A, B, C.
On A colour in a pair of edges which are parallel.
On B colour in a pair of edges which are perpendicular.
On C colour in a pair of edges which are neither parallel nor
intersect each other.

10. Sit back to back with a partner. Look at one of the models
below but don't tell your partner which one. Tell your partner
how to make the model. Now swap over. With practice you
can design harder models of your own.

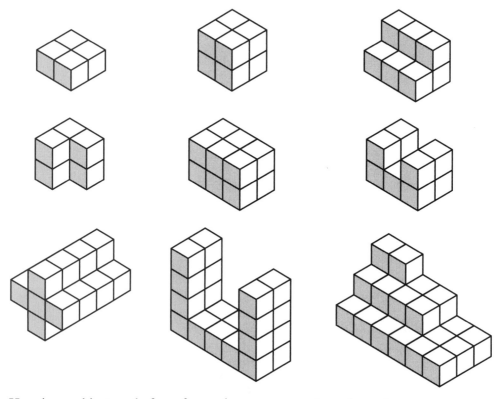

11. Here is an object made from four cubes.
  (a) Copy the drawing on isometric paper.
     (Make sure you have the paper the
     right way round.)

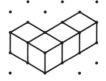

  (b) Make as many *different* objects as you can using four cubes.
     Draw each object on isometric paper.

Nets for making shapes

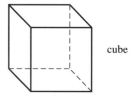
cube

● If the cube shown was made of cardboard, and you cut along some of the edges and laid it out flat, you would have a *net* of the cube.

  There is more than one net of a cube as you will see in the exercise below.

● To make a cube from card you need to produce the net shown below complete with the added 'tabs' for glueing purposes.

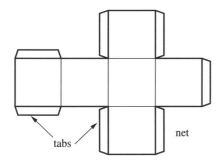

tabs   net

● In this section you will make several interesting 3D objects. You will need a pencil, ruler, scissors and either glue (Pritt Stick) or Sellotape.
  Score all lines before cutting out the net. This makes assembly of the object easier. Don't forget the tabs!

Exercise 3

1. Here are several nets which may or may not make cubes. Draw the nets on squared paper, cut them out and fold them to see which ones do make cubes.

(a)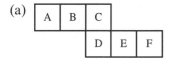

(b)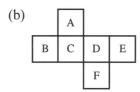

(c)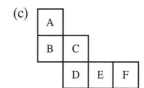

(d)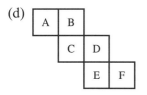

(e)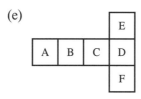

2. For the nets, which *did* make cubes in Question **1**, state which of the faces B, C, D, E or F was opposite face A on the cube.

3. Each diagram below shows *part* of the net of a cube. Each net needs one more square to complete the net.

(a) 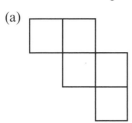   (b)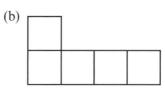

Cut out each of the shapes given and then draw the four possible nets which would make a cube with each one.

4. Draw a net for each of the following:
(a) a closed cuboid measuring 5 cm × 3 cm × 2 cm
(b) a square-based pyramid.

5. Some interesting objects can be made using triangle dotty paper. The basic shape for the nets is an equilateral triangle. With the paper as shown the triangles are easy to draw.

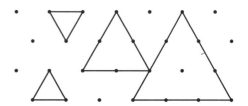

Make the sides of the triangles 3 cm long so that the objects are easy to make. Here is the net of a tetrahedron. Draw it and then cut it out.

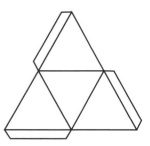

6. Here are two more.
(a) Octahedron (octa: eight; hedron: faces)   (b) Icosahedron (an object with 20 faces)

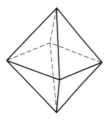   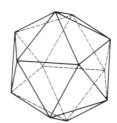

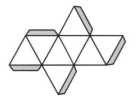   

1.5 Decimals 1

- Decimals are used with money and with measurements of lengths, weights, times.

  The number 3·745 is 'three point seven four five', *not* 'three point seven hundred and forty-five'.

  £1·67 is spoken as 'one pound sixty-seven'.
  £2·05 is spoken as 'two pounds and five pence'.

- The diagram below shows numbers we would see if we could 'zoom in' on an imaginary ruler.

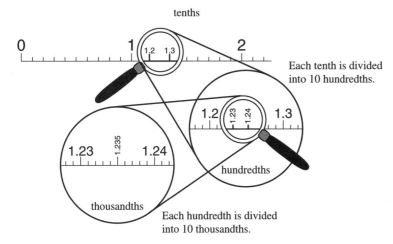

The numbers between 1·2 and 1·3 go up by 0·01 at a time:
  1·21, 1·22, 1·23, 1·24 ...
The numbers between 1·23 and 1·24 go up by 0·001 at a time:
  1·231, 1·232, 1·233, 1·234, 1·235 ...

- Here are some decimal numbers.

Number	Hundreds H	Tens T	Units U	•	Tenths $\frac{1}{10}$	Hundredths $\frac{1}{100}$	Thousandths $\frac{1}{1000}$
538·1	5	3	8	•	1		
42·63		4	2	•	6	3	
0·04			0	•	0	4	
7·125			7	•	1	2	5

Ordering decimals

Consider these three decimals ...

   0·09, 0·101, 0·1.

Which is the correct order from lowest to highest?

- When ordering decimals it is always helpful to write them with the same number of figures after the decimal point.

0·09   ⟶ 0·090   Empty spaces can be
0·101 ⟶ 0·101   filled with zeros.
0·1   ⟶ 0·100

Now we can clearly see the correct order of these decimals from lowest to highest ... 0·090, 0·1, 0·101.

Exercise 1

In Questions **1** to **16** answer True (T) or False (F).

1. 0·7 is less than 0·71   **2.** 0·61 is more than 0·16.

3. 0·08 is more than 0·008   **4.** 0·5 is equal to 0·500

5. 0·613 is less than 0·631   **6.** 7·0 is equal to 0·7.

7. 6·2 is less than 6·02   **8.** 0·09 is more than 0·1.

9. 2·42 is equal to 2·420   **10.** 0·63 is less than 0·36

11. 0·01 is more than 0·001   **12.** 0·78 is less than 0·793

13. 8 is equal to 8·00   **14.** 0·4 is more than 0·35

15. 0·07 is less than 0·1   **16.** 0·1 is equal to $\frac{1}{10}$.

17. Here is a pattern of numbers based on 3. ⟶

   Write a similar pattern based on 7 and extend it from 70 000 000 down to 0·0007. Write the numbers in figures and in words

three thousand	3000
three hundred	300
thirty	30
three	3
nought point three	0·3
nought point nought three	0·03

18. What does the digit 7 in 3·271 represent? And the 2? And the 1?

19. What does the digit 3 in 5·386 represent? And the 6? And the 8?

20. Write the decimal number equivalent to:
   (a) three tenths   (b) seven hundredths
   (c) eleven hundredths   (d) four thousandths
   (e) sixteen hundredths   (f) sixteen thousandths.

21. Write down the single operation needed [+,−] when you change:
    (a) 5·32 to 5·72   (b) 11·042 to 11·047
    (c) 0·592 to 0·392   (d) 0·683 to 0·623.

Exercise 2

In Questions **1** to **20**, arrange the numbers in order of size, smallest first.

1. 0·21, 0·31, 0·12.   **2.** 0·04, 0·4, 0·35.

3. 0·67, 0·672, 0·7.   **4.** 0·05, 0·045, 0·07.

5. 0·1, 0·09, 0·089.   **6.** 0·75, 0·57, 0·705.

7. 0·41, 0·041, 0·14.   **8.** 0·809, 0·81, 0·8.

9. 0·006, 0·6, 0·059.   **10.** 0·15, 0·143, 0·2.

11. 0·04, 0·14, 0·2, 0·53.   **12.** 1·2, 0·12, 0·21, 1·12.

13. 2·3, 2·03, 0·75, 0·08.   **14.** 0·62, 0·26, 0·602, 0·3.

15. 0·5, 1·3, 1·03, 1·003.   **16.** 0·79, 0·792, 0·709, 0·97.

17. 1·23, 0·321, 0·312, 1·04. **18.** 0·008, 0·09, 0·091, 0·075.

19. 2·05, 2·5, 2, 2·046.   **20.** 1·95, 9·51, 5·19, 5·1.

21. Here are numbers with letters
    (a) Put the numbers in order, smallest first. Write down just the letters.
    (b) Finish the sentence using letters and numbers of your own. The numbers must increase from left to right.

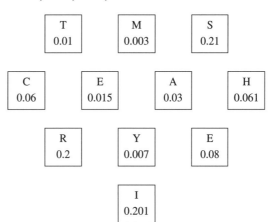

T	M	S
0.01	0.003	0.21

C	E	A	H
0.06	0.015	0.03	0.061

R	Y	E
0.2	0.007	0.08

I
0.201

22. Increase the following numbers by $\frac{1}{10}$th:
    (a) 3·27   (b) 14·8   (c) 0·841

23. Increase the following numbers by $\frac{1}{100}$th:
    (a) 11·25   (b) 1·294   (c) 0·382

24. Increase the following numbers by $\frac{1}{1000}$th:
    (a) 3·142   (b) 2·718   (c) 1·414

25. Write the following amounts in pounds:
    (a) 11 pence.   (b) 2 pence.   (c) 5 pence.
    (d) 10 pence.   (e) 20 pence.   (f) 50 pence.

Find the number which the arrow is pointing to on each of the scales.

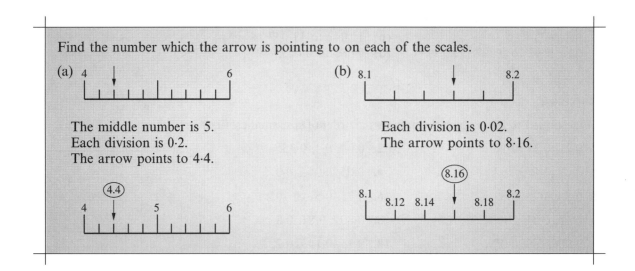

(a)

The middle number is 5.
Each division is 0·2.
The arrow points to 4·4.

(b)

Each division is 0·02.
The arrow points to 8·16.

Exercise 3

Work out the value indicated by the arrow.

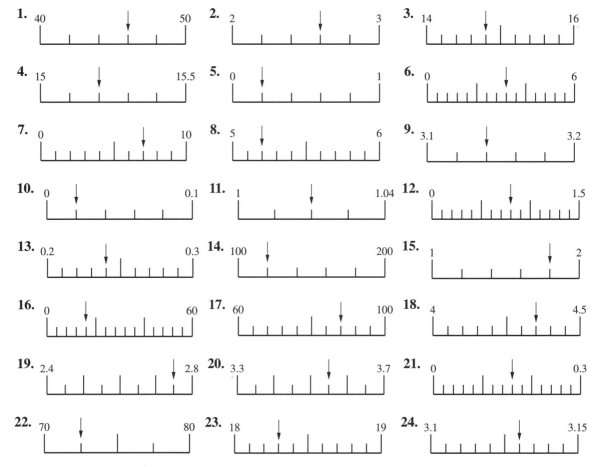

Adding and subtracting decimals

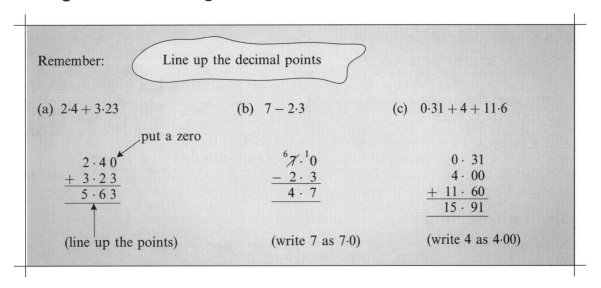

Remember: Line up the decimal points

(a) $2·4 + 3·23$

put a zero

$$\begin{array}{r} 2·4\,0 \\ +\ 3·2\,3 \\ \hline 5·6\,3 \\ \hline \end{array}$$

(line up the points)

(b) $7 - 2·3$

$$\begin{array}{r} {}^{6}7·{}^{1}0 \\ -\ 2·3 \\ \hline 4·7 \\ \hline \end{array}$$

(write 7 as 7·0)

(c) $0·31 + 4 + 11·6$

$$\begin{array}{r} 0·31 \\ 4·00 \\ +\ 11·60 \\ \hline 15·91 \\ \hline \end{array}$$

(write 4 as 4·00)

Exercise 4

1. $5 + 0·26$
2. $2·9 + 4·37$
3. $8·62 + 7·99$
4. $0·078 + 2·05$
5. $10·04 + 3·005$
6. $13·47 + 27·084$
7. $1·97 + 19·7$
8. $4·56 + 7·890$
9. $456·7 + 8·901$
10. $16·374 + 0·947 + 27$
11. $3·142 + 2·71 + 8$
12. $0·03 + 11 + 8·74$

13. $29·6 - 14$
14. $59·2 - 34·8$
15. $81·8 - 29·9$
16. $8 - 2·7$
17. $6·7 - 4·29$
18. $47·2 - 27·42$
19. $94·63 - 5·9$
20. $2·97 - 1·414$
21. $25·52 - 1·436$
22. $3·142 - 1·414$
23. $2·718 - 1·732$
24. $12 - 3·74$

25. Find the missing digits

(a)
$$\begin{array}{r} \boxed{}·5\,\boxed{} \\ -\ 4·\boxed{}\,3 \\ \hline 3·7\,3 \\ \hline \end{array}$$

(b)
$$\begin{array}{r} 4·\boxed{}\,7 \\ +\ \boxed{}·9\,\boxed{} \\ \hline 9·0\,3 \\ \hline \end{array}$$

(c)
$$\begin{array}{r} 3·1\,7\,\boxed{} \\ -\ \boxed{}·4\,\boxed{}\,8 \\ \hline 0·\boxed{}\,4\,8 \\ \hline \end{array}$$

26. David has £3·20 and wants to buy articles costing £1·10, 66 p, £1·99 and 45 p. How much more money does he need?

27. Which six different coins make £1·78?

28. Jane went to a shop and bought a book for £2·95 and a compact disc for £10·95. She paid with a £50 note. What change did she receive?

1.6 Rounding off

Here are cuttings from two newspapers:

A. '1074 bus shelters were vandalised last
   year at a total cost of £517,638.'

B. '1000 bus shelters were vandalised at a
   cost of over £500,000.'

In B the figures have been *rounded off* because the reporter thinks
that his readers will not be interested in the exact numbers in the
report.

Rules for rounding

- Rounding to the nearest whole number.

  If the first digit after the decimal point
  is *5 or more* round *up*.
  Otherwise round down.

  $$57\cdot3 \rightarrow 57$$
  $$89\cdot8 \rightarrow 90$$
  $$5\cdot5 \rightarrow 6$$

- Rounding to the nearest 100.

  If the digit in the tens column
  is 5 or more round up.
  Otherwise round down.

  $$593 \rightarrow 600$$
  $$247 \rightarrow 200$$
  $$2643 \rightarrow 2600$$

- Rounding to the nearest 10.

  If the digit in the units column
  is 5 or more round up.
  Otherwise round down.

  $$27 \rightarrow 30$$
  $$42 \rightarrow 40$$
  $$265 \rightarrow 270$$

- Rounding to the nearest 1000.

  If the digit in the hundreds column
  is 5 or more round up.
  Otherwise round down.

  $$1394 \rightarrow 1000$$
  $$502 \rightarrow 1000$$
  $$11\,764 \rightarrow 12\,000$$

Exercise 1

1. Round off these numbers to the nearest 10.
   (a) 73   (b) 58   (c) 24   (d) 99
   (e) 56   (f) 127   (g) 242   (h) 18
   (i) 29   (j) 589   (k) 37   (l) 51

2. Round off these numbers to the nearest 100.
   (a) 584   (b) 293   (c) 607   (d) 914
   (e) 285   (f) 655   (g) 222   (h) 1486

3. Round off these numbers to the nearest 1000.
   (a) 4555   (b) 757   (c) 850   (d) 2251
   (e) 614   (f) 2874   (g) 25712   (h) 13568

4. Work out these answers on a calculator and then round off the
    answer to the *nearest whole number*.
    (a) 235 ÷ 17   (b) 4714 ÷ 58   (c) 2375 ÷ 11   (d) 999 ÷ 17
    (e) 5·62 × 7·04   (f) 19·3 × 1·19   (g) 53·2 × 2·3   (h) 12·6 × 0·93
    (i) 119·6 ÷ 5·1   (j) 109 ÷ 0·7   (k) 63·4 ÷ 11   (l) 1·92 ÷ 0·09

Decimal places

- Using a calculator to work out 25 ÷ 9, the
  answer is 2·777777.
  On a number line we can see that the answer
  is nearer to 2·8 than to 2·7. We will *round off*
  the answer to 2·8 correct to 1 *decimal place*.

  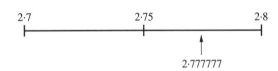

- Using a calculator to work out 11% of 21·23,
  the answer is 2·3353.
  On a number line we can see that the answer
  is nearer to 2·3 than to 2·4. So the answer is
  2·3, correct to 1 decimal place (1 d.p. for
  short).

- Suppose the calculator shows 1·75. This number is exactly half
  way between 1·7 and 1·8. Do we round up or not?
  The rule for rounding off to 1 decimal place is:

  > If the figure in the 2nd decimal place is 5 or more, round
  > up. Otherwise do not.

  Examples: 3·7538 = 3·8 to 1 d.p.
                   ↑
              14·287 = 14·3 to 1 d.p.
                 ↑
              17·9582 = 18·0 to 1 d.p. (We need the zero!)
                 ↑

  > Rounding off to 2 decimal places: If the figure in the 3rd decimal
  > place is 5 or more, round up. Otherwise do not round up.

  Examples: 15·6251   = 15·63 to 2 d.p.
                   ↑
              0·7936   = 0·79 to 2 d.p.
                 ↑

Exercise 2

1. Round these numbers to 1 decimal place.
   (a) 2·41   (b) 8·94   (c) 4·65   (d) 12·47

2. Round these numbers to 2 decimal places.
   (a) 1·924   (b) 4·065   (c) 9·997   (d) 65·374

3. Write the following numbers correct to 1 decimal place.
   (a) 18·7864   (b) 3·55   (c) 17·0946   (d) 0·7624
   (e) 5·421   (f) 11·27   (g) 10·252   (h) 7·084

4. Write the following numbers correct to 2 decimal places.
   (a) 3·75821   (b) 11·64412   (c) 0·38214   (d) 138·2972
   (e) 11·444   (f) 7·058   (g) 6·5781   (h) 5·3092

5. Write the following numbers correct to the number of decimal
   places indicated.
   (a) 8·4165 (3 d.p.)   (b) 0·7446 (2 d.p.)   (c) 18·2149 (3 d.p.)
   (d) 18·0612 (1 d.p.)   (e) 0·07451 (3 d.p.)   (f) 0·0312 (2 d.p.)
   (g) 1·355 (2 d.p.)   (h) 9·974 (1 d.p.)   (i) 0·45555 (3 d.p.)

6. Work out the following on a calculator and write the answer
   correct to 2 decimal places.
   (a) 11 ÷ 7   (b) 213 ÷ 11   (c) 1·4 ÷ 6   (d) 29 ÷ 13
   (e) 1·3 × 0·95   (f) 1·23 × 3·71   (g) 97 ÷ 1·3   (h) 0·95 × 8·3

7. Measure the lines below and give the lengths in cm correct to one decimal place.

   (a) ——————————————————————————————

   (b) ——————————

   (c) ————————————————————————————————————

   (d) ——————————————————————

   (e) ——

8. Measure the dimensions of the rectangles below.
   (a) Write down the length and width in cm, correct to one
       decimal place.
   (b) Work out the area of each rectangle and give the answer in
       cm², correct to one decimal place.

   (i)   (ii)

Calculating with estimates, checking results

- Hazim worked out 38.2×10.78 and wrote down 41.1796. He can check his answer by working with estimates.
  Instead of 38.2 use 40, instead of 10.78 use 10.

  So $40 \times 10 = 400$.

  Clearly Hazim's answer is wrong. He put the decimal point in the wrong place.

- Here are three more calculations with estimates.

  (a) 27.2×51.7 (b) $78.9 \div 1.923$ (c) 12% of £411.55
  $\approx 30 \times 50$ $\approx 80 \div 2$ $\approx$ 10% of £400
  ≈ 1500 ≈ 40 $\approx$ £40

Exercise 3

Do not use a calculator. Decide, by estimating, which of the three answers is closest to the exact answer. Write the calculation and the approximate answer for each question (use $\approx$).

	Calculation	A	B	C
1.	102.6×9.7	90	500	1000
2.	7.14×11.21	30	70	300
3.	1.07×59.2	6	60	200
4.	2.21×97.8	200	90	20
5.	8.95×42.1	200	400	4000
6.	4.87×6.18	15	10	30
7.	789×12.3	8000	4000	800
8.	978×9.83	1 million	100 000	10 000
9.	1.11×28.7	20	30	60
10.	9.8×82463	8 million	1 million	800 000
11.	$307.4 \div 1.97$	50	100	150
12.	$81.2 \div 0.99$	8	0.8	80
13.	$6121 \div 102.4$	60	300	600
14.	$59.71 \div 3.14$	10	20	180
15.	$1072 \div 987.2$	0.2	1	10
16.	$614 - 297.4$	300	100	3000
17.	$0.104 + 0.511$	0.06	0.1	0.6
18.	$8216.1 + 1.44$	800	4000	8000
19.	51% of £8018.95	£40	£400	£4000
20.	9% of £205.49	£10	£20	£200

21. A new band's first demo tape was sold at £2·95 per copy. Estimate the total cost of 47 copies.

22. David has to pay £208·50 per month for 2 years towards the cost of his car. Estimate the total cost of his payments.

23. Two hundred and six people share the cost of hiring a train. Roughly how much does each person pay if the total cost was £61 990?

In Questions **24** and **25** there are six calculations and six answers. Write down each calculation and insert the correct answer from the list given. Use estimation.

24. (a) $6·9 \times 7·1$ (b) $9·8 \div 5$ (c) $21 \times 10·2$
    (d) $0·13 + 15·2$ (e) $3114 \div 30$ (f) $4.03 \times 1·9$

Answers: 1·96, 15·33, 48·99, 103·8, 7·657, 214·2.

25. (a) $103·2 \div 5$ (b) $7·2 \times 7·3$ (c) $4·1 \times 49$
    (d) $3·57 \div 3$ (e) $36·52 \div 4$ (f) $1·4 \div 10$

Answers: 52·56, 1·19, 9·13, 200·9, 20·64, 0·14.

1.7 Area and perimeter

We use area to describe how much *surface* a shape has.

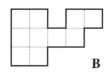

B contains 10 squares.
B has an area of 10 squares.

C has an area of $12\frac{1}{2}$ squares.
D has an area of 12 squares.

Rectangles

A 2 cm by 3 cm rectangle may be split into 6 squares as shown.

The area of each square is one square centimetre (1 cm^2), so the area of the rectangle is 6 cm^2.

This result can be obtained by multiplying the *length* by the *width*.

Area of rectangle $= (3 \times 2) \text{ cm}^2$
$= 6 \text{ cm}^2$

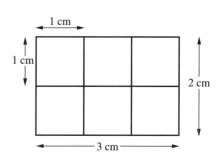

Exercise 1

Calculate the total area of each shape. The lengths are in cm.

1.

2.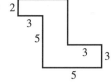

3.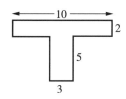

4.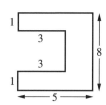

5.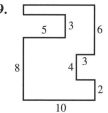

6.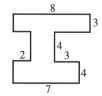

7.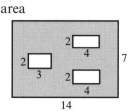

8.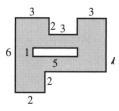

9.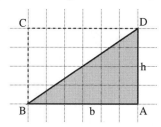

10.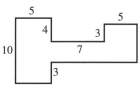

11. Find the shaded area

12.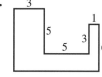

Triangles

(a) This triangle has base *b*, height *h* and a right angle at A.

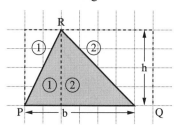

Area of rectangle ABCD = $b \times h$
By symmetry,
area of triangle ABD = area of triangle CDB.

$\therefore$ Area of triangle ABD = $\dfrac{b \times h}{2}$

(b) Here triangle PQR is drawn inside a rectangle.

Area of triangle PQR = area ① + area ②
Area of rectangle = (2 × area ①) + (2 × area ②)

$\therefore$ Area of triangle PQR = $\dfrac{b \times h}{2}$

Notice that this is the same formula as above.

Exercise 2

Find the area of each shape. In questions **1** to **8** give the answer in
square units.

1.   **2.** 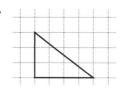   **3.** 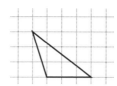   **4.**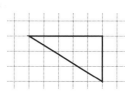

5.   **6.** 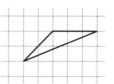   **7.**   **8.**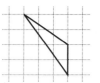

In questions **9** to **15** the lengths are in cm.

9. 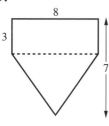   **10.** 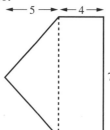   **11.** 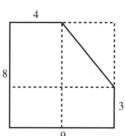   **12.**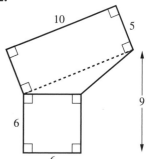

13.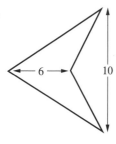

14. Find the shaded area.

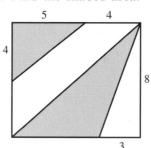

15. Find the shaded area.

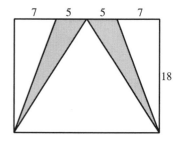

In Questions **16** to **23** the area is written inside the shape. Calculate
the length of the side marked x.

16.   **17.** 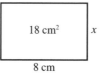   **18.**   **19.**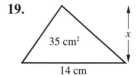

20.

21.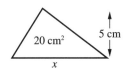

22.

23.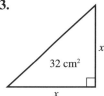

Irregular shapes

It is not easy to find the exact area of the triangle shown because we do not know either the length of the base or the height.

We could measure both lengths but this would introduce a small error due to the inevitable inaccuracy of the measuring.

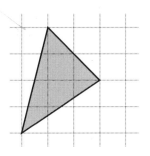

- A good method is to start by drawing a rectangle around the triangle. The corners of the triangle lie either on the sides of the rectangle or at a corner of the rectangle.

  Calculate the area of the rectangle.
  In this example: Area of rectangle $= 3 \times 4$
  $= 12$ square units.

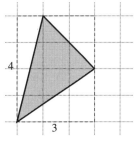

- Now find the areas of the three triangles marked A, B and C. This is easy because the triangles each have a right angle.
  Use the symbol '$\triangle$A' to mean 'triangle A'

  Area of $\triangle A = \dfrac{4 \times 1}{2} = 2$ square units

  Area of $\triangle B = \dfrac{2 \times 2}{2} = 2$ square units

  Area of $\triangle C = \dfrac{3 \times 2}{2} = 3$ square units

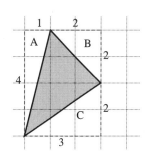

  Now we can find the area of the required triangle by subtracting the areas of $\triangle A$, $\triangle B$ and $\triangle C$ from the area of the rectangle.

  Area of shaded triangle $= 12 - [2 + 2 + 3]$
  $= 5$ square units.

Exercise 3

Find the area of each shape.

1.

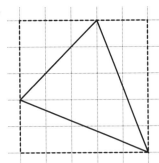

2.

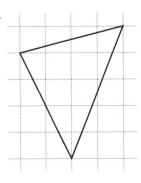

3.

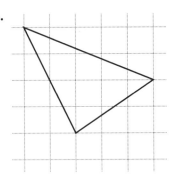

4.

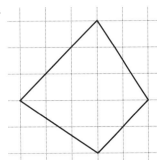

5.

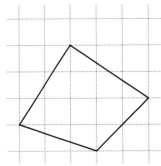

6.

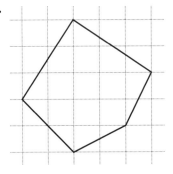

For Questions **7** to **13** draw axes with *x* and *y* from 0 to 10.
Plot the points given, join them up in order

7. (1, 7), (3, 2), (7, 6).

8. (4, 2), (6, 8), (1, 3).

9. (1, 2), (3, 6), (7, 5), (5, 3).

10. (3, 1), (8, 3), (5, 6), (1, 4)

11. (2, 0), (7, 1), (8, 4), (5, 5), (1, 3)

12. (3, 1), (6, 0), (9, 2), (7, 5), (3, 6), (1, 4)

13. (2, 3), (5, 1), (11, 5), (9, 7), (5, 8), (2, 8), (0, 6), (2, 3).

14. A triangle and a square are drawn on dotty paper with dots 1 cm apart. What is the area of the shaded region?

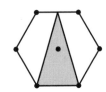

15. A triangle is drawn inside a regular hexagon. What is the area of the triangle as a fraction of the area of the hexagon?

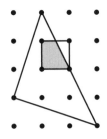

Perimeter

The perimeter of a shape is the distance around its outline.

(a) The perimeter of this rectangle
     is $4 + 10 + 4 + 10 = 28$ cm

(b) The perimeter of this triangle
     is $7 + 5 + 9 = 21$ cm.

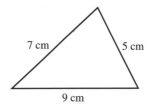

Exercise 4

1. Measure the sides of these shapes and work out the perimeter of
each one.

(a)

(b)

(c)

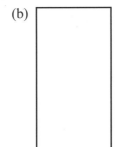

2. Find the perimeter of these pictures.

(a)

(b)

(c)

3. Find the perimeters of these shapes

    (a) rectangle 7·5 cm by 4 cm

    (b) square of side 6 cm

    (c) equilateral triangle of side 7 cm

    (d) rectangle 3·5 cm by 2·5 cm

    (e) square of side 20 m

    (f) regular hexagon of side 5 cm

The shapes in Questions **4** to **11** consist of rectangles joined together.
Find the missing lengths and then work out the perimeter of each
shape. The lengths are in cm.

4.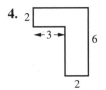

5.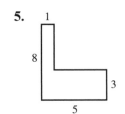

6.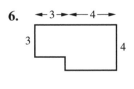

7.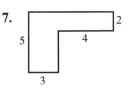

8.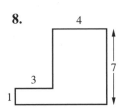

9.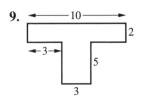

10.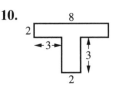

11.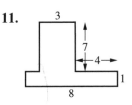

Questions **12** onwards are about perimeter *and* area.

12. Here are four shapes made with centimetre squares.

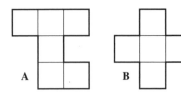 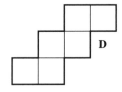 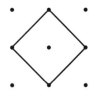

A   B   C   D

(a) Which shape has an area of $5\,\text{cm}^2$?
(b) Which two shapes have the same perimeter?

13. Each of the shapes here has an
area of $2\,\text{cm}^2$.
(a) On square dotty paper draw three
more shapes with area $2\,\text{cm}^2$
(b) Draw three shapes with area $3\,\text{cm}^2$.
(c) Draw one shape with area $4\,\text{cm}^2$
and perimeter $10\,\text{cm}$.

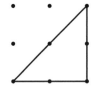

14. A picture frame has its length
twice its height.
The total length of wood
used in the frame is $132\,\text{cm}$.
Work out the length
of the frame.

height

length

15. Here are five shapes made from equilateral triangles of side 1 cm.

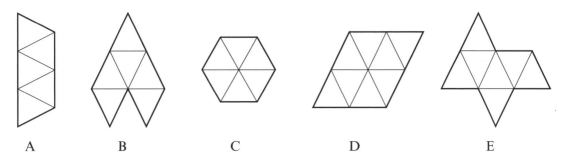

| A | B | C | D | E |

(a) Which shape has the longest perimeter?
(b) Which shape has the smallest area?
(c) Which shape has the same perimeter as D?

16. The perimeter of a rectangular lawn is 40 m. The shortest side is 7 m. How long is the longest side?

17.* The diagram shows the areas of 3 faces of a rectangular box. What are the measurements of the box?

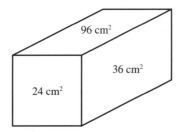

Area and perimeter: an investigation

A • Draw *four* different rectangles which all have a *perimeter* of 24 cm.

B • Draw *three* different rectangles which all have an *area* of 24 cm².

C • Draw at least four rectangles which have a perimeter of 20 cm.
  • Work out the area of each rectangle.
  • Which of your rectangles has the largest area?

D • The perimeter of a new rectangle is 32 cm.
  • Try to *predict* what the sides will be for the rectangle with the largest possible area.
  • Now check to see if your prediction was correct.

E* • Explain why you cannot find a rectangle with perimeter 32 cm which has the *smallest* possible area. [Neither length nor width can be zero.]

Area problems

Exercise 5

1. The diagram shows a picture 10 cm by 6 cm
   surrounded by a border 4 cm wide.
   What is the area of the border?

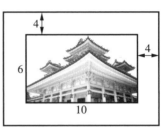

2. A floor measuring 4 m by 5 m is to be covered by square tiles
   measuring 50 cm by 50 cm. How many tiles are needed?

3. How many panes of glass 30 cm by 20 cm can be cut from a sheet
   which is 1 metre square?

4. Find the shaded area. All the lengths are in cm.

(a)

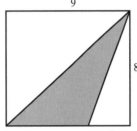

(b)

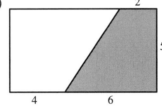

5. A rectangular field measures 500 m by 1 km. Find the area of the
   field in hectares. $\left(1 \text{ hectare} = 10\,000 \text{ m}^2\right)$

6. A rectangular field 300 m long has an area of 6 hectares.
   Calculate the width of the field.

7. Farmland is sold at £2500 per hectare. How much would you
   pay for a rectangular piece of farmland measuring 300 m by
   400 m?

8. A line starts at A and goes along
   the dotted lines to B. It divides the
   area of the rectangle into two
   halves.
   (a) Draw a rectangle like the one
   here and draw a line from C
   to D which divides the area of
   the rectangle into two halves.
   (b) Draw a second rectangle and
   draw a line from C to D which
   divides the area of the
   rectangle into two parts so
   that one part has *twice* the
   area of the other part.

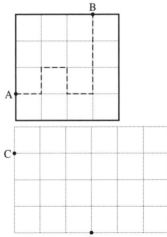

9. A flag has a sloping strip drawn across. Calculate the area of the shaded strip.

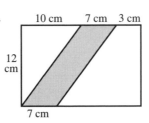

10. A rectangle has a perimeter of 28 m and a length of 6·5 m. What is its area?

11. The field shown is sold at auction for £55 250. Calculate the price *per acre* which was paid.
[1 acre = 4840 square yards]

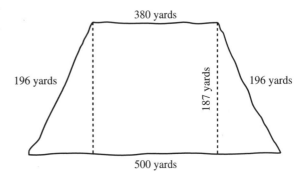

12. A groundsman has enough grass seed to cover three hectares. [1 hectare = $10\,000\,\text{m}^2$]. A tennis court measures 15 m by 40 m. How many courts can he cover with seed?

13. A rectangular field 350 m long has an area of 7 hectares. Calculate the perimeter of the field.

14. A waterproofing spray is applied to the outside of the 4 walls, including the door, and the roof of the garage shown.
(a) Calculate the total area to be sprayed.
(b) The spray comes in cans costing £1·95 and each can is enough to cover $4\,\text{m}^2$. How much will it cost to spray this garage? [Assume you have to buy full cans].

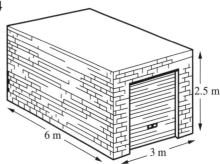

15.

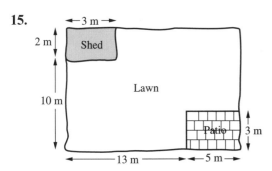

A gardener is using moss killer on his lawn. The instructions say that 4 measures of the mosskiller, in water, will treat $10\,\text{m}^2$ of lawn. The box contains 250 measures and costs £12·50.
Find the area of the lawn and hence the cost of the moss killer required.

Part 2

2.1 Fractions

Equivalent fractions

- In the diagram, $\frac{3}{6}$ of the shape is shaded. If you look at it a different way you can see that $\frac{1}{2}$ of the shape is shaded.

  The two fractions $\frac{3}{6}$ and $\frac{1}{2}$ are the same.

  We say they are equivalent.

  We normally use the simpler fraction which in this case is $\frac{1}{2}$.

- In this diagram, $\frac{4}{12}$ of the shape is shaded.

  A simpler fraction, which is the same as $\frac{4}{12}$, is $\frac{1}{3}$.

  You can *cancel* $\frac{4}{12}$ by dividing 4 and 12 by 4.

  So $\dfrac{\cancel{4}^{\,1}}{\cancel{12}_{\,3}} = \dfrac{1}{3}$.

Exercise 1

In Questions **1** to **9** write down the fraction shaded. If possible write the fraction in a simpler form.

1.

2.

3.

4.

5.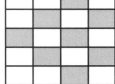

6.

7.   **8.**   **9.**

In Questions **10** to **25** fill in the missing numbers

10. $\dfrac{4}{8} = \dfrac{\square}{2}$ **11.** $\dfrac{6}{8} = \dfrac{\square}{4}$ **12.** $\dfrac{8}{12} = \dfrac{\square}{3}$ **13.** $\dfrac{2}{10} = \dfrac{\square}{5}$

14. $\dfrac{9}{12} = \dfrac{3}{\square}$ **15.** $\dfrac{15}{30} = \dfrac{1}{\square}$ **16.** $\dfrac{3}{9} = \dfrac{1}{\square}$ **17.** $\dfrac{9}{15} = \dfrac{\square}{5}$

19. $\dfrac{3}{7} = \dfrac{\square}{14}$ **20.** $\dfrac{3}{5} = \dfrac{\square}{10}$ **21.** $\dfrac{1}{4} = \dfrac{\square}{8}$ **22.** $\dfrac{3}{10} = \dfrac{\square}{30}$

23. $\dfrac{9}{24} = \dfrac{\square}{8}$ **24.** $\dfrac{5}{7} = \dfrac{25}{\square}$ **25.** $\dfrac{16}{24} = \dfrac{2}{\square}$

In Questions **26** to **33** find the odd one out.

26. (a) 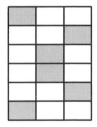   (b)   (c)

27. (a) 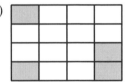   (b)   (c)

28. $\dfrac{2}{3}, \dfrac{4}{9}, \dfrac{4}{6}$ **29.** $\dfrac{1}{5}, \dfrac{3}{15}, \dfrac{3}{10}$ **30.** $\dfrac{3}{4}, \dfrac{8}{12}, \dfrac{6}{9}$

31. $\dfrac{2}{5}, \dfrac{6}{15}, \dfrac{4}{10}$ **32.** $\dfrac{5}{8}, \dfrac{6}{10}, \dfrac{12}{20}$ **33.** $\dfrac{3}{8}, \dfrac{5}{12}, \dfrac{6}{16}$

Proper and improper fractions

- A *proper* fraction is one in which the *numerator* (top number) is less than the *denominator* (bottom number).

  The fractions $\frac{1}{2}, \frac{2}{3}, \frac{3}{4}$ and $\frac{99}{100}$ are all examples of *proper* fractions.

- An *improper* fraction is one in which the *numerator* is larger than the *denominator*. They are sometimes called 'top-heavy' fractions.

  The fractions $\frac{3}{2}, \frac{4}{3}, \frac{8}{5}$ and $\frac{100}{33}$ are all examples of *improper* fractions.

- A *mixed number* is one which contains both a whole number and a fraction. *Improper* fractions can be changed into *mixed numbers* and vice versa.

 $3\frac{1}{2} = \frac{7}{2}$

 $\frac{16}{3} = 5\frac{1}{3}$

Exercise 2

Change the following improper fractions to mixed numbers or whole numbers where applicable.

1. $\frac{7}{2}$ **2.** $\frac{5}{3}$ **3.** $\frac{7}{3}$ **4.** $\frac{5}{4}$ **5.** $\frac{8}{3}$

6. $\frac{8}{6}$ **7.** $\frac{9}{3}$ **8.** $\frac{9}{2}$ **9.** $\frac{9}{4}$ **10.** $\frac{10}{2}$

11. $\frac{10}{6}$ **12.** $\frac{10}{7}$ **13.** $\frac{13}{8}$ **14.** $\frac{35}{15}$ **15.** $\frac{42}{21}$

16. $\frac{120}{10}$ **17.** $\frac{22}{7}$ **18.** $\frac{15}{9}$ **19.** $\frac{12}{5}$ **20.** $\frac{150}{100}$

In Questions **21** to **35** change the mixed numbers to improper fractions.

21. $1\frac{1}{4}$ **22.** $1\frac{1}{3}$ **23.** $2\frac{1}{4}$ **24.** $2\frac{2}{3}$ **25.** $1\frac{7}{8}$

26. $1\frac{2}{3}$ **27.** $3\frac{1}{7}$ **28.** $2\frac{1}{6}$ **29.** $4\frac{3}{4}$ **30.** $7\frac{1}{2}$

31. $3\frac{5}{8}$ **32.** $4\frac{2}{5}$ **33.** $3\frac{2}{5}$ **34.** $8\frac{1}{4}$ **35.** $1\frac{3}{10}$

Fraction of a number

- The dungeon of a castle contained 135 prisoners of whom $\frac{4}{5}$ were innocent of any crime.
  How many innocent prisoners were there?

- We need to work out $\frac{4}{5}$ of 135.
  $$\frac{1}{5} \text{ of } 135 = 135 \div 5$$
  $$= 27$$
  $$\text{So } \frac{4}{5} \text{ of } 135 = 27 \times 4$$
  $$= 108$$

  There were 108 innocent prisoners in the dungeon.

- Note that $\frac{2}{5}$ of 15, $\frac{2}{5} \times 15$ and $15 \times \frac{2}{5}$ are all the same calculation.

Exercise 3

Work out

1. $\frac{2}{5}$ of 100   **2.** $\frac{3}{4}$ of 40   **3.** $\frac{2}{3}$ of 15

4. $\frac{5}{6}$ of 24   **5.** $\frac{3}{5}$ of 260   **6.** $\frac{3}{4}$ of 92

7. $\frac{5}{8}$ of £496   **8.** $\frac{2}{7}$ of £3500   **9.** $\frac{4}{5}$ of 80 kg

10. $\frac{3}{5} \times 60$ **11.** $36 \times \frac{2}{9}$ **12.** $60 \times \frac{7}{20}$

13. Paul's new jeans are 96 cm long when they leave the shop. After washing they shrink to $\frac{11}{12}$ of their previous length.
  What is the new length of the jeans?

14. What fraction of £1 is 27 p?
What fraction of 1 m is 97 cm?
What fraction of 1 kg is 250 g?
What fraction of 1 km is 1 m?
What fraction of one year is one day?
What fraction of one year is December?

15. Richard has a packet of 32 Polos.
For some unknown reason Richard gives $\frac{3}{8}$
of his Polos to his sister Jane.
Generous Jane then gives $\frac{1}{4}$ of her share to
a friend and eats the rest.
Richard meanwhile eats $\frac{2}{5}$ of his remaining
Polos.
(a) How many Polos does Richard have
left at the end?
(b) How many Polos does Jane eat?

16. The petrol tank of a car holds 60 litres. How much *more* petrol
can be put into the tank when it is $\frac{5}{8}$ full?

17. A 'super bouncy' ball rises to $\frac{7}{10}$ of its previous height on each
bounce. One of these balls is dropped from a height of 4 m.
(a) How high will it rise after one bounce?
(b) How high will it rise after the second bounce?

18. Draw a 4 × 5 rectangle.
Use different colours to show
$\frac{1}{2}$, $\frac{1}{4}$, $\frac{1}{5}$ and $\frac{1}{20}$ of the whole rectangle.
Parts must not overlap.

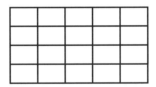

19. Draw a 3 × 4 rectangle. Divide it into four parts using four
different fractions, each with numerator 1.

20. Draw a 5 × 6 rectangle. Divide it into three parts using three
different fractions, each with numerator 1.

Adding and taking away

- Fractions can be added when they have the same denominator (bottom number).

- Here are some easy ones.

$\frac{1}{5} + \frac{2}{5} = \frac{3}{5}$, $\frac{2}{7} + \frac{3}{7} = \frac{5}{7}$, $\frac{1}{10} + \frac{5}{10} = \frac{6}{10}$

- In these questions one of the fractions has to be changed to an equivalent fraction

(a) $\frac{1}{2} + \frac{1}{4}$

$\quad = \frac{2}{4} + \frac{1}{4}$

$\quad = \frac{3}{4}$

(b) $\frac{1}{6} + \frac{1}{3}$

$\quad = \frac{1}{6} + \frac{2}{6}$

$\quad = \frac{3}{6}$

(c) $\frac{5}{8} - \frac{1}{4}$

$\quad = \frac{5}{8} - \frac{2}{8}$

$\quad = \frac{3}{8}$

Exercise 4

Work out

1. $\frac{1}{5} + \frac{2}{5}$
2. $\frac{2}{7} + \frac{1}{7}$
3. $\frac{1}{6} + \frac{4}{6}$
4. $\frac{1}{8} + \frac{3}{8}$

5. $\frac{2}{9} + \frac{3}{9}$
6. $\frac{3}{10} + \frac{4}{10}$
7. $\frac{3}{11} + \frac{2}{11}$
8. $\frac{1}{25} + \frac{2}{25}$

In Questions **9** to **24** change one of the fractions to an equivalent fraction. [e.g. $\frac{1}{2} = \frac{2}{4}$]

9. $\frac{1}{4} + \frac{1}{2}$
10. $\frac{1}{8} + \frac{1}{4}$
11. $\frac{3}{8} + \frac{1}{2}$
12. $\frac{1}{16} + \frac{1}{2}$

13. $\frac{3}{4} - \frac{1}{2}$
14. $\frac{5}{8} - \frac{1}{4}$
15. $\frac{1}{4} - \frac{1}{8}$
16. $\frac{5}{8} - \frac{1}{2}$

17. $\frac{1}{6} + \frac{2}{3}$
18. $\frac{4}{5} + \frac{1}{10}$
19. $\frac{2}{5} + \frac{3}{10}$
20. $\frac{1}{6} + \frac{1}{3}$

21. $\frac{7}{8} - \frac{1}{2}$
22. $\frac{2}{3} - \frac{1}{6}$
23. $\frac{1}{10} - \frac{1}{20}$
24. $\frac{3}{4} - \frac{3}{8}$

25. (a) 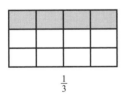 $\frac{1}{3}$ $+$ 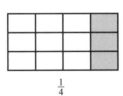 $\frac{1}{4}$ $=$ 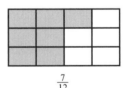 $\frac{7}{12}$

(b) Draw similar diagrams to show that $\frac{2}{3} + \frac{1}{4} = \frac{11}{12}$.

26. The fraction sum $\frac{1}{3} + \frac{4}{6}$ is made from four different digits and the sum is 1.

Find other fraction sums using four different digits so that the sum is 1.

2.2 Coordinates

- To get to the point P on this grid we go **across** 1 and **up** 3 from the bottom corner.
  The position of P is (1, 3).
  The numbers 1 and 3 are called the **coordinates** of P.
  The coordinates of Q are (4, 2).
  The *origin* is at (0, 0).

  We call the first coordinate the *x*-coordinate and the second coordinate the *y*-coordinate.

- The *across* coordinate is always *first* and the *up* coordinate is *second*.
  Remember: 'Along the corridor and up the stairs'.

- Notice also that the *lines* are numbered, *not* the squares.

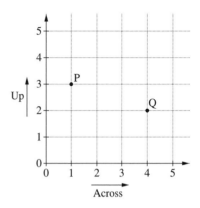

Exercise 1

1. Write down the coordinates of all the points marked like this: A(5, 1) B(1,4)

   Don't forget the brackets.

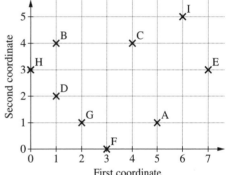

2. The map below shows a remote Scottish island used for training by the S.A.S.

   Write down the coordinates of the following places:
   (a) Rocket launcher
   (b) H.Q.
   (c) Hospital A
   (d) Rifle range
   (e) Officers' mess
   (f) Radar control

3. Make a list of the places which are at the following points:
   (a) (2, 8)   (b) (7, 8)   (c) (3, 3)
   (d) (6, 4)   (e) (2, 6)   (f) (6, 2)
   (g) (2, 4)   (h) (9, 1)

4. Make up your own map and mark points of interest.

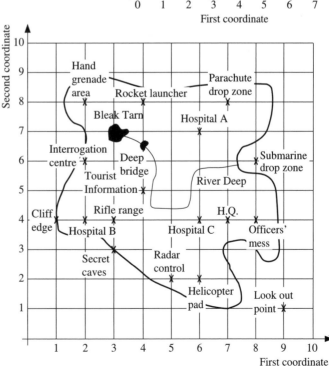

Negative coordinates

The x axis can be extended to the left and the y axis can be extended downwards to include the negative numbers -1, -2, -3 etc.

The name 'FALDO' can be found using the letters in the following order:
$(2, 3)$, $(-2, -1)$, $(-1, 2)$, $(2, -2)$, $(-2, -3)$.

Similarly the coordinates of the points which spell out the word 'LOAD' are $(-1, 2)$, $(-2, -3)$, $(-2, -1)$, $(2, -2)$

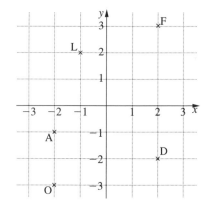

Exercise 2

The letters from A to Z are shown on the grid.
Coded messages can be sent using coordinates.

For example $(-4, -2)$ $(-4, 2)$ $(-4, 2)$ $(4, 2)$ reads 'FOOD'.

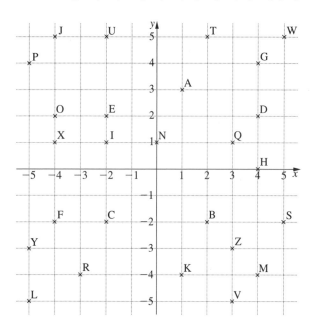

Decipher the following messages

1. $(5, 5)$ $(4, 0)$ $(1, 3)$ $(2, 5)$ # $(4, 2)$ $(-4, 2)$ # $(-5, -3)$
$(-4, 2)$ $(-2, 5)$ # $(-2, -2)$ $(1, 3)$ $(-5, -5)$ $(-5, -5)$ #
$(1, 3)$ # $(4, -4)$ $(1, 3)$ $(0, 1)$ # $(5, 5)$ $(-2, 1)$ $(2, 5)$ $(4, 0)$ #
$(1, 3)$ # $(5, -2)$ $(-5, 4)$ $(1, 3)$ $(4, 2)$ $(-2, 2)$ # $(-2, 1)$
$(0, 1)$ # $(4, 0)$ $(-2, 1)$ $(5, -2)$ # $(4, 0)$ $(-2, 2)$ $(1, 3)$
$(4, 2)$? # $(4, 2)$ $(-4, 2)$ $(-2, 5)$ $(4, 4)$!

2. Change the seventh word to: (5, 5) (−2, 1) (2, 5) (4, 0)
    (−4, 2) (−2, 5) (2, 5).
    Change the last word to: (4, 2) (−4, 2) (−2, 5) (4, 4)
    (−5, −5) (1, 3) (5, −2).

3. (5, 5) (4, 0) (1, 3) (2, 5) # (4, 2) (−4, 2) # (−5, −3)
    (−4, 2) (−2, 5) # (−2, −2) (1, 3) (−5, −5) (−5, −5) #
    (1, 3) # (4, 2) (−2, 2) (1, 3) (4, 2) # (−5, 4) (1, 3) (−3, −4)
    (−3, −4) (−4, 2) (2, 5) ? # (−5, 4) (−4, 2) (−5, −5) (−5, −3)
    (4, 4) (−4, 2) (0, 1) !

4. (5, 5) (−2, 1) (2, 5) (4, 0) # (5, 5) (4, 0) (1, 3) (2, 5) #
    (4, 2) (−4, 2) # (−5, −3) (−4, 2) (−2, 5) # (5, −2) (2, 5)
    (−2, 5) (−4, −2) (−4, −2) # (1, 3) # (4, 2) (−2, 2) (1, 3)
    (4, 2) # (−5, 4) (1, 3) (−3, −4) (−3, −4) (−4, 2)
    (2, 5) ? # (−5, 4) (−4, 2) (−5, −5) (−5, −3) (−4, −2) (−2, 1)
    (−5, −5) (−5, −5) (1, 3) !

Coordinate pictures

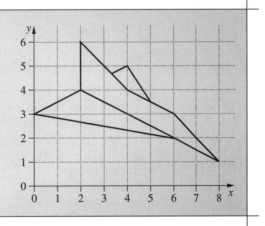

Plot the points below and join them up in order.
(a) (2, 4), (8, 1), (6, 3), (4, 4),
    (2, 6), (2, 4), (0, 3), (6, 2).
(b) (5, 3½), (4, 5), (3¼, 4⅔).

Exercise 3

Plot the points given and join them up in order. Write down what
you have drawn in each question.

1. Draw axes with values from 0 to 15.
    (8, 1), (10, 1), (11, 3), (11, 3½), (12, 4½), (12, 7),
    (14, 9), (14, 10), (13, 10), (11, 12), (10, 14),
    (10, 14½), (8, 14), (6½, 14½), (6½, 15), (4, 15),
    (3, 14), (1, 13), (1, 11), (2, 9), (3, 8½), (4, 9),
    (6, 9), (6, 8), (7, 6), (6½, 5), (7, 4), (8, 1).

2. Draw axes with values from 0 to 14.
    (a) (6, 13), (1, 3), (2, 1), (12, 1), (8, 9), (6, 5),
        (4, 5), (8, 13), (6, 13), (8, 13), (13, 3), (12, 1).
    (b) (1, 3), (9, 3), (7, 7), (6, 5), (8, 5)
    Colour in the shape.

3. Draw axes with values from 0 to 18.
  (a) (0, 3), (1, 4), (2, 6), (4, 8), (6, 8), (8, 9), (12, 9),
      (13, 11), (12, 12), (12, 14), (14, 12), (15, 12),
      (17, 14), (17, 12), (16, 11), (17, 10), (17, 9),
      (16, 9), (15, 8), (14, 9), (13, 9)
  (b) (16, 9), (16, 7), (14, 5), (14, 1), (15, 1), (15, 6),
      (13, 4), (13, 1), (12, 1), (12, 4), (11, 5), (9, 5),
      (9, 6$\frac{1}{2}$), (9, 4), (8, 3), (8, 1), (7, 1), (7, 4), (6, 6),
      (6, 4), (5, 3), (5, 1), (6, 1), (6, 3), (7, 4), (6, 6),
      (6, 7), (3, 2), (1, 2), (0, 3).

4. Draw axes with values from 0 to 10.
  (a) (3, 2), (4, 2), (5, 3), (3, 5), (3, 6), (2, 7), (1, 6),
      (1, 8), (2, 9), (3, 9), (5, 7), (4, 6), (4, 5), (6, 4),
      (8, 4), (8, 5), (6, 7), (5, 7).
  (b) (7, 4), (9, 2), (8, 1), (7, 3), (5, 3).
  (c) (1, 6), (2, 8), (2, 9), (2, 7).
  (d) Draw a dot at (3, 8).

In Questions **5** and **6** you will draw a picture and then alter it by
changing the coordinates according to different rules.

5. Draw axes with x from 0 to 18 and y from 0 to 9.
  (a) Plot the following points and join them up in order.
      (1, 2), (3, 3), (6, 3), (6, 2), (4, 1), (1, 1), (1, 2),
      (4, 2), (4, 1), (4, 2), (6, 3).
  (b) Multiply all the coordinates by 3, plot the new points and
      join them up to draw a new picture.
  (c) For each of the original points add 10 to the x coordinate
      and keep the same y coordinate.
      So, for example, (1, 2) becomes (11, 2) and (3, 3) becomes
      (13, 3). Plot the new points and join them up.
  (d) In parts (b) and (c) describe what has happened to the first
      picture.

6. Draw axes with both x and y from 0 to 12.
  (a) Plot the following points and join them up in order.
      (5, 11), (5, 10), (6, 8), (7, 9), (7, 10), (6, 12), (4, 12),
      (3, 11), (0, 10), (1, 9), (3, 9), (1, 9), (4, 8), (5, 7),
      (8, 8), (7, 9).
      Draw a dot at (3$\frac{1}{2}$, 10$\frac{1}{2}$).
  (b) Plot a new picture by swopping the x and y coordinates.
      So: instead of (5, 11) plot (11, 5);
           instead of (5, 10) plot (10, 5) and so on.

      Describe what has happened to the first picture.

Complete the shape

Two sides of a rectangle are drawn.

Find (a) the coordinates of the fourth vertex of the rectangle

(b) the coordinates of the centre of the rectangle.

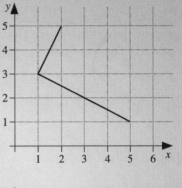

The complete rectangle is shown.
(a) Fourth vertex is at (6, 3)
(b) Centre of rectangle is at $(3\frac{1}{2}, 3)$

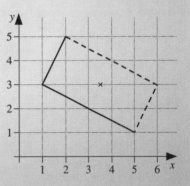

Exercise 4

1. The graph shows several incomplete quadrilaterals. Copy the diagram and complete the shapes.
   (a) Write down the coordinates of the fourth vertex of each shape.
   (b) Write down the coordinates of the centre of each shape.

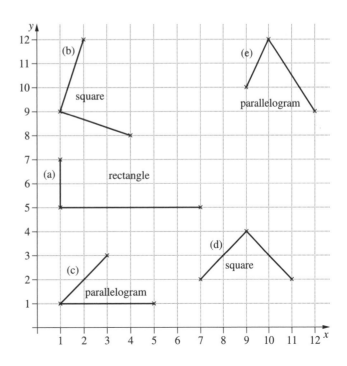

2. You are given the vertices but not the sides of two parallelograms P and Q.

For each parallelogram find *three* possible positions for the fourth vertex.

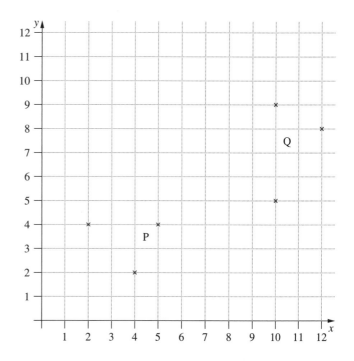

3.

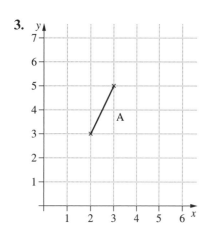

The crosses mark two vertices of an isosceles triangle A.

Find as many points as you can, with whole number coordinates, for the third vertex of the triangle.
[There are 12 possible points.]

4. The diagram shows one side of an isosceles triangle B.
   (a) Find *six* possible points, with whole number coordinates, for the third vertex of the triangle.
   (b) Explain how you could find the coordinates of several more positions for the third vertex.

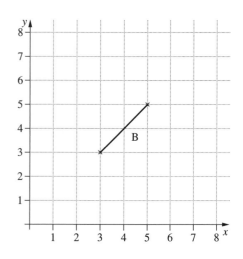

5. Copy the graph shown.
   (a) A, B and F are three corners of a square.
       Write down the coordinates of the other
       corner.
   (b) B, C and D are three corners of another
       square. Write down the coordinates of the
       other corner.
   (c) D, E and F are three corners of a
       rectangle. Write down the coordinates of
       the other corner.

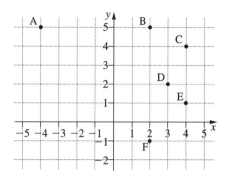

6. Draw a grid with values from −5 to 5. Plot the three points
   given and then find the coordinates of the point which makes a
   square when the points are joined up.
   (a) (−4, 0) (−1, 0) (−4, −3)
   (b) (2, −2) (5, 0) (0, 1)
   (c) (−5, 4) (−4, 1) (−1, 2)

7. A trapezium has one   A kite has two pairs
   pair of parallel sides.   of adjacent equal sides.

The graph shows three incomplete
shapes. Copy the diagram and
show two possible positions
for the fourth vertex of each
shape.
Write down the coordinates of
the points you find.

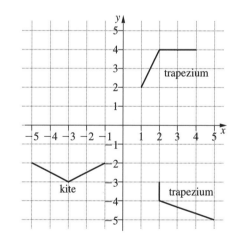

2.3 Rules of algebra

Using letters for numbers

Many problems in mathematics are easier to solve when letters are used instead of numbers. This is called using *algebra*.

It is important to remember that the *letters stand for numbers*.

- Here is a square with sides of length l cm
  The perimeter of the square in cm is $l + l + l + l$.
  If we use p cm to stand for the perimeter,
  we can write $\qquad p = l + l + l + l$
  or $\qquad\qquad\quad p = 4l \qquad$ (This means $4 \times l$)

- Suppose there are a number of people in a room. Call this number N. If one more person enters the room there will be $N + 1$ people in the room. $N + 1$ is an *expression*. An expression has no equals sign whereas an equation does have an equals sign.

- Suppose there are x cows in a field. After the farmer puts 3 more cows in the field there are $x + 3$ cows in the field.

$x + 3$ and $l - 5$ are *expressions*

- Suppose a piece of wood is l centimetres long.
  If you cut off 5 cm the length left is $l - 5$ cm.

- Suppose there are y people on a bus. At a bus stop n more people get on the bus. Now there are $y + n$ people on the bus.

- If I start with a number N and then double it, I will have $2N$. If I then add 7 I will have $2N + 7$.

- When you multiply, write the number before the letter. So write $2N$ *not* $N2$.

Exercise 1

In Questions **1** to **10** find the expression I am left with.

1. I start with M and then double it.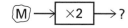

2. I start with N and then add 6.

3. I start with e and then take away 3.

4. I start with d and then add 10.

5. I start with N and then multiply by 3.

6. I start with x, double it and then add 3.

7. I start with y, double it and then and then take away 7.

8. I start with k, treble it and then add 10.

9. I start with s and multiply by 100.

10. I start with t, multiply it by 6 and then add 11.

11. (a) The perimeter p of the square is
$$p = x + x + x + x$$
or $\quad p = 4x$.

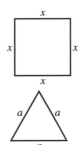

(b) Find the perimeter, p of this triangle. Write '$p = \ldots$'

In Questions **12** to **17** find the perimeter p of the shape.

12.

13.

14.

15.

16.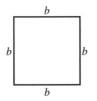

17.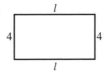

18. Draw and label a rectangle whose perimeter p is given by the formula $\quad p = 2t + 2m$.

19. Draw and label a triangle whose perimeter is given by the formula $\quad p = 2y + 7$.

20. Draw and label a pentagon (5 sides) whose perimeter p is given by the formula $\quad p = 2a + 3b$.

Exercise 2

In Questions **1** to **8** find what expression I am left with.

1. I start with x, add y and then take away 3.

2. I start with N, double it and then add T.

3. I start with p, add t and then take away x.

4. I start with b, treble it and then add c.

5. I start with M, divide it by 2 and then add 7.

6. I start with $3x$, take away z and then add 3.

7. I start with $5N$, double it and then add M.

8. I start with p, treble it and then take away $2x$.

9. A piece of string is $l$cm long. If I cut off a piece 4cm long, how much string remains?

10. A piece of rope is 25 m long. How much remains after I cut off a piece of length x m?

11. When a man buys a small tree it is h cm tall. During the year it grows a further t cm and then he cuts off 30 cm. How tall is it now?

12. A brick weighs w kg. How much do six bricks weigh?

13. A man shares a sum of N pence equally between four children. How much does each child receive?

14. On Monday there are n people in a cinema. On Friday there are three times as many people plus another 50. How many people are there in the cinema on Friday?

15. A prize of £x is shared equally between you and four others. How much does each person receive?

Simplifying expressions

The expression $5a + 2a$ can be *simplified* to $7a$. This is because $5a + 2a$ means five a's plus two a's, which is equivalent to seven a's.

(It can also be remembered as '5 *apples* + 2 *apples* = 7 *apples*'.)

Similarly, the expression $7c - 3c$ can be simplified to $4c$.

The expression $10x + x$ can be thought of as $10x + 1x$ which can be simplified to $11x$.

Similarly, $9a - a$ can be thought of as $9a - 1a$ which can be simplified to $8a$.

Notice that when we simplify an expression we are not finding its value when a is a particular number. We are just rewriting the expression in a simpler form.

Some expressions cannot be simplified.

The expression $7x + 2x$ consists of two *terms*, $7x$ and $2x$.

The expression $5x + 3y$ consists of two *terms*, $5x$ and $3y$.

   $7x$ and $2x$ are called *like* terms.
   $5x$ and $3y$ are called *unlike* terms.

An expression which is the sum or difference of two terms can only be simplified if the terms are *like* terms.

Exercise 3

Simplify as many of the following expressions as possible. This exercise could be done orally.

1. $7x - 2x$ **2.** $4a + 5a$ **3.** $3a + 2b$ **4.** $9y - 2y$

5. $5x + 4x$ **6.** $5c - 2d$ **7.** $4x + 3$ **8.** $9d + d$

9. $13y - y$ **10.** $6d - 4$ **11.** $6x + 3y$ **12.** $4h + 2h$

13. $7y - 5y$ **14.** $13x - 9x$ **15.** $7a + a$ **16.** $3a + b$

17. $4 - 2x$ **18.** $7d - 3d$ **19.** $10a - 4a$ **20.** $17t - 2t$

21. $19b + 3b$ **22.** $9c + 5c$ **23.** $5c - c$ **24.** $5c - 5$

25. $9a + a$ **26.** $9a + 9$ **27.** $11b - 11$ **28.** $11b - b$

Collecting like terms

- This pentagon has three sides of length a and two sides of length l. The perimeter of the shape is $a + a + a + l + l$. We can simplify this expression to $3a + 2l$.

  This is called *collecting like terms*.

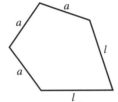

- We follow the conventions below when collecting like terms

  $4 + m + 3 + 3m = 4m + 7$ ← collect in alphabetical order, with letter terms before numbers

  $s + 4 + s + 2 + t = 2s + t + 6$ ←

  $4p - 4$ can not be simplified.

  $3x + y - 3x = y$ ← do not write 0_x do not write $1y$,

- The sign in *front* of the term is part of the term. If we change the order of terms the sign in *front* of each term *stays* with the term. We can emphasise this fact by drawing loops around each term to include the sign.

(a) Simplify $7x + 5y + 2x - 3y$

$$(7x)(+5y)(+2x)(-3y) = (7x)(+2x)(+5y)(-3y)$$ $\begin{bmatrix} \text{group together} \\ \text{like terms} \end{bmatrix}$

$$= 9x + 2y$$

$\begin{bmatrix} \text{no sign} \\ \text{means } + \end{bmatrix}$

(b) Simplify $5a - 2x - a + 2x$

$$(5a)(-2x)(-a)(+2x) = (5a)(-a)(-2x)(+2x)$$ $\begin{bmatrix} \text{group together} \\ \text{like terms} \end{bmatrix}$

$$= 4a$$

Exercise 4

Simplify the following expressions as far as possible by collecting like terms.

1. $7x + 3y + 2x + 5y$
2. $9x + 2y + 3x + y$
3. $5a + 6y - 2a - 4y$
4. $11t + 7 - t - 4$
5. $8y + 3 + y + 7$
6. $9x + 2b - 8x + 7b$
7. $6a + 10 - 2a - 2$
8. $6h - 2y + 3h + 9y$
9. $8y - 3 + y + 9$
10. $4x + 10 - x + 3$
11. $x + 12y + 3x - 2y$
12. $7y + 5 + 7y - 4$
13. $3a - 2c + 5c - 2a$
14. $5x + 2y + 7y + 5x$
15. $7d - 4 + 10 - 6d$
16. $5a + 2c - 2a - 5d$
17. $10x + 7 - 4x + x$
18. $6x - 2y + x + 4$
19. $11y + 3 + 2y - 2$
20. $a - 4c + 2a + 10c$
21. $8d - 5 - 7d + 9$
22. $4a - 11 + 2 + 6a$
23. $14a + 13c - 2a - 8c$
24. $2 + 3y + 7 - 2y$
25. $4y - 2x + 8y + 5x$
26. $6c + 13d - 7d + 4c$
27. $8a + 5y + 2a - y$
28. $9a + c - 8a + c$
29. $5x + 11y - 2y + 9$
30. $6a + 3x - 2a + 10a$

Order of operations

Algebraic operations follow the same conventions and order as numerical operations.

- In the expression $3 + 4n$, the multiplication is performed first.
- In the expression $5 + x^2$, x is squared first and then added to 5.
- In the expression $3(n + 5)$, the operation inside the bracket is performed first.

Inverses

- We know that $3 + 6 = 6 + 3$ and that $a + b = b + a$.
  Also if $a + b = 10$, then $a = 10 - b$.

- We know that $3 \times 5 = 5 \times 3$ and that $a \times b = b \times a$.
  If $a \times b = 30$, then $a = \dfrac{30}{b}$ and $b = \dfrac{30}{a}$.

Exercise 5

In Questions **1** to **12** write down each statement and say whether it is 'True' or 'False' for all values of the symbols used.

1. $n + n = 2n$
2. $n \times n \times n = 3n$
3. $a \times a = a^2$
4. $cd = dc$
5. $p + q = q + p$
6. $n^2 + n^2 = 2n^2$
7. $m - n = n - m$
8. $a \times 4 = 4a$
9. $3n - n = 3$
10. $n \div 2 = 2 \div n$
11. $2n^2 = (2n)^2$
12. $\frac{1}{2}$ of $h = \dfrac{h}{2}$

13. Copy and complete

    (a) If $m + n = 100$, then $m = \boxed{} - \boxed{}$

    (b) If $a \times b = 15$, then $a =$

    (c) If $c - d = 20$, then $c =$

14. Simplify the following expressions.

(a) $a + 3 + 4a - 3$ (b) $n - 2 + 2n$ (c) $m + n + p + n$

(d) $\dfrac{a}{a}$ (e) $\dfrac{3n}{3}$ (f) $\dfrac{a^2}{a}$

15. Think of two pairs of values for a and b for each equation.

(a) $a + b = 20$ (b) $ab = 100$ (c) $a^2 b = 8$

16. Find the value of each expression, when $n = 3$.

(a) $3n + 2$ (b) $2 + n^2$ (c) $5(n + 1)$
(d) $4(4 + n)$ (e) $(2n)^2$ (f) $2n^2$

Number walls: an investigation

Here we have three bricks with a number written inside each one.

A wall is built by putting more bricks on top to form a sort of pyramid.

The number in each of the new bricks is found by adding together the numbers in the two bricks below like this:

Here is another wall.

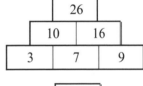

A • If you re-arrange the numbers at the bottom, does it affect the total at the top?
   • What is the largest total you can get using the same numbers?
   • What is the smallest total?
   • *How* do you get the largest total?

B • What happens if the bottom numbers are
    (a) the same? (e.g. 5, 5, 5, 5)
    (b) consecutive? (e.g. 2, 3, 4, 5)
   • Write down any patterns or rules that you notice.

C ● What happens if you use different numbers at random? (eg 7, 3, 5, 11)
  ● Given 4 numbers at the bottom, can you find a way to predict the top number without finding all the bricks in between?

D ● Can you find a rule with 3 bricks at the bottom, or 4 bricks? Can algebra help? [Hint: see diagram]

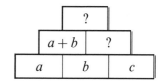

Balance puzzles

In balance puzzles the scales balance exactly.

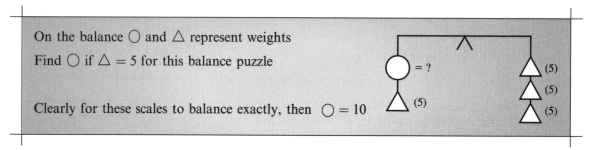

Exercise 6

Copy each diagram and find the value of the required symbol.

1. Find ☐ if △ = 4.   **2.** Find ◯ if △ = 10.   **3.** Find ◯ if ☐ = 4.

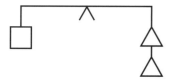      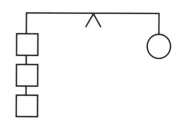

4. Find ☐ if △ = 12.   **5.** Find △ if ☐ = 2.   **6.** Find △ if ◯ = 6.

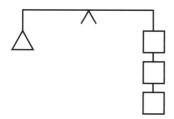   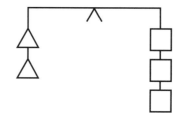   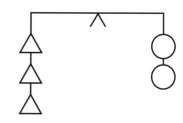

7. Find ☐ if ○ = 8.

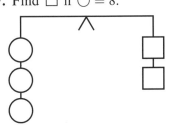

8. Find △ if ☐ = 15.

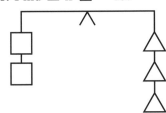

9. Find △ if ○ = 14.

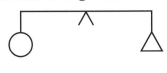

10. Find ☐ if ○ = 8.

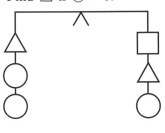

11. Find ○ if △ = 6.

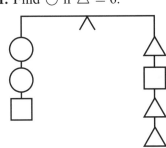

12. Find ○ if ☐ = 5.

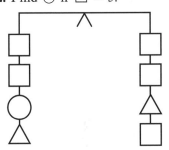

Exercise 7

Copy each diagram and find the value of the unknown symbols.

1. ○ = 10, find △ and ☐.

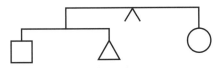

2. △ = 8, find ○ and ☐.

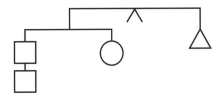

3. ☐ = 14, find ○ and △.

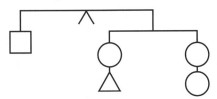

4. ☐ = 6, find ○ and △.

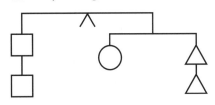

5. ○ = 8, find ☐ and △.

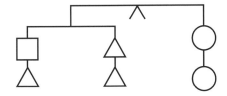

6. ☐ = 4, find ○ and △.

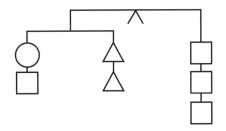

7. △ = 4, find ◯ and □.

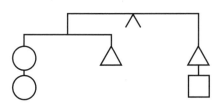

8. ◯ = 10, find △ and □.

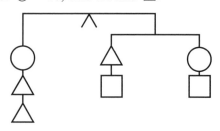

9. △ = 5, find ◯ and □.

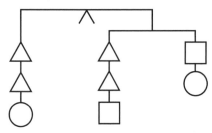

10. □ = 3, find ◯ and △.

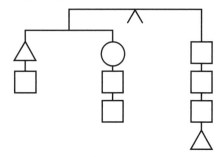

11. □ = 6, find △ and ◯.

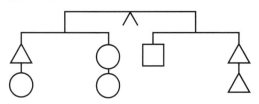

12. ◯ = 5, find □ and △.

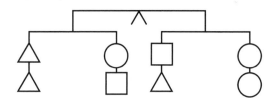

13. △ = 4, find ◯ and □.

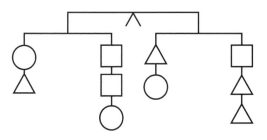

14. ◯ = 8, find □ and △.

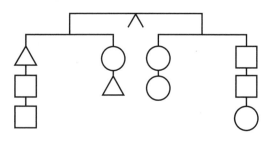

15. □ = 4, find ◯ and △.

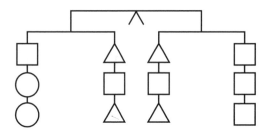

16. ◯ = 3, find ✳.

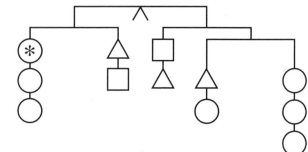

2.4 Percentages

Common percentages

- Some percentages are used a lot and you should learn them.

$$10\% = \frac{10}{100} = \frac{1}{10}, \quad 30\% = \frac{30}{100} = \frac{3}{10}, \quad 70\% = \frac{7}{10}, \quad 90\% = \frac{9}{10}, \quad 20\% = \frac{20}{100} = \frac{1}{5},$$

$$40\% = \frac{40}{100} = \frac{2}{5}, \quad 60\% = \frac{3}{5}, \quad 80\% = \frac{4}{5}, \quad 25\% = \frac{1}{4}, \quad 50\% = \frac{1}{2},$$

$$75\% = \frac{3}{4}, \quad 33\tfrac{1}{3}\% = \frac{1}{3}, \quad 66\tfrac{2}{3}\% = \frac{2}{3}$$

 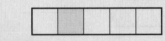

$$\frac{1}{4} = 25\% \qquad\qquad \frac{1}{5} = 20\% \qquad\qquad \frac{3}{10} = 30\%$$

Exercise 1

1.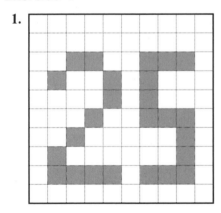

   In this square, 25 out of 100 squares are shaded to show 25%.
   Draw your own numbers (like 17, 21 or 33) and shade in the correct number of squares to show the percentage. Try to draw the numbers the same size.

2. The diagram shows the percentage of people who took part in activities offered at a sports centre on a Friday night.

   (a) What percentage went swimming?
   (b) What percentage played squash?
   (c) What percentage played a racket sport?
   (d) What percentage did not play football?
   (e) What percentage played activities involving a ball?

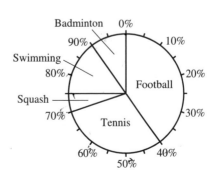

3. For each shape write
  (a) what fraction is shaded   (b) what percentage is shaded.

A 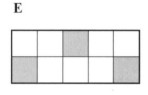   **B** 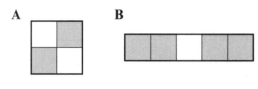   **C** 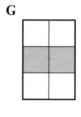   **D**

E 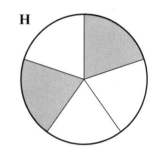   **F** 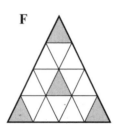   **G** 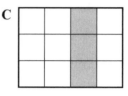   **H**

4. Copy these and fill in the spaces.
  (a) $30\% = \frac{}{10}$ (b) $\frac{3}{4} = \quad \%$ (c) $\frac{1}{3} = \quad \%$
  (d) $1\% = \frac{}{100}$ (e) $80\% = -$ (f) $\frac{1}{10} = \quad \%$

5. These pictures show how much petrol is in a car. E is Empty and F is Full.
  What percentage of a full tank is in each car?

  (a)    (b)

  (c)    (d)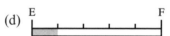

  (e)

6. What percentage could be used in each sentence?
  (a) Three quarters of the pupils at a school had school dinners.
  (b) Three out of five workers voted for a strike.
  (c) Nicki got 15 out of 20 in the spelling test.
  (d) One in three cats prefer 'Whiskas'.
  (e) Half of the customers at a supermarket thought that prices were too high.
  (f) One in four mothers think children are too tidy at home.

7. Draw three diagrams of your own design, like those in Question **3** and shade in:
  (a) 30%   (b) 75%   (c) $66\frac{2}{3}\%$

Percentage of a number

(a) Work out 25% of £60.
25% is the same as $\frac{1}{4}$, $\frac{1}{4}$ of £60 is £15.

(b) In a sale, prices are reduced by 20%. Find the 'sale price' of the dress shown.

20% is the same as $\frac{1}{5}$
$\frac{1}{5}$ of £40 = £8.

Sale price = £40 − £8
= £32.

£40

Exercise 2

1. Work out
   (a) 20% of £50   (b) 75% of £12   (c) 10% of £90
   (d) 25% of £4000   (e) $33\frac{1}{3}$% of £90   (f) 30% of £40

2. Now do these
   (a) 90% of £100   (b) 40% of $30   (c) $66\frac{2}{3}$% of £12
   (d) 50% of $1200   (e) 1% of £300   (f) 5% of £100

3. Kate earns £15 for doing a paper round. How much *extra* does she earn when she gets a 20% rise?

4. Full marks in a maths test is 60. How many marks did Tim get if he got 60%?

5. Of the 240 children at a school, 75% walk to school. How many children walk to school?

6. Find the actual cost of the following items in a sale. The normal prices are shown.

(a) £60

25% off
marked price

(b)  £15

50% off!

(c) £24

$33\frac{1}{3}$% off
normal
price

(d) 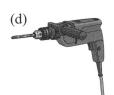 £40

10%
discount
off price

(e) £80

75% off!

(f) £25

40%
discount
off price

7. In many countries Value Added Tax [V.A.T.] is charged at $17\frac{1}{2}\%$. Here is a method for finding $17\frac{1}{2}\%$ of £4000 without a calculator.

$17\frac{1}{2}\%$ of £4000:
$$10\% = £400$$
$$5\% = £200$$
$$2\frac{1}{2}\% = £100$$
$$\overline{17\frac{1}{2}\% = £700}$$

Use this method to work out:

(a) $17\frac{1}{2}\%$ of £6000   (b) $17\frac{1}{2}\%$ of £440   (c) $17\frac{1}{2}\%$ of £86

8. The price of a car was £6600 but it is increased by $17\frac{1}{2}\%$. What is the new price?

9. The price of a boat was £36 000 but it is increased by 5%. What is the new price?

10. In a sale the price of a shirt costing £12 is reduced by 25%. Find the reduced price of the shirt.

(a) Work out 16% of £15.   (b) Work out 23% of £350
                                               (Quick way)
16% of £15   23% = 0·23 as a decimal (since $23\% = \frac{23}{100}$)

$= \frac{16}{100} \times \frac{15}{1}$ So 23% of £350 = 0·23 × 350

$= \frac{240}{100} = £2·40$ = £80·50

Exercise 3

1. Work out

(a) 55% of £310   (b) 24% of £44   (c) 19% of £1120
(d) 6% of £406   (e) 5% of £12·60   (f) 120% of £400

2. Give the correct units in your answers to the following:

(a) 18% of 28 km   (b) 97% of 4000 kg   (c) 35% of 400 m
(d) 62% of $35 000   (e) 11·2% of 710 km   (f) 7·2% of $155

3. Using a calculator we find that 13·2% of £12·65 = £1·6698.

This answer has to be rounded off to the nearest penny, since the penny is the smallest unit of currency.
So 13·2% of £12·65 = £1·67, to the nearest penny.

Work out, to the nearest penny:
(a) 8% of £11·64   (b) 37% of £9·65
(c) 3·5% of £13·80   (d) 12% of £24·52
(e) $3\frac{1}{2}\%$ of £11·11   (f) 115% of £212·14

4. It is possible to do some 'easy' percentages in your head.
Remember $10\% = \frac{1}{10}$, $25\% = \frac{1}{4}$, $33\frac{1}{3}\% = \frac{1}{3}$ etc.

Work these out in your head:
(a) 10% of £230   (b) 25% of £880
(c) 80% of £5000   (d) $33\frac{1}{3}\%$ of £120
(e) 5% of £2000   (f) 75% of £12

5. A joint of meat originally weighs 3·4 kg. During cooking the
weight goes down by 15%.
What is the loss of weight of the meat?

6. The number of children having school dinners is 640. When
chips are not on the menu, the number goes down by 5%. How
many fewer children have school dinners?

7. A worm weighs 24 g. After providing lunch for a starling, the
weight of the worm is decreased by 8%. By how much does the
weight of the worm decrease?

8. In a restaurant a service charge of 10% is added to the price of a
meal. What is the service charge on a meal costing £28·50?

9. At a garage 140 cars were given a safety test and
65% of the cars passed the test.
(a) How many passed the test?
(b) How many failed the test?

10. Of the 980 children at a school 45% cycle to school, 15% go by
bus and the rest walk.
(a) How many cycle to school?
(b) How many walk to school?

11. A lottery prize of £65 000 is divided between Steve, Pete and Phil
so that Steve receives 22%, Pete receives 32% and Phil the rest.
How much money does Phil receive?

2.5 Mental arithmetic

Mental calculation strategies

In this section we will look at strategies for adding and subtracting numbers mentally. The introduction is followed by 12 questions to practise the new techniques.

A. 'Easy-to-add' numbers

When numbers are added the order of the numbers does not matter:

$$23 + 17 \qquad = 17 + 23$$
$$41 + 9 + 110 = 110 + 9 + 41$$

Many pairs of numbers are easy to add together mentally

e.g. $17 + 23 = 40, \qquad 18 + 32 = 50, \qquad 33 + 7 = 40$

Practice questions
Look for 'easy-to-add' pairs of numbers in the following. If necessary change the order of the numbers in your head and then write down the answer without working.

1. $5 + 17 + 15$	**2.** $8 + 27 + 12$	**3.** $17 + 13 + 16$
4. $22 + 48 + 11$	**5.** $9 + 87 + 11$	**6.** $19 + 41 + 37$
7. $17 + 15 + 25$	**8.** $18 + 2 + 57$	**9.** $16 + 3 + 24$
10. $90 + 110 + 58$	**11.** $75 + 37 + 25$	**12.** $215 + 49 + 51$

B. Splitting the numbers

- $23 + 48$: $20 + 40 = \ 60$ and $3 + 8 = 11$
      So $23 + 48 = \ 60 + 11 = 71$

- $255 + 38$: $250 + 30 = 280$ and $5 + 8 = 13$
      So $225 + 38 = 280 + 13 = 293$

- Other way
   $23 + 48 = \ 23 + 40 + 8 = \ 63 + 8 = 71$
   $255 + 38 = 255 + 30 + 8 = 285 + 8 = 293$

   $576 - 43 = 576 - 40 - 3 = 536 - 3 = 533$
   $95 - 48 = \ 95 - 40 - 8 = \ 55 - 8 = 47$

Practice questions

1. $34 + 47$	**2.** $65 + 28$	**3.** $78 + 23$	**4.** $57 + 24$
5. $88 - 31$	**6.** $97 - 42$	**7.** $84 + 17$	**8.** $82 - 35$
9. $66 + 37$	**10.** $58 + 34$	**11.** $62 - 44$	**12.** $206 + 105$

C. Add/subtract
9, 19, 29 … 11, 21, 31, …, adjusting by one.

- $54 + 19 = 54 + 20 - 1 = 63$
- $77 + 41 = 77 + 40 + 1 = 118$
- $63 + 59 = 63 + 60 - 1 = 122$
- $54 - 31 = 54 - 30 - 1 = 23$
- $77 - 39 = 77 - 40 + 1 = 38$
- $95 - 29 = 95 - 30 + 1 = 66$

Practice questions
1. $67 + 21$	**2.** $37 + 51$	**3.** $36 + 39$	**4.** $76 + 29$
5. $45 + 29$	**6.** $70 - 21$	**7.** $80 - 41$	**8.** $44 + 58$
9. $33 + 96$	**10.** $91 - 37$	**11.** $53 + 41$	**12.** $48 - 23$

D. Doubling large numbers: work from the left
- double 63 = double 60 + double 3 = $120 + 6 = 126$
- double 79 = double 70 + double 9 = $140 + 18 = 158$
- double 127 = double 100 + double 20 + double 7 = $200 + 40 + 14 = 254$
- double 264 = double 200 + double 60 + double 4 = $400 + 120 + 8 = 528$

Practice questions
1. double 54	**2.** double 38	**3.** double 67	**4.** double 73
5. double 28	**6.** double 79	**7.** double 115	**8.** double 126
9. double 87	**10.** double 66	**11.** double 237	**12.** double 342

E. (a) Multiplying by doubling and then halving
- 23×5 $23 \times 10 = 230$ $230 \div 2 = 115$
- 7×45 $7 \times 90 = 630$ $630 \div 2 = 315$
- 11×15 $11 \times 30 = 330$ $330 \div 2 = 165$

(b) To multiply by 50, multiply by 100, then halve the result.
- 23×50 $23 \times 100 = 2300$ $2300 \div 2 = 1150$
- 38×50 $38 \times 100 = 3800$ $3800 \div 2 = 1900$

(c) To multiply by 25, multiply by 100, then divide by 4
- 44×25 $44 \times 100 = 4400$ $4400 \div 4 = 1100$
- 56×25 $56 \times 100 = 5600$ $5600 \div 4 = 1400$

Practice questions

1. 22×50	**2.** 32×50	**3.** 24×25	**4.** 16×25
5. 8×35	**6.** 8×15	**7.** 7×45	**8.** 9×35
9. 14×50	**10.** 13×20	**11.** 18×50	**12.** 12×25
13. 12×25	**14.** 44×50	**15.** 26×50	**16.** 22×15

Mental arithmetic tests

There are several sets of mental arithmetic questions in this section. It is intended that a teacher will read out each question twice, with all pupils' books closed. The answers are written down without any written working. Only a pencil or pen may be used.

Test 1

1. Add together five, four and nineteen.

2. Write the number that is eight less than three hundred.

3. What is five hundred and forty six to the nearest hundred?

4. What is nine multiplied by six?

5. Write the number eight thousand and six in figures.

6. Write nought point seven as a fraction.

7. Change seven and a half metres into centimetres.

8. What is four point six multiplied by one thousand?

9. How many thirds are there in two whole ones?

10. Twenty six per cent of the people in a survey did not like cheese. What percentage liked cheese?

11. The side of a square is five centimetres. What is the area of the square?

12. A bus journey starts at six fifty. It lasts for thirty five minutes. At what time does it finish?

13. At mid-day the temperature is seven degrees celsius. By midnight it has fallen twelve degrees. What is the temperature at midnight?

14. How many groups of 5 can be made from 100?

15. Write down a factor of twenty seven, which is greater than one.

16. What is six thousand divided by ten?

17. What number is eight squared?

18. How many seventeens are there in three hundred and forty?

19. What is the difference between 3·3 and 5·5?

20. How much does each person receive when a prize of £200 is shared between 5 people?

21. How many more than 27 is 40?

22. Twenty per cent of a number is twelve. What is the number?

23. Find the change from a £10 note if you spend £3·20.

24. How many altogether are 7, 6 and 5?

25. What is the remainder when 40 is divided by 7?

Test 2

1. What are two eighteens?

2. Add together 7, 8 and 9.

3. Divide 8 into 48.

4. Multiply 15 by 40.

5. Write $\frac{3}{4}$ as a percentage.

6. Work out 13 divided by 10 as a decimal.

7. What number is 40 less than 75?

8. Share a cost of £56 between 7 people.

9. What four coins make 67p?

10. What is the product of 60 and 3?

11. I have 2 dogs and 5 cats. What fraction of my pets are cats?

12. What is the cost of 2 C.D.s at £6·99 each?

13. Subtract the sum of 7 and 8 from 40.

14. One quarter of a number is 3·5. What is the number?

15. I have one 10p, three 5p and one 50p coin. How much money do I have?

16. Lemons cost 12p each. What is the cost of 7 lemons?

17. Apples cost 75p for five. What is the cost of one apple?

18. A bunch of grapes costs 64p. What is the change from £1?

19. How many 20p coins do I need for £2·80?

20. A shirt costs £15·95 new. I get a discount of £4. How much do I pay?

21. I share 60 sweets equally among 5 people. How many sweets does each receive?

22. The area of a square is 36 cm². How long is each side?

23. What must I spend from £20 to leave £14·50?

24. How many millimetres are there in 10 metres?

25. Write 5.30 a.m. in 24 hour clock time.

Test 3

1. What is the perimeter of a square with sides 8 cm?

2. Write one fifth as a percentage.

3. What number is half way between 4·2 and 4·8?

4. I have six 20p, one 5p and one 2p coin. How much do I have?

5. A poster costs three pounds. Andrew saves sixty pence per week. How many weeks will it be before he can buy it?

6. Screws cost 8 pence each. What is the cost of 25 screws?

7. Hooks cost 70 pence for five. What is the cost of 1 hook?

8. A pair of earrings costs £1·23. What is the change from £2?

9. How many 5p coins do I need for 85p?

10. A drill costs £34 new. I get a discount of £8·50. How much do I pay?

11. A T.V. programme starts at 9.50 and ends at 10.40. How long is the programme?

12. I travel at 60 m.p.h. for 4 hours. How far do I travel?

13. Work out ten per cent of £65.

14. Susie has 3 red pens and 4 black pens. What fraction of her pens are black?

15. Jacqui make a phone call from 18.40 until 19.21. How long is the call in minutes?

16. What five coins make 62p?

17. Write the number fifty thousand and six in figures.

18. The product of two numbers is thirty nine. One of the numbers is three. What is the other?

19. Change four and a half metres into centimetres.

20. Subtract 18 from 150.

21. Write three fifths as a decimal.

22. Increase forty pounds by 25 percent.

23. I buy three magazines at 99p each. What change do I get from £10?

24. How many lengths of 8 cm can be cut from 50 cm?

25. How many minutes are there in $2\frac{3}{4}$ hours?

Test 4

1. What are 37 twos?

2. What is the smaller angle between the hands of a clock at 8 o'clock?

3. Two angles of a triangle are 55° and 30°. What is the third angle?

4. What is 50% of £44?

5. How many 5p coins are needed to make £10?

6. A car costing £8500 is reduced by £120. What is the new price?

7. What number is twice as big as sixty-nine?

8. On a tray fourteen out of fifty peaches are rotten. What percentage is that?

9. Add together 11, 18 and 9.

10. A C.D. cost £13·55. Find the change from a £20 note.

11. What five coins make 51p?

12. What is $\frac{2}{3}$ of £186?

13. Write one twentieth as a decimal.

14. How many minutes are there between 8.15 p.m. and 10.20 p.m.?

15. A pools prize of six million pounds is shared equally between one hundred people. How much does each person receive?

16. If June 14th is a Tuesday what day of the week is June 23rd?

17. True or false: 1 kg is about 2 pounds?

18. How many millimetres are there in 3·5 metres?

19. A daily newspaper costs 25p from Monday to Saturday and 45p on Sunday. What is the total cost for the seven days?

20. Write $\frac{3}{4}$ as a decimal.

21. A clock ticks once every second. How many times does it tick between six o'clock and seven o'clock?

22. Add eleven to nine times eight

23. A rectangular piece of wood measures 15 cm by 10 cm. What is its area?

24. An egg box holds six eggs. How many boxes are needed for 100 eggs?

25. How many 19p stamps can I buy for a pound?

Test 5

1. By how much is three kilos more than 800 grams?

2. How many 20p coins do I need to make £400?

3. How many square centimetres are there in one square metre?

4. How much more than £108 is £300?

5. Two angles of a triangle are 44° and 54°. What is the third angle?

6. Work out 10% of £5000.

7. My watch reads ten past eight. It is 15 minutes fast. What is the correct time?

8. A 50p coin is 2 mm thick. What is the value of a pile of 50p coins 2 cm high?

9. Add together £2·35 and £4·15.

10. A ship was due at noon on Friday but arrived at 8.00 a.m. on Saturday. How many hours late was the ship?

11. By how much is half a metre longer than 1 millimetre? (answer in mm).

12. What number is thirty-five more than eighty?

13. How many minutes are there in two and a half hours?

14. From nine times seven take away five.

15. A T.V. show lasting 45 minutes starts at 10 minutes to eight. When does it finish?

16. A train travels at an average speed of 48 mph. How far does it travel in 2 hours?

17. What is the perimeter of a square of side 14 cm?

18. A string of length 390 cm is cut in half. How long is each piece?

19. A half is a quarter of a certain number. What is the number?

20. A man died in 1993 aged 58. In what year was he born?

21. *Roughly* how many millimetres are there in one foot?

22. Write down ten thousand pence in pounds.

23. What is a quarter of two hundred and ten?

24. Find two ways of making 66p using five coins.

25. John weighs 8 stones and Jim weighs 80 kg. Who is heavier?

Test 6

1. What number is 10 less than nine thousand?

2. I want to buy 4 records, each costing £4·49. To the nearest pound, how much will my bill be?

3. How many magazines costing 95p can I buy with £10?

4. What is the total of 57 and 963?

5. What is a half of a half of 10?

6. True or false: 3 feet is slightly longer than 1 metre.

7. A triangle has a base 4 cm and a height of 10 cm. What is its area?

8. What number is exactly mid-way between 3·7 and 3·8?

9. Work out two squared plus three squared.

10. The pupils in Darren's class are given lockers numbered from 32 to 54. How many pupils are there in Darren's class?

11. Write 7 divided by 100 as a decimal.

12. Jane is 35 cm taller than William, who is 1·34 metres tall. How tall is Jane?

13. A toy train travels 6 metres in two seconds. How far will it go in one minute?

14. Which is larger: 2 cubed or 3 squared?

15. What number is next in the series 1, 2, 4, 8, . . . ?

16. Write the number '$2\frac{1}{2}$ million' in figures.

17. Joe borrowed £4·68 from his father. He paid him back with a £10 note. How much change did he receive?

18. What is a tenth of 2·4?

19. I think of a number and subtract 6. The result is equal to 7 times 3. What is the number?

20. Write down the next prime number after 32.

21. How much longer is 7·5 metres than 725 centimetres?

22. How many lines of symmetry does a square have?

23. What is a quarter of a half?

24. Work out 200 times 300.

25. How many edges does a cube have?

2.6 Mathematical puzzles

Crossnumbers

Make four copies of the pattern below and complete the puzzles using the clues given. To avoid confusion it is better not to write the small reference numbers 1, 2–18 on your patterns.

Part **A** [No calculators]

Across	Down
1. $499 + 43$	**1.** 1% of 5700
3. 216×7	**2.** $600 - 365$
5. $504 \div 9$	**4.** 6^3
6. $8214 - 3643$	**7.** $4488 \div 6$
8. Half of 192	**8.** $30^2 + 3 \times 6$
9. 20% of 365	**9.** $10\,000 - 2003$
10. Prime number between 30 and 36	**11.** $4 \times 4 \times 4 \times 4$
11. $213 + 62 + 9$	**12.** $58{\cdot}93 \times (67 + 33)$
13. $406 \div 7$	**14.** $1136 - 315$
15. 316×23	**16.** $11^2 - 10^2$
17. $1000 - 731$	
18. Next prime number after 200	

In parts **B**, **C** and **D** a calculator may be used [where absolutely necessary!] Write any decimal points on the lines between squares.

Part **B**

Across	Down
1. $9 \times 10 \times 11$	**1.** $\dfrac{5 \times 6 \times 7 \times 8}{2} - 11 \times 68$
3. Ninety less than ten thousand	**2.** 26% as a decimal
5. $\left(7\frac{1}{2}\right)^2$ to the nearest whole number	**4.** $0 \cdot 1^2$
6. $140 \cdot 52 \div 0 \cdot 03$	**7.** Next in the sequence $102\frac{1}{2}$, 205, 410
8. Last two digits of 99^2	**8.** $1 - 0 \cdot 97$
9. $3^2 + 4^2 + 5^2 + 6^2$	**9.** 52% of £158·50
10. Angle between the hands of a clock at 2.00 pm	**11.** $0 \cdot 0854 \div (7 - 6 \cdot 99)$
11. Eight pounds and eight pence	**12.** $10^3 + 11^3$
13. Next prime number after 89	**14.** $3 \times 5 \times 7^2$
15. 11% of 213	**16.** Half of a third of 222
17. 3·1 m plus 43 cm, in cm	
18. Area of a square of side 15 cm.	

Part **C**

Across	Down
1. Next square number after 144	**1.** $1\frac{4}{5}$ as a decimal
3. 5·2 m written in mm	**2.** $\dfrac{12^2 + 352}{1 \cdot 4 + 0 \cdot 2}$
5. Total of the numbers on a dice	**4.** 66% as a decimal
6. $0 \cdot 1234 \div 0 \cdot 01^2$	**7.** Days in a year minus 3
8. Ounces in a pound	**8.** Number of minutes between 1322 and 1512
9. Inches in a yard	**9.** Seconds in an hour
10. $3^4 + 56 \cdot 78 \times 0$	**11.** Double 225 plus treble 101
11. Next in the sequence 1, 2, 6, 24, 120	**12.** A quarter to midnight on the 24 h clock
13. One foot four inches, in inches	**14.** $2^3 \times 3 \times 5^2$
15. 234 m written in km	**16.** $\left(5\frac{1}{3}\right)^2$ to the nearest whole number
17. $\frac{1}{25}$ as a decimal	
18. [Number of letters in 'ridiculous']^2	

Part **D**

Across	Down

Across

1. 20% of 15% of £276
3. $81 \cdot 23 \times 9 \cdot 79 \times 11 \cdot 2$, to the nearest thousand
5. Three dozen
6. $1 \cdot 21$ m in mm
8. Solve $2x - 96 = 72$
9. Inches in two feet
10. $6 \cdot 6 \div 0 \cdot 1$
11. $\frac{1}{4} - \frac{1}{5}$ as a decimal
13. Volume of a cube of side 4 units
15. $555 + 666 + 777$
17. A gross
18. $\left(19\frac{1}{4}\right)^2$ to the nearest whole number

Down

1. Next in the sequence 25, 36, 49, 64
2. $900 - \left(\dfrac{17 \times 12}{3}\right)$
4. $0 \cdot 2 \times 0 \cdot 2$
7. Solve $x^3 = 1$ million
8. $9 - 0 \cdot 36$
9. $8^3 + 9^3 + 10^3$
11. 99% as a decimal
12. 20% of 2222
14. $0 \cdot 2055 \div 0 \cdot 0005$
16. 4 score plus ten

Puzzles

1. The totals for the rows and columns are given. Unfortunately some of the totals are hidden by ink blots. Find the values of the letters.

(a)

A	A	A	A	28
A	B	C	A	27
A	C	D	B	30
D	B	B	B	▓
▓	25	30	24	

(b)

A	B	A	B	B	18
B	B	E	C	D	21
A	B	B	A	B	18
C	B	C	B	C	19
E	B	D	E	D	26
27	10	25	23	17	

This one is more difficult

(c)

A	A	A	A	24
C	A	C	D	13
A	B	B	A	18
B	B	D	C	12
▓	18	15	18	

(d)

A	B	B	A	22
A	A	B	B	22
A	B	A	B	22
B	B	A	B	17
27	17	22	17	

2. In these triangle puzzles the numbers a, b, c, d are connected as follows:

$$a \times b = c$$
$$c \times b = d$$

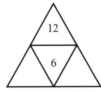 For example:

Copy and complete the following triangles:

(a)

(b)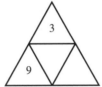

(c)

(d)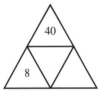

(e)

(f)

3. What is the largest possible number of people in a room if no two people have a birthday in the same month?

4. The letters A, B, C, D, E appear once in every row, every column and each main diagonal of the square. Copy the square and fill in the missing letters

				B
D				
				E
A	D			

5. Two different numbers on this section of a till receipt are obscured by food stains. What are the two numbers?

tapes at £ ●.99 :£87.89

6. Draw four straight lines which pass through all 9 points, without taking your pen from the paper and without going over any line twice. [Hint: Lines can extend beyond the square].

● ● ●

● ● ●

● ● ●

7. Draw six straight lines to pass through all 16
   points, subject to the same conditions as in
   question 6.

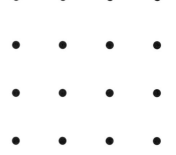

8. King Henry has 9 coins which look identical but in fact one of
   them is an underweight fake. Describe how he could discover
   the fake using just *two* weighings on an ordinary balance.

9. Write the digits 1 to 9 so that
   all the answers are correct.

$$\Box - \Box = \Box$$
$$\Box \div \Box = \Box$$
$$\Box + \Box = \Box$$

In Questions **10** and **11** each letter stands for a *different* single digit
from 0 to 9. The first digit of a number is never zero.

10. (a) M E
         M E +
       ‾‾‾‾‾‾
         A M
    [Find two solutions]

    (b) K L M
            L M
         M L M +
       ‾‾‾‾‾‾‾‾‾
         L M M

    (c) N A V E   Work out E, V, A and S. You will find
         W A V E   that N, W and R can each have three
         R A V E +   different values.
       ‾‾‾‾‾‾‾‾‾‾‾‾
         S E V E

11. Some of these questions have more than one solution.
    (a) O N E   (b) C U T   (c) S O N
         O N E +   C O T   S U N
       ‾‾‾‾‾‾‾‾‾   I F +   I S +
         T W O   ‾‾‾‾‾‾‾‾‾   ‾‾‾‾‾‾‾‾‾
                             O A T   O W N

    (d) T O U R   (e) F O U R
         S O U R   F I V E +
         R O A R +   ‾‾‾‾‾‾‾‾‾‾‾
       ‾‾‾‾‾‾‾‾‾‾‾   N I N E
         P E R R

Part 3

3.1 Properties of numbers

Prime numbers

A prime number is divisible by just two different numbers: by itself and by one.

Notice that one is not a prime number.

The first five prime numbers are 2, 3, 5, 7, 11.

Mathematicians have been fascinated by the study of prime numbers for hundreds of years. Nowadays computers are used to test for prime numbers. Many prime numbers have been found which are *thousands* of digits long.

Factors

- The number 12 can be written as two numbers multiplied together in three different ways

$$\boxed{1 \times 12} \qquad \boxed{2 \times 6} \qquad \boxed{3 \times 4}$$

The numbers 1, 12, 2, 6, 3, 4 are all the *factors* of 12.

- $\boxed{1 \times 8} = 8 \qquad \boxed{2 \times 4} = 8$

The factors of 8 are 1, 2, 4, 8.

- It is sometimes useful to write a number as a product of its *prime factors*.

  Eg $540 = 2 \times 2 \times 3 \times 3 \times 3 \times 5$
  $ = 2^2 \times 3^3 \times 5$

This is called prime factor decomposition.

Exercise 1

Write down all the factors of the following numbers

1. 6	**2.** 4	**3.** 10	**4.** 7	**5.** 15
6. 18	**7.** 24	**8.** 21	**9.** 36	**10.** 40
11. 32	**12.** 31	**13.** 60	**14.** 63	**15.** 85

16. Factors of a number which are also prime numbers are called prime factors. We can find these prime factors using a 'factor tree'

(a) Here is a factor tree for 60   (b) Here is a factor tree for 24

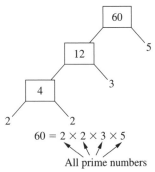

$$60 = 2 \times 2 \times 3 \times 5$$

All prime numbers

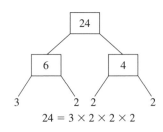

$$24 = 3 \times 2 \times 2 \times 2$$

(c) You can turn the diagram upside down and then draw a trunk around the number and branches to give a real 'tree shape'. Some people like to draw the prime factors inside apples, pears, bananas and so on.

(d) Draw a factor tree for 36.

In Questions **17** to **28** draw a factor tree for each number.

17. 28	**18.** 32	**19.** 34	**20.** 81
21. 84	**22.** 216	**23.** 294	**24.** 200
25. 1500	**26.** 2464	**27.** 4620	**28.** 98 175

29. The number 345 has 3 and 5 as factors.
Write another three-digit number which has 3 and 5 as factors.

30. The number 432 has 2 and 9 as factors.
Write another three-digit number which has 2 and 9 as factors.

31.* Which number less than 100 has the most prime factors?

32.* Which number less than 1000 has the most *different* prime factors? (You cannot repeat a factor.)

33.* What is the smallest whole number which is exactly divisible by all the numbers from 1 to 10 inclusive?

Multiples

The *multiples* of 5 divide by 5 with no remainder.
The first four multiples of 5 are 5, 10, 15, 20.
The first four multiples of 6 are 6, 12, 18, 24.

Exercise 2

Write down the first four multiples of:

1. 3	**2.** 4	**3.** 2	**4.** 7	**5.** 10

Write down the first six multiples of:

6. 5	**7.** 8	**8.** 9	**9.** 11	**10.** 20

11. Find which numbers the following sets are multiples of
    (a) 8, 12, 20, 28
    (b) 25, 30, 55, 60
    (c) 14, 21, 35, 70

In Questions **12** to **16** find the 'odd one out'. (The number which is not a multiple of the number given.)

12. Multiples of 6: 18, 24, 32, 48, 54.

13. Multiples of 11: 33, 77, 101, 132.

14. Multiples of 10: 5, 10, 20, 30, 60.

15. Multiples of 9: 18, 27, 45, 56, 72.

16. Multiples of 7: 49, 77, 91, 105, 18.

17. Find three numbers that are multiples of both 3 and 4.

18. Find three numbers that are multiples of both 2 and 5.

19. Find three numbers that are multiples of 2, 3 and 5.

20. Find two numbers that are multiples of 2, 4 and 6.

L.C.M. and H.C.F.

(a) The first few multiples of 4 are   4, 8, 12, 16, (20), 24, 28 …
    The first few multiples of 5 are   5, 10, 15, (20), 25, 30, 35 …

    The *Lowest Common Multiple* (L.C.M.) of 4 and 5 is 20.
    It is the lowest number which is in both lists.

(b) The factors of 12 are   1, 2, 3, (4), 6, 12

    The factors of 20 are   1, 2, (4), 5, 10, 20

    The *Highest Common Factor* (H.C.F.) of 12 and 20 is 4.
    It is the highest number which is in both lists.

Exercise 3

1. (a) Write down the first four multiples of 2.
    (b) Write down the first four multiples of 5.
    (c) Write down the L.C.M. of 2 and 5.

2. (a) Write down the first four multiples of 4.
    (b) Write down the first four multiples of 12.
    (c) Write down the L.C.M. of 4 and 12.

3. Find the L.C.M. of
   - (a) 6 and 9
   - (b) 8 and 12
   - (c) 14 and 35
   - (d) 2, 4 and 6
   - (e) 3, 5 and 10
   - (f) 4, 7 and 9

4. The table shows the factors and common factors of 24 and 36.

number	factors	common factors
24	1, 2, 3, 4, 6, 8, 12, 24	} 1, 2, 3, 4, 6, 12
36	1, 2, 3, 4, 6, 9, 12, 18, 36	

   Write down the H.C.F. of 24 and 36.

5. Find the H.C.F. of
   - (a) 12 and 18
   - (b) 22 and 55
   - (c) 45 and 72
   - (d) 12, 18 and 30
   - (e) 36, 60 and 72
   - (f) 20, 40 and 50

6. Given that $1386 = 2 \times 3 \times 3 \times 7 \times 11$ and $858 = 2 \times 3 \times 11 \times 13$, find the highest common factor of 1386 and 858. (i.e. the highest number that goes into 1386 and 858.]

7. If $1170 = 2 \times 3 \times 3 \times 5 \times 13$ and $10\,725 = 3 \times 5 \times 5 \times 11 \times 13$, find the highest common factor of 1170 and 10 725.

Square numbers and cube numbers

Exercise 4

1.

  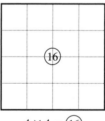

$1 \times 1 = \textcircled{1}$ $2 \times 2 = \textcircled{4}$ $3 \times 3 = \textcircled{9}$ $4 \times 4 = \textcircled{16}$

   (a) The first four *square* numbers are 1, 4, 9, 16.
   (b) Draw diagrams with labels to show the next three square numbers.

2. A square number is obtained by multiplying a number by itself.
   3×3 is written 3^2 (We say '3 squared...')
   4×4 is written 4^2

   Work out
   - (a) 5^2
   - (b) 8^2
   - (c) 10^2
   - (d) 1^2

3. Work out
   - (a) $3^2 + 4^2$
   - (b) $1^2 + 2^2 + 3^2$
   - (c) $9^2 + 10^2$

4. (a) Write down this sentence and fill in the missing numbers

$$1 \qquad\qquad = 1 \qquad = 1^2$$

$$1 + 3 \qquad\qquad = 4 \qquad = 2^2$$

$$1 + 3 + 5 \qquad = \boxed{} \qquad = \boxed{}^2$$

$$1 + 3 + 5 + 7 \quad = \boxed{} \qquad = \boxed{}^2$$

(b) Write down the next five lines of the sequence.

5. What number when multiplied by itself gives the following
(a) 49 (b) 81 (c) 144

6. The *square root* of a number is the number which is multiplied by itself to give that number. The symbol for square root is $\sqrt{}$.
So $\sqrt{9} = 3$, $\sqrt{16} = 4$, $\sqrt{100} = 10$
Work out
(a) $\sqrt{25}$ (b) $\sqrt{81}$ (c) $\sqrt{49}$ (d) $\sqrt{1}$

7. Copy the following and fill in the spaces

(a) $7^2 = 49$, $\sqrt{49} = \boxed{}$ (b) $14^2 = 196$, $\sqrt{196} = \boxed{}$

(c) $21^2 = 441$, $\sqrt{\boxed{}} = 21$ (d) $3{\cdot}3^2 = 10{\cdot}89$, $\sqrt{\boxed{}} = 3{\cdot}3$

8. *Lagrange's theorem.* A famous mathematician called Lagrange proved that every whole number could be written as the sum of four or fewer square numbers.

For example: $\quad 21 = 16 + 4 + 1$
$$19 = 16 + 1 + 1 + 1$$
$$35 = 25 + 9 + 1$$

Check that the theorem applies to the following numbers.

(a) 10 (b) 24 (c) 47
(d) 66 (e) 98 (f) 63
(g) 120 (h) 141 (i) 423

If you can find a number which needs more than four squares you will have disproved Lagrange's theorem and a new theorem will be named after you.

9. The numbers 1, 8, 27 are the first three *cube* numbers.

$1 \times 1 \times 1 = 1^3 = 1$ (we say '1 cubed')
$2 \times 2 \times 2 = 2^3 = 8$ (we say '2 cubed')
$3 \times 3 \times 3 = 3^3 = 27$ (we say '3 cubed')

The odd numbers can be added in groups to give an interesting sequence:

$1 \qquad\qquad = 1 \qquad = 1^3$
$3 + 5 \qquad\quad = 8 \qquad = 2^3$
$7 + 9 + 11 \quad = 27 \qquad = 3^3$

Write down the next three rows of the sequence to see if the sum of each row always gives a cube number.

10. The number 324 is a square number [$324 = 18 \times 18$].
In its prime factors, $324 = 2 \times 2 \times 3 \times 3 \times 3 \times 3$.
If we take half of the twos and half of the threes we have
$2 \times 3 \times 3$, which is 18.
We say that 18 is the *square root* of 324.
Find the square roots of these numbers (without a calculator!)

(a) 196 ($= 2 \times 2 \times 7 \times 7$)   (b) 256 ($= 2 \times 2 \times 2 \times 2 \times 2 \times 2 \times 2 \times 2$)
(c) 576   (d) 1936
(e) 38 025

11. In its prime factors, $588 = 2 \times 2 \times 3 \times 7 \times 7$.
What is the smallest number by which you can multiply 588 so
that the answer is a square number?

12. Write 8820 in its prime factors. What is the smallest number by
which you can multiply 8820 so that the answer is a square
number?

Finding prime numbers

Exercise 5

1. Find the two numbers in each line which are prime.
(a) 14, 17, 21, 27, 29, 39
(b) 41, 45, 49, 51, 63, 67
(c) 2, 57, 71, 81, 91, 93

2. The prime numbers up to 100 or 200 can be found as
follows:

- Write the numbers in 8 columns (leave space
  underneath to go up to 200 later).
- Cross out 1 and draw circles around 2, 3, 5 and 7.
- Draw 4 vertical lines to cross out the even numbers
  (apart from 2).
- Draw 6 diagonal lines to cross out the multiples of 3.
- Draw 2 diagonal lines to cross out the multiples of 7.
- Cross out any numbers ending in 5.
- Draw circles around all the numbers which have not
  been crossed out. These are the prime numbers.
  Check that you have 25 prime numbers up to 100.

3. Selmin looked at her circled prime numbers and she
thought she noticed a pattern. She thought that all the
prime numbers in columns A and B could be written as
the sum of two square numbers.
For example $17 = 1^2 + 4^2$
$41 = 4^2 + 5^2$

Was Selmin right? Can *all* the prime numbers in columns A and
B be written like this?

4. Extend the table up to 200 and draw in more lines to cross out multiples of 2, 3 and 7. You will also have to cross out any multiples of 11 and 13 which would otherwise be missed. (Can you see why?)

Does the pattern which Selmin noticed still work?

5. Write down two prime numbers which add up to another prime number. Do this in three ways.

6. How many prime numbers are even?

7. Find three prime numbers which add up to another prime number.

Testing for prime numbers

(a) Is 307 a prime number?

You might think that we need to test whether 307 is divisible by 2, 3, 4, 5, 6, 7, 8, ...306. This would be both tedious and unnecessary.

In fact, if 307 is divisible by any number at all it will certainly be divisible by a prime number less than $\sqrt{307}$.

Since $\sqrt{307}$ is about 17·5, we only need to test whether 307 is divisible by 2, 3, 5, 7, 11, 13, 17.

Using a calculator, we find that 307 is not divisible by any of these, so we know that 307 *is* a prime number.

(b) Is 689 a prime number?

Since $\sqrt{689} \approx 26·2$, we only need to test whether 689 is divisible by 2, 3, 5, 7, 11, 13, 17, 19, 23.

Using a calculator we find that 689 is divisible by 13. We do not need to go any further than this.

We now know that 689 is *not* a prime number.

Exercise 6

1. Use your calculator to find which of the following are prime numbers.

(a) 293   (b) 407   (c) 799   (d) 335

(e) 709   (f) 1261   (g) 923   (h) 1009

2. One very large prime number is $2^{86243} - 1$.

The number has 25 962 digits.

(a) How long would it take to write out this number, assuming that you could maintain a rate of 1 digit every second? Give your answer in hours, minutes and seconds.

(b) How many pages would you need to write out this number if you could write 50 digits on a line and 30 lines on a page?

Satisfied numbers

The number 4 is an even number *and* a square number. It *satisfies* both categories.

1. Copy the grid below and use a pencil for your answers (so that you can rub out mistakes.)

Write the numbers from 1 to 9, one in each box, so that all the numbers satisfy the conditions for both the row and the column.

	Number between 5 and 9	Square number	Prime number
Factor of 6	6	?	?
Even number	?	?	?
Odd number	?	?	?

2. Copy the grid and write the numbers from 1 to 9, one in each box.

	Prime number	Multiple of 3	Factor of 16
Number greater than 5			
Odd number			
Even number			

3. This one is more difficult. Write the numbers from 1 to 16, one in each box. There are several correct solutions. Ask a friend to check yours.

	Prime number	Odd number	Factor of 16	Even number
Numbers less than 7				
Factor of 36				
Numbers less than 12				
Numbers between 11–17				

4. Design a grid with categories of your own and ask a friend to solve it.

Happy numbers

- (a) Take any number, say 23.
  (b) Square the digits and add: $2^2 + 3^2 = 4 + 9 = 13$
  (c) Repeat (b) for the answer: $1^2 + 3^2 = 1 + 9 = 10$
  (d) Repeat (b) for the answer: $1^2 + 0^2 = 1$

  23 is a so-called 'happy' number because it ends in one.

- Take another number, say 7.

  Write 7 as 07 to maintain the pattern of squaring and adding the digits.

  Here is the sequence:

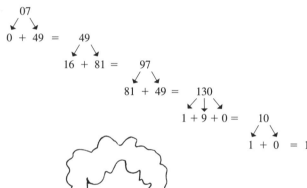

So 7 is a happy number also.

With practice you may be able to do the arithmetic in your head and write: $07 \rightarrow 49 \rightarrow 97 \rightarrow 130 \rightarrow 10 \rightarrow 1$.

You may find it helpful to make a list of the square numbers 1^2, 2^2, 3^2, ... 9^2.

- Your task is to find all the happy numbers from 1 to 100 and to circle them on a grid like the one shown.
  This may appear to be a very time-consuming and rather tedious task!
  But remember: Good mathematicians always look for short cuts and for ways of reducing the working.

  So think about what you are doing and good luck!
  As a final check you should find that there are 20 happy numbers from 1 to 100.

1	2	3	4	5	6	7	8	9	10
11	12	13	14	15	16	17	18	19	20
21	22	23	24	25	26	27	28	29	30
31	32	33	34	35	36	37	38	39	40
41	42	43	44	45	46	47	48	49	50
51	52	53	54	55	56	57	58	59	60
61	62	63	64	65	66	67	68	69	70
71	72	73	74	75	76	77	78	79	80
81	82	83	84	85	86	87	88	89	90
91	92	93	94	95	96	97	98	99	100

3.2 Order of operations

- Mathematicians all over the world regularly exchange their ideas and the results of their theories, even though much of the time they are unable to speak the same language! They can communicate mathematically because it has been agreed that everyone follows certain rules.

- Consider the possible answers to this question:
  'What is five add seven multiplied by three?'

  By adding first, we obtain: $5 + 7 \times 3$
  $$= 12 \times 3$$
  $$= 36$$

  By multiplying first, we obtain: $5 + 7 \times 3$
  $$= 5 + 21$$
  $$= 26$$

  As it stands both answers make perfect sense, though if we could all come up with different answers to the same mathematical question life would be rather stressful as people would have to argue constantly over who is correct.

- The table below shows the order in which everyone must do the given mathematical operations to ensure we all agree.

B rackets	( )	do first	'B'
I ndices	x^y	do next	'I'
D ivision M ultiplication	÷ ×	do this pair next	'D' 'M'
A ddition S ubtraction	+ −	do this pair next	'A' 'S'

Remember the word 'B I D M A S'.

(a) $40 \div 5 \times 2$
$$= 8 \times 2$$
$$= 16$$

(b) $9 + 8 - 7$
$$= 17 - 7$$
$$= 10$$

(c) $5 + 2 \times 3$
$$= 5 + 6$$
$$= 11$$
× before +

(d) $10 - 8 \div 2$
$$= 10 - 4$$
$$= 6$$
÷ before −

Exercise 1

Work out the following. Show every step in your working.

1. $5 + 3 \times 2$	**2.** $4 - 1 \times 3$	**3.** $7 - 4 \times 3$
4. $2 + 2 \times 5$	**5.** $9 + 2 \times 6$	**6.** $13 - 11 \times 1$
7. $7 \times 2 + 3$	**8.** $9 \times 4 - 12$	**9.** $2 \times 8 - 7$
10. $4 \times 7 + 2$	**11.** $13 \times 2 + 4$	**12.** $8 \times 5 - 15$
13. $6 + 10 \div 5$	**14.** $7 - 16 \div 8$	**15.** $8 - 14 \div 7$
16. $5 + 18 \div 6$	**17.** $5 + 18 \div 6$	**18.** $6 - 12 \div 4$
19. $20 \div 4 + 2$	**20.** $15 \div 3 - 7$	**21.** $24 \div 6 - 8$
22. $30 \div 6 + 9$	**23.** $8 \div 2 + 9$	**24.** $28 \div 7 - 4$
25. $13 + 3 \times 13$	**26.** $9 + 26 \div 13$	**27.** $10 \times 8 - 70$
28. $96 \div 4 - 4$	**29.** $36 \div 9 + 1$	**30.** $1 \times 2 + 3$

(a) $8 + 3 \times 4 - 6$
$= 8 + (3 \times 4) - 6$
$= 8 + 12 - 6$
$= 14$

$\times$ and $\div$
before
$+$ and $-$

(b) $3 \times 2 - 8 \div 4$
$= (3 \times 2) - (8 \div 4)$
$= 6 - 2$
$= 4$

(c) $\dfrac{8 + 6}{2} = \dfrac{14}{2}$
$= 7$
A horizontal line acts as a bracket.

Notice that we have put brackets in to make the working easier.

Exercise 2

Evaluate the following. Show every step in your working.

1. $2 + 3 \times 4 + 1$	**2.** $4 + 8 \times 2 - 10$	**3.** $7 + 2 \times 2 - 6$
4. $25 - 7 \times 3 + 5$	**5.** $17 - 3 \times 5 + 9$	**6.** $11 - 9 \times 1 - 1$
7. $1 + 6 \div 2 + 3$	**8.** $6 + 28 \div 7 - 2$	**9.** $8 + 15 \div 3 - 5$
10. $5 - 36 \div 9 + 3$	**11.** $6 - 24 \div 4 + 0$	**12.** $8 - 30 \div 6 - 2$
13. $3 \times 4 + 1 \times 6$	**14.** $4 \times 4 + 14 \div 7$	**15.** $2 \times 5 + 8 \div 4$
16. $21 \div 3 + 5 \times 4$	**17.** $10 \div 2 + 1 \times 3$	**18.** $15 \div 5 + 18 \div 6$
19. $5 \times 5 - 6 \times 4$	**20.** $2 \times 12 - 4 \div 2$	**21.** $7 \times 2 - 10 \div 2$
22. $35 \div 7 - 5 \times 1$	**23.** $36 \div 3 - 1 \times 7$	**24.** $42 \div 6 - 56 \div 8$
25. $72 \div 9 + 132 \div 11$	**26.** $19 + 35 \div 5 - 16$	**27.** $50 - 6 \times 7 + 8$
28. $30 - 9 \times 2 + 40$	**29.** $4 \times 11 - 28 \div 7$	**30.** $13 \times 11 - 4 \times 8$

In Questions **31** to **50** remember to perform the operation in the brackets first.

31. $3 + (6 \times 8)$

32. $(3 \times 8) + 6$

33. $(8 \div 4) + 9$

34. $3 \times (9 \div 3)$

35. $(5 \times 9) - 17$

36. $10 + (12 \times 8)$

37. $(16 - 7) \times 6$

38. $48 \div (14 - 2)$

39. $64 \div (4 \times 4)$

40. $81 + (9 \times 8)$

41. $67 - (24 \div 3)$

42. $(12 \times 8) + 69$

43. $(6 \times 6) + (7 \times 7)$

44. $(12 \div 3) \times (18 \div 6)$

45. $(5 \times 12) - (3 \times 9)$

46. $(20 - 12) \times (17 - 9)$

47. $100 - (99 \div 3)$

48. $1001 + (57 \times 3)$

49. $(3 \times 4 \times 5) - (72 \div 9)$

50. $(2 \times 5 \times 3) \div (11 - 5)$

51. $\dfrac{15 - 7}{2}$

52. $\dfrac{160}{7 + 3}$

53. $\dfrac{19 + 13}{6 - 2}$

54. $\dfrac{5 \times 7 - 9}{13}$

Indices

Remember BIDMAS: **B** rackets
I ndex
D ivide
M ultiply
A dd
S ubtract

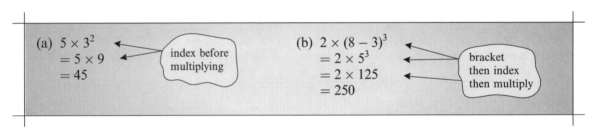

(a) 5×3^2
$= 5 \times 9$
$= 45$

index before multiplying

(b) $2 \times (8 - 3)^3$
$= 2 \times 5^3$
$= 2 \times 125$
$= 250$

bracket then index then multiply

Exercise 3

Evaluate the following, showing all your working.

1. 2^4

2. 3^3

3. 0^5

4. $10 + 3^3$

5. $4^2 - 8$

6. $32 - 5^2$

7. $3 + 3^2$

8. 8^2

9. 5×4^2

10. $3^2 \times 2$

11. 62×2^3

12. $5^3 \times 1$

13. $1^4 \times 3^4$

14. $(1 + 1)^3$

15. $(1 + 2)^3$

16. $(5 - 4)^3$

17. $4 \times (3 + 1)^2$

18. $(9 - 5)^4 \div 4$

19. $2 \times (3^2 - 1)$

20. $(5^2 + 5^2) \div 5$

21. $2 \times (6 - 3)^2$

22. $5 \times (2 \times 1)^3$

23. 3×2^3

24. $20 - 4^2$

Working backwards

Exercise 4

Copy each question and write brackets so that each calculation gives
the correct answer.

1. $3 + 4 \times 5 = 35$
2. $6 + 9 \times 7 = 69$
3. $7 \times 2 + 3 = 17$
4. $9 + 12 \times 5 = 105$
5. $6 \times 8 - 2 = 36$
6. $3 \times 8 - 6 = 18$
7. $19 - 6 \times 3 = 39$
8. $27 - 9 \div 3 = 24$
9. $51 \div 3 + 4 = 21$
10. $7 \times 24 - 5 = 133$
11. $6 + 14 \div 2 = 10$
12. $11 + 6 \times 4 = 68$
13. $12 \times 8 - 9 \times 7 = 33$
14. $8 \times 9 - 4 \times 7 = 44$
15. $5 \times 6 - 4 \div 2 = 13$
16. $81 \div 9 \times 12 - 4 = 72$
17. $3 + 5 \times 9 - 7 = 16$
18. $16 - 10 \div 18 \div 6 = 2$
19. $6 + 7 - 1 \div 2 = 6$
20. $5 + 7 \div 3 \times 0 = 0$

Jumble the numbers

Exercise 5

Using each number once, find the calculation which gives the correct
answer.

For example:

Numbers	Answer	Calculation
5, 3, 6	3	$(6 - 5) \times 3 = 3$

	Numbers			Answer	Calculation		Numbers			Answer	Calculation
1.	2	4	8	6		**2.**	2	3	5	21	
3.	7	2	3	3		**4.**	9	2	4	7	
5.	8	4	5	20		**6.**	20	2	3	6	
7.	7	2	4	30		**8.**	7	22	6	20	
9.	6	4	3	8		**10.**	8	40	3	8	
11.	8	36	4	5		**12.**	7	49	2	14	
13.	21	14	11	24		**14.**	16	3	9	57	
15.	12	4	16	7		**16.**	24	42	6	24	
17.	18	5	13	25		**18.**	40	6	16	4	
19.	7	8	6	50		**20.**	13	8	4	44	
21.	4	3	9	12		**22.**	7	9	3	21	
23.	45	4	3	11		**24.**	121	11	7	77	

25. Make up your own question to try on a friend.
    You may use as many numbers as you like.

3.3 Using a calculator

Money and time on a calculator

- To work out £27·30 ÷ 7, key in $\boxed{27\cdot3}$ $\boxed{\div}$ $\boxed{7}$ $\boxed{=}$
  The answer is 3·9. *Remember* this means £3·90.

- A machine takes 15 minutes to make one toy. How long will it take to make 1627 toys?
  15 minutes is one quarter of an hour and $\frac{1}{4} = 0\cdot25$ as a decimal.

  Key in $\boxed{0\cdot25}$ $\boxed{\times}$ $\boxed{1627}$ $\boxed{=}$.

  The answer is 406·75.
  It will take 406·75 hours or 406 hours 45 minutes.

- 6 minutes is $\frac{6}{60}$ of an hour. $\frac{6}{60} = \frac{1}{10} = 0.1$ hours.
  Similarly 27 minutes $= \frac{27}{60}$ of an hour. $\frac{27}{60} = 0\cdot45$ hours.

Exercise 1

1. Work out the following and give your answer in *pounds*.
   (a) £1·22 × 5   (b) £153·60 ÷ 24   (c) £12·35 − £7·65
   (d) 20p × 580   (e) 6p × 2155   (f) £10 ÷ 250

2. Write these time intervals in hours as decimals.
   (a) 2 h 30 min   (b) 4 h 15 min   (c) 3 h 45 min
   (d)   6 min   (e)   12 min   (f)   54 min
   (g) 5 h 24 min   (h) 1 h 20 min   (i) 3 h 40 min

3. Work out the following and give your answer in *hours*.
   (a) 2 h 45 min × 9   (b) 3 h 20 min × 9   (c) 14 h 30 min ÷ 5
   (d) 24 min × 15   (e) 27 min × 22   (f) 18 min × 58

4. Convert the following into hours.

   (a) 435 minutes   (b) 980 minutes   (c) 1350 minutes
   (d) 144 minutes   (e) 216 minutes   (f) 460 minutes

> 6 min $= \dfrac{6}{60}$ hour
>
> $= 0\cdot1$ hour
>
> 15 min $= \dfrac{15}{60}$ hour
>
> $= 0\cdot25$ hour

Order of operations

Where there is a mixture of operations to be performed to avoid uncertainty you must follow these rules:
(a) work out brackets first
(b) work out indices next
(c) work out ÷, × before +, −

Remember: 'BIDMAS' from Section 3.2 in this book.

It is good practice to check your answers by estimation or by performing the inverse operation.

Exercise 2

Use a calculator and give the answer correct to one decimal place.

1. 2.5×1.67

2. $19.6 - 3.7311$

3. 0.792^2

4. $0.13 + 8.9 - 3.714$

5. $2.4^2 - 1.712$

6. $5.3 \times 1.7 + 3.7$

7. $0.71 \times 0.92 - 0.15$

8. $9.6 \div 1.72$

9. $8.17 - 1.56 + 7.4$

10. $\dfrac{6.3}{1.84}$

11. $\dfrac{19.7}{8.24} + 1.97$

12. $\dfrac{2.63}{1.9} - 0.71$

In Questions **13** to **30** remember 'BIDMAS'.

13. $2.5 + 3.1 \times 2.4$

14. $7.81 + 0.7 \times 1.82$

15. $8.73 + 9 \div 11$

16. $11.7 \div 9 - 0.74$

17. $7 \div 0.32 + 1.15$

18. $2.6 + 5.2 \times 1.7$

19. $2.9 + \dfrac{8.3}{1.83}$

20. $1.7^2 + 2.62$

21. $5.2 + \dfrac{11.7}{1.85}$

22. $9.64 + 26 \div 12.7$

23. $1.27 + 3.1^2$

24. $4.2^2 \div 9.4$

25. $0.151 + 1.4 \times 9.2$

26. 1.7^3

27. $8.2 + 3.2 \times 3.3$

28. $3.2 + \dfrac{1.41}{6.72}$

29. $\dfrac{1.9 + 3.71}{2.3}$

30. $\dfrac{8.7 - 5.371}{1.14}$

Using brackets

Most calculators (apart from those given away free with a packet of 'Honey Nut Loops') have brackets buttons like these $\boxed{[(\_\_\_}$, $\boxed{\_\_\_)]}$.

When you press the left hand bracket button $\boxed{[(\_\_\_}$ you may see

$\boxed{\text{[01} \qquad \text{0.}}$ ignore this.

When the right hand bracket button is pressed you will see that the calculation inside the brackets has been performed. Try it.

Don't forget to press the $\boxed{=}$ button at the end to give the final answer.

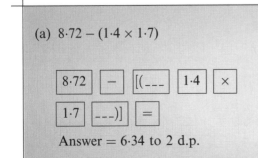

(a) $8.72 - (1.4 \times 1.7)$

$\boxed{8.72}$ $\boxed{-}$ $\boxed{[(\_\_\_}$ $\boxed{1.4}$ $\boxed{\times}$
$\boxed{1.7}$ $\boxed{\_\_\_)]}$ $\boxed{=}$

Answer $= 6.34$ to 2 d.p.

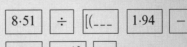

(b) $\dfrac{8.51}{(1.94 - 0.711)}$

$\boxed{8.51}$ $\boxed{\div}$ $\boxed{[(\_\_\_}$ $\boxed{1.94}$ $\boxed{-}$
$\boxed{0.711}$ $\boxed{\_\_\_)]}$ $\boxed{=}$

Answer $= 6.92$ to 2 d.p.

Exercise 3

Work out and give the answer correct to 2 decimal places.

1. $18 \cdot 41 - (7 \cdot 2 \times 1 \cdot 3)$

2. $11 \cdot 01 + (2 \cdot 6 \div 7)$

3. $(1 \cdot 27 + 5 \cdot 6) \div 1 \cdot 4$

4. $9 \cdot 6 + (11 \cdot 2 \div 4)$

5. $(8 \cdot 6 \div 3) - 1 \cdot 4$

6. $11 \cdot 7 - (2 \cdot 6 \times 2 \cdot 7)$

7. $7 \cdot 41 - \left(\dfrac{7 \cdot 3}{1 \cdot 4} \right)$

8. $\left(\dfrac{8 \cdot 91}{1 \cdot 7} \right) - 2 \cdot 63$

9. $\dfrac{1 \cdot 41}{(1 \cdot 7 + 0 \cdot 21)}$

10. $(1 \cdot 56 + 1 \cdot 9) \div 2 \cdot 45$

11. $3 \cdot 2 \times (1 \cdot 9 - 0 \cdot 74)$

12. $8 \cdot 9 \div (1 \cdot 3 - 0 \cdot 711)$

13. $(8 \cdot 72 \div 1 \cdot 4) \times 1 \cdot 49$

14. $(2 \cdot 67 + 1 \cdot 2 + 5) \times 1 \cdot 13$

15. $23 - (9 \cdot 2 \times 1 \cdot 85)$

16. $\dfrac{(8 \cdot 41 + 1 \cdot 73)}{1 \cdot 47}$

17. $\dfrac{7 \cdot 23}{(8 \cdot 2 \times 0 \cdot 91)}$

18. $\dfrac{(11 \cdot 4 - 7 \cdot 87)}{17}$

In Questions **19** to **40** use the $\boxed{x^2}$ button where needed.

19. $2 \cdot 6^2 - 1 \cdot 4$

20. $8 \cdot 3^2 \times 1 \cdot 17$

21. $7 \cdot 2^2 \div 6 \cdot 67$

22. $(1 \cdot 4 + 2 \cdot 67)^2$

23. $(8 \cdot 41 - 5 \cdot 7)^2$

24. $(2 \cdot 7 \times 1 \cdot 31)^2$

25. $8 \cdot 2^2 - (1 \cdot 4 + 1 \cdot 73)$

26. $\dfrac{2 \cdot 6^2}{(1 \cdot 3 + 2 \cdot 99)}$

27. $4 \cdot 1^2 - \left(\dfrac{8 \cdot 7}{3 \cdot 2} \right)$

28. $\dfrac{(2 \cdot 7 + 6 \cdot 04)}{(1 \cdot 4 + 2 \cdot 11)}$

29. $\dfrac{(8 \cdot 71 - 1 \cdot 6)}{(2 \cdot 4 + 9 \cdot 73)}$

30. $\left(\dfrac{2 \cdot 3}{1 \cdot 4} \right)^2$

31. $9 \cdot 72^2 - (2 \cdot 9 \times 2 \cdot 7)$

32. $(3 \cdot 3 + 1 \cdot 3^2) \times 9$

33. $(2 \cdot 7^2 - 2 \cdot 1) \div 5$

34. $\left(\dfrac{2 \cdot 84}{7} \right) + \left(\dfrac{7}{11 \cdot 2} \right)$

35. $\dfrac{(2 \cdot 7 \times 8 \cdot 1)}{(12 - 8 \cdot 51)}$

36. $\left(\dfrac{2 \cdot 3}{1 \cdot 5} \right) - \left(\dfrac{6 \cdot 3}{8 \cdot 9} \right)$

37. $(1 \cdot 31 + 2 \cdot 705) - 1 \cdot 3^2$

38. $(2 \cdot 71 - 0 \cdot 951) \times 5 \cdot 62$

39. $\dfrac{(8 \cdot 5 \times 1 \cdot 952)}{(7 \cdot 2 - 5 \cdot 96)}$

40. $\left(\dfrac{80 \cdot 7}{30 \cdot 3} \right) - \left(\dfrac{11 \cdot 7}{10 \cdot 2} \right)$

Calculator words

- When you hold a calculator display upside down some numbers

  appear to form words: 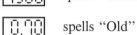 spells "Gosh"

  $\boxed{0.70}$ spells "Old"

  (ignoring the decimal point)

Exercise 4

Translate this passage using a calculator and the clues below:

" ①___ !" shouted Olag out of the window of his ②___ . "I need

some ③___ / ④___ for my dinner. Do you ⑤___ them?"

" ⑥___ did" ⑦___ / ⑧___ "I even took off the ⑨___ for free.

⑩___ / ⑪___ / ⑫___ they were. The problem is that all the ⑬___

were eaten in the ⑭___ , mostly by ⑮___ . ⑯___ / ⑰___ such a

⑱___ / ⑲___ lately. ⑳___ and ㉑___ are always ㉒___ because of

the amount of ㉓___ they drink every night"

" ㉔___ well, he is the ㉕___ I suppose" Olag grumbled "Roast ㉖___

again tonight then ..."

Clues to passage

①: $2(9-4)$

②: $(3 \div 40) + 0{\cdot}0011$

③: $\frac{3}{8} - (39{\cdot}2 \div 10^4)$

④: $5 \times 12 \times 100 - 7$

⑤: $(90 \times 80) + (107 \times 5)$

⑥: $\sqrt{0{\cdot}01} \times 10$

⑦: $(68 + 1{\cdot}23) \div 200$

⑧: $101^2 - (5 \times 13) - 2$

⑨: $750^2 + (296\,900 \div 20)$

⑩: $2^3 \times 5^2 \times 3 + 16{\cdot}3 + 1{\cdot}7$

⑪: $(70\,000 \div 2) + (3 \times 2)$

⑫: $11\,986 \div 2$

⑬: $(600^2 - 6640) \div 10$

⑭: $200^2 - 685$

⑮: $(0{\cdot}5^2 \times 0{\cdot}6)$

⑯: $\sqrt{289} \times 2$

⑰: $836{\cdot}4 \div 17 + 1{\cdot}8$

⑱: $30^2 + 18$

⑲: $5^3 \times 64{\cdot}6$

⑳: $(63\,508 \times 5) - 3$

㉑: $\sqrt{(1160 - 4)}$

㉒: $1{\cdot}3803 \times 0{\cdot}25$

㉓: $(32 \times 10^3) + 8$

㉔: $2^3 \times 5$

㉕: $(5^3 \times 2^2 \times 11) + 8$

㉖: $7 \times 10^7 - 9\,563\,966$

Using the memory

We will use the following memory keys: $\boxed{\text{Min}}$ Puts a number into the memory.

$\boxed{\text{MR}}$ Recalls a number from the memory.

To *clear* the memory we will press $\boxed{0}$ $\boxed{\text{Min}}$.

Many calculators will keep a number stored in the memory even when they are switched off. A letter 'M' on the display shows that the memory does contain a number.

The $\boxed{\text{Min}}$ key is very useful because it *automatically* clears any number already in the memory when it puts in the new number.

So if you pressed $\boxed{13\cdot2}$ $\boxed{\text{Min}}$ $\boxed{6\cdot5}$ $\boxed{\text{Min}}$, the number in the memory would be 6·5. The 13·2 is effectively 'lost'.

Work out, correct to 2 decimal places.

(a) $\dfrac{8\cdot97}{1\cdot6 - 0\cdot973}$

Work out the bottom line first.

$\boxed{1\cdot6}$ $\boxed{-}$ $\boxed{0\cdot973}$ $\boxed{=}$ $\boxed{\text{Min}}$

$\boxed{8\cdot97}$ $\boxed{\div}$ $\boxed{\text{MR}}$ $\boxed{=}$

Answer = 14·31 to 2 d.p.

(b) $8\cdot51 - \left(\dfrac{3\cdot24}{1\cdot73}\right)$

Work out the brackets first.

$\boxed{3\cdot24}$ $\boxed{\div}$ $\boxed{1\cdot7}$ $\boxed{=}$ $\boxed{\text{Min}}$

$\boxed{8\cdot51}$ $\boxed{-}$ $\boxed{\text{MR}}$ $\boxed{=}$

Answer = 6·64 to 2 d.p.

A very common error occurs when people forget to press the $\boxed{=}$ button at the end of the calculation.

Exercise 5

Work out and give the answer correct to 2 decimal places.

1. $\dfrac{5\cdot63}{2\cdot8 - 1\cdot71}$

2. $\dfrac{11\cdot5}{5\cdot24 + 1\cdot57}$

3. $\dfrac{8\cdot27}{2\cdot9 \times 1\cdot35}$

4. $\dfrac{3\cdot7 - 2\cdot41}{1\cdot9 + 0\cdot72}$

5. $\dfrac{8\cdot5 + 9\cdot3}{12\cdot9 - 8\cdot72}$

6. $\dfrac{0\cdot97 \times 3\cdot85}{1\cdot24 + 4\cdot63}$

7. $14\cdot5 - \left(\dfrac{1\cdot9}{0\cdot7}\right)$

8. $8\cdot41 - 3\cdot2 \times 1\cdot76$

9. $11\cdot62 - \dfrac{6\cdot3}{9\cdot8}$

10. $\dfrac{9\cdot84 \times 0\cdot751}{6\cdot3 \times 0\cdot95}$

11. $5\cdot62 + 1\cdot98 + \dfrac{1\cdot2}{4\cdot5}$

12. $8\cdot5 - \dfrac{8\cdot9}{11\cdot6}$

13. $\dfrac{6\cdot3}{4\cdot2} + \dfrac{8\cdot2}{11\cdot9}$

14. $\dfrac{8\cdot43 + 1\cdot99}{9\cdot6 - 1\cdot73}$

15. $\dfrac{17\cdot6}{8\cdot4} - \dfrac{1\cdot92}{8\cdot41}$

16. $25\cdot1 - 4\cdot2^2$

17. $(9\cdot8 - 4\cdot43)^2$

18. $18\cdot7 - 2\cdot33^2$

19. $8\cdot21^2 + 1\cdot67^2$

20. $9\cdot23^2 - 7\cdot42^2$

21. $16\cdot1 - 1\cdot1^2$

22. $\dfrac{16\cdot1}{4\cdot7} - 1\cdot8^2$

23. $\left(\dfrac{17\cdot2}{9\cdot8} - 1\cdot2\right)^2$

24. $9\cdot9 - 8\cdot3 \times 0\cdot075$

25. $1\cdot21 - \dfrac{9}{14^2}$

26. $3\cdot7^2 + \dfrac{11\cdot4}{1\cdot7}$

27. $\dfrac{11\cdot7 - 3\cdot73}{2\cdot45^2}$

28. $\dfrac{8\cdot94}{4\cdot8 + 1\cdot7^2}$

29. $\dfrac{3\cdot21^2}{8\cdot2 - 4\cdot11}$

30. $\dfrac{116\cdot7}{8\cdot1^2 + 32}$

31. $8\cdot7 + \dfrac{8\cdot2}{9\cdot7} + \dfrac{4\cdot1}{5\cdot6}$

32. $8\cdot5 - (1\cdot6^2 + 1\cdot9^2)$

33. $8\cdot3 + \dfrac{1\cdot9}{8\cdot4} - \dfrac{1\cdot7}{6\cdot5}$

34. $3\cdot2 + \left(3\cdot2 + \dfrac{1\cdot4}{5}\right)^2$

35. $\dfrac{3\cdot4}{1\cdot6} + \left(\dfrac{2\cdot1}{1\cdot3}\right)^2$

36. $\left(8\cdot2 - \dfrac{1}{8\cdot2}\right) \times 8\cdot2$

3.4 Metric and Imperial units

Originally measurements were made by using appropriately sized bits of human being. The inch was measured using the thumb, (hence we still sometimes say 'rule of thumb' when we mean rough measurement), the foot by using the foot.

After the French Revolution in 1789 the standard unit of length became the metre and the unit of mass became the kilogram. All the smaller and larger units are obtained by dividing or multiplying by ten, a hundred, a thousand and so on.

Here is a table with details of the most commonly used units for length, mass and volume.

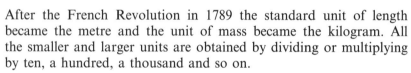

Metric units		**Imperial units**
Length	10 mm = 1 cm	12 inches = 1 foot
	100 cm = 1 m	3 feet = 1 yard
	1000 m = 1 km	1760 yards = 1 mile
Mass	1000 mg = 1 g	16 ounces = 1 pound
	1000 g = 1 kg	14 pounds = 1 stone
	1000 kg = 1 tonne	2240 pounds = 1 ton
Volume	1000 ml = 1 litre	8 pints = 1 gallon
	1 ml = 1 cm^3	

Exercise 1

Copy and complete

1. 57 cm =   m
2. 1·3 km =   m
3. 0·24 kg =   g
4. 600 g =   kg

5. 17 mm =   cm
6. 3000 kg =   t
7. 0·6 m =   cm
8. 14 mm =   cm

9. 2000 ml =   ℓ
10. 305 g =   kg
11. 80 cm =   m
12. 200 mm =   m

13. 2·5 t =   kg
14. 2·4 m =   mm
15. 20 g =   kg
16. 4·5 ℓ =   ml

17. 2 ℓ =   cm³
18. 5·5 m =   cm
19. 56 mm =   m
20. 7 g =   kg

Questions **21** to **30** involve imperial units

21. 3 feet =   inches
22. 5 yards =   feet

23. 2 pounds =   ounces
24. 9 stones =   pounds

25. 24 inches =   feet
26. $\frac{1}{2}$ pound =   ounces

27. 2 feet 6 inches =   inches
28. 1 ton =   pounds

29. 8 stones 4 pounds =   pounds
30. 5 feet 2 inches =   inches

Questions **31** to **45** involve a mixture of metric and imperial units.

31. 0·032 kg =   g
32. 6 feet =   yards
33. 8 ounces =   pound

34. 1 mile =   feet
35. 235 mm =   cm
36. 0·42 t =   kg

37. 11·1 cm =   m
38. $\frac{1}{4}$ pound =   ounces
39. 7 litres =   ml

40. 4 yards =   feet
41. 7 mm =   cm
42. 2 gallons =   pints

43. 400 m =   km
44. 5 gallons =   pints
45. 10 miles =   yards

Converting between metric and imperial units

- It is sometimes necessary to convert imperial units into metric units and vice versa.
  Try to remember the following *approximate equivalents*:

1 inch ≈ 2·5 cm	1 kg ≈ 2·2 pounds
1 foot ≈ 30 cm	30 g ≈ 1 ounce
1 km ≈ $\frac{5}{8}$ mile	1 gallon ≈ 4·5 litres

  [The '≈' sign means 'is approximately equal to'.]

- Here are some familiar objects to help you remember.

A one pound coin has a mass of about 10 grams.

A standard bag of sugar has a mass of 1 kg.

A 'tall' adult man is about 6 feet tall. [180 cm]

Exercise 2

Copy each sentence and choose the number which is the best estimate.

1. The Prime Minister is about [1 m, 6 feet, 8 feet] tall.

2. An egg weighs about [$\frac{1}{2}$ oz, 60 g, 1 kg].

3. The distance from London to Dover is about [60 miles, 300 km, 10 miles].

4. A bag of crisps weighs about [25 g, 100 g, 1 lb].

5. The thickness of a pound coin is about [1 mm, 3 mm, 6 mm].

6. The perimeter of the classroom is about [30 m, 10 m, $\frac{1}{10}$ mile].

7. A can of coke contains about [500 ml, 2 litres, 20 ml].

8. The width of one of my fingers is about [1 mm, 5 mm, 10 mm].

9. Suppose you have just won a prize which is one million grams of gold! Which of the following would you need to take away your prize?
(a) A large suitcase
(b) A van
(c) Two large delivery lorries

10. Work out:
(a) 3 m + 65 cm [in cm]   (b) 5 km + 25 m [in m]   (c) 04 kg + 300 g [in g]
(d) 5 cm + 5 mm [in mm]   (e) 6 cm + 6 mm [in cm]   (f) 7 m + 18 cm [in m]

Exercise 3

Copy and complete using the approximate conversions given above.

1. 3 kg ≈   pounds   **2.** 10 inches ≈   cm   **3.** 4 gallons ≈   litres

4. 24 km ≈   miles   **5.** 5 feet ≈   cm   **6.** 80 kg ≈   pounds

7. 4 inches ≈   cm   **8.** 10 gallons ≈   litres   **9.** 6 feet 2 inches ≈   cm

10. All the teachers at Gibson Academy must be at least 5 feet 6 inches tall. Mr Swan is 1·70 m tall. Is he tall enough to teach at Gibson Academy?

11. A boxer must weigh no more than 10 stones just before his fight. With two days to go he weighs 65 kg.
Roughly how much weight in pounds does he have to lose to get down to the 10 stone limit?

12. A car manual states that 2 gallons of oil must be put into the engine before it is started. Roughly how much will it cost if oil costs £1·20 per litre?

13. If the speed limit on a road in Holland is 80 km/h, what is the equivalent speed limit in m.p.h.?

14. The perimeter of a farm is about 40 km. What is the approximate perimeter of the farm in miles?

15. Here are scales for changing:
    A kilograms and pounds,
    B litres and gallons.
    In this question give your answers to the *nearest whole number*.
    (a) About how many kilograms are there in 6 pounds?
    (b) About how many litres are there in 3·3 gallons?
    (c) About how many pounds are there in 1·4 kilograms?

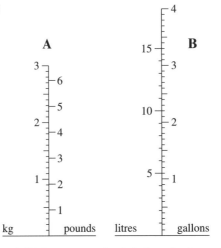

16. A carpenter requires a 12 mm drill for a certain job but he has only the imperial sizes $\frac{1}{4}$, $\frac{1}{2}$ and $\frac{3}{4}$ inch.
    Which of these drills is the closest in size to 12 mm?

17. At a charity cake sale all the proceeds were collected in 10p coins and then the coins were arranged in a long straight line for a newspaper photo.
    If the diameter of a 10p coin is just under one inch and the line of coins was 50 metres long, roughly how much money was raised?

18.* Grass seed should be sown at the rate of $\frac{3}{4}$ of an ounce per square yard. One packet of seed contains 3 lb of seed. How many packets of seed are needed for a rectangular garden measuring 60 feet by 36 feet? [3 feet = 1 yard, 16 ounces = 1 lb]

Changing units

When a problem has quantities measured in different units the first thing you must do is change some of the units so that all quantities are in the same units.

● Find the area of the rectangular table top shown.

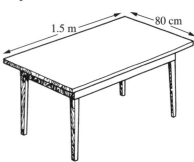

Write 80 cm as 0·8 m.

Area of table $= 1·5 \times 0·8$.
$\qquad\qquad = 1·2 \, \text{m}^2$.

- A piece of metal weighing 2 kg is melted down and cast into small cubes each weighing 50 g.
  How many cubes can be made?
  Write 2 kg as 2000 g.

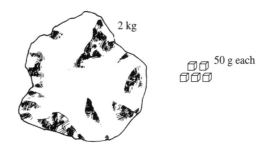

  Number of cubes = 2000 ÷ 50.
  $\qquad\qquad\qquad\qquad$ = 40.

- A *very* common error occurs where the units of an area are changed.

Here is a square of side 1 m. 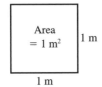 The same square has sides of 100 cm.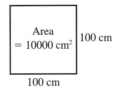

So 1 m² = 10 000 cm²   [NOT 100 cm²!].

Exercise 4

1. Find the area of each shape in m².

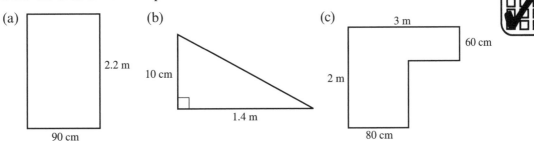

(a)   2.2 m   90 cm

(b)   10 cm   1.4 m

(c)   3 m   60 cm   2 m   80 cm

2. An urn containing 56 litres of water is used to fill cups of capacity 140 ml. How many cups can be filled?

3. A shopping bag weighing 65 g contains the following items:
- 3 bags of flour weighing 1·2 kg each
- 1 tube of toothpaste weighing 200 g
- 15 packets of crisps each weighing 25 g.

Find the total weight of the bag and its contents in kg.

4. A large lump of 'Playdoh' weighing 3·6 kg is cut up into 800 identical pieces. Find the weight of each piece in grams.

5. In an equatorial forest a young tree grows at a constant rate of 18 cm per day. How much in mm does it grow in one minute?

6. A solid gold coin weighing 0·84 kg is melted down and cast into tiny coins each weighing 150 mg.
How many small coins can be made?

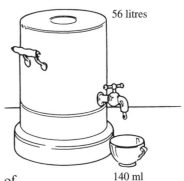

7. Every face of the rectangular block shown is painted. The tin of paint used contains enough paint to cover an area of $8\,m^2$. How many blocks can be painted completely?

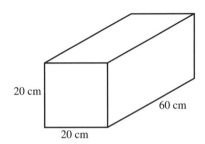

20 cm

60 cm

20 cm

8. Water is leaking from a tap at a rate of $1{\cdot}2\,cm^3$ per second. How many litres of water will leak from the tap in a seven day week?

9. Calculate the area of each shape in cm^2.

(a)

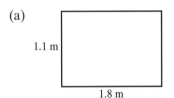

1.1 m

1.8 m

(b)

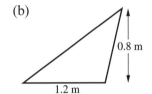

0.8 m

1.2 m

(c)

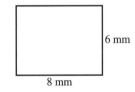

6 mm

8 mm

10. The diagram shows the outline of a strip of farmland.
   (a) Calculate the area of the field in hectares. [1 hectare = $10\,000\,m^2$]
   (b) The field is sprayed with a pesticide and it takes 3 seconds to spray $100\,m^2$. How many hours will it take to spray the entire field?

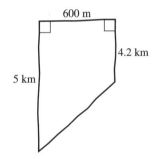

600 m

4.2 km

5 km

11. The waterfall with the greatest flow of water in the world is the 'Guaira' between Brazil and Paraguay. Its estimated average flow is $13\,000\,m^3$ per second. The dome of St Paul's Cathedral has a capacity of $7800\,m^3$. How long would it take the waterfall to fill the dome?

12. In the U.K. about $90\,000$ tonnes of tobacco are smoked as cigarettes each year.
   (a) If one cigarette weighs $0{\cdot}9\,g$, work out how many cigarettes are smoked in the U.K. every year. [You can work out the answer without a calculator].
   (b) If a packet of 20 cigarettes costs £4, how much is spent in the U.K. on cigarettes every year?

3.5 Handling data

Newspapers regularly present the results of surveys or research in the form of pie charts.

Most computers are programmed so that they can easily display information in interesting charts, possibly in colour or with a '3-D' effect.

It is a good idea to use colours freely in your own work and sometimes people make charts more eye-catching by drawing small pictures to illustrate the sectors.

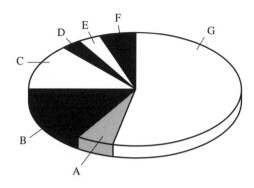

Pie charts

In a pie chart a circle is divided into sectors to display information. Pie charts are often used to show the results of a survey. The sectors of the circle show what *fraction* of the total is in each group.

A farmer divides his land into three parts. He uses 5 acres for corn, 3 acres for carrots and 2 acres for pigs.

(a) Add the three parts: $5 + 3 + 2 = 10$ acres
(b) 10 acres $= 360°$
$$1 \text{ acre} = \frac{360}{10}$$
$$= 36°$$
(c) For corn, 5 acres $= 5 \times 36° = 180°$
For carrots, 3 acres $= 3 \times 36° = 108°$
For pigs, 2 acres $= 2 \times 36° = 72°$

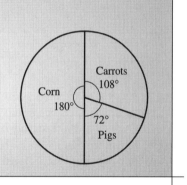

- This pie chart shows the afterschool activities of 200 pupils.
  (a) The number of pupils $= \frac{36}{360} \times 200 = 20$ pupils doing drama
  (b) the number of pupils $= \frac{144}{360} \times 200 = 80$ doing sport
  (c) the number of pupils $= \frac{45}{360} \times 200 = 25$ doing computing

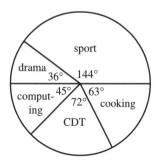

Exercise 3

1.  The pie chart shows the contents of a bar of chocolate.
(a) What fraction of the contents is chocolate?
(b) What fraction of the contents is toffee?
(c) If the total weight of the packet is 400 g, what is the weight of nuts?

2. In a survey children said what pets they had at home.
(a) What fraction of the children had a hamster?
(b) What fraction of the children had a dog?
(c) 40 children took part in the survey.
    How many of these children had a pet spider?

3. In another survey children were asked what *pests* they had at home. $\frac{1}{3}$ of the children said, 'my sister'.
What angle would you draw for the 'my sister' sector on a pie chart?

4. The pie chart shows the results of a survey in which 80 people were asked how they travelled to work. Copy this table and fill it in.

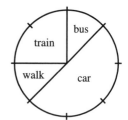

Method	car	walk	train	bus
Number of people				

5. Lara had £24 to spend on presents. The pie chart shows how much she spent on each person.
How much did she spend on:
(a) her mum   (b) her dad
(c) her brother   (d) her grandma
(e) her friend   (f) her auntie?
[Make sure that your answers add up to £24.]

6. Six hundred families travelling home on a ferry were asked to name the country in which they had spent most of their holiday. The pie chart represents their answers.

(a) How many stayed longest (i) in Portugal?
                            (ii) in Spain?

(b) What angle represents holidays in Switzerland?

(c) How many families stayed longest in Switzerland?

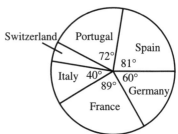

7. A 'Chewit' bar contains these four ingredients:

    Oats   6 g
    Barley   9 g
    Sugar   3 g
    Rye   18 g

   (a) Work out the total weight of the ingredients.
   (b) Work out the angle on a pie chart for 1 g of the ingredients
      [i.e. $360° \div$ (total weight)].
   (c) Work out the angle for each ingredient and draw a pie chart.

In Questions **8**, **9**, **10** work out the angle for each sector and draw a pie chart.

8. Number of programmes per night.

Programme	Frequency
News	2
Soap	5
Comedy	4
Drama	5
Film	2

9. Pupils' favourite sports.

Sport	Frequency
Rugby	5
Football	7
Tennis	4
Squash	2
Athletics	3
Swimming	3

10. Periods per subject.

Subject	Frequency
Maths	5
English	5
Science	6
Humanities	4
Arts	4
Others	16

11. At the 'Crooked Corkscrew' last Friday, 120 customers ordered meals.

    40 ordered beefburger
    20 ordered ham salad
    16 ordered curry
    25 ordered cod
    19 ordered chicken.

Draw a pie chart to show this information.

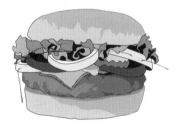

12. In a survey the children at a school were asked to state their favourite sport in the Olympics.
   (a) Estimate what fraction of the children chose gymnastics.
   (b) There are 120 children in the school. Estimate the number of children who chose athletics.
   (c) 15% of the children chose swimming. How many children was that?

13. A hidden observer watched Stephen in a 60 minute maths lesson. This is how he spent his time:

Looking for a calculator	8 minutes
Sharpening a pencil	7 minutes
Talking	32 minutes
Checking the clock	2 minutes
Working	4 minutes
Packing up	7 minutes

Draw an accurate pie chart to illustrate Stephen's lesson.

14. The pie chart illustrates the sales of four brands of petrol.
   (a) What percentage of total sales does BP have?
   (b) If Shell accounts for 35% of total sales, calculate the angles x and y.

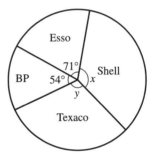

15. In a survey 320 on an aircraft and 800 people on a ferry were asked to state their nationality.

Aircraft
320
people

Ferry
800
people

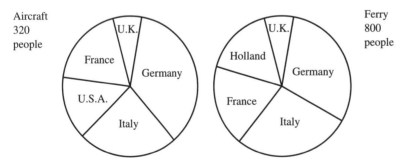

   (a) Roughly what percentage of the people on the aircraft were from the U.K.?
   (b) Roughly how many people from France were on the ferry?
   (c) Jill looked at the charts and said 'There were about the same number of people from Italy on the aircraft and on the ferry'. Explain why Jill is wrong.

Bar charts and bar-line graphs

When you do a survey the information you collect is called *data*.
This data is usually easier for someone else to understand if you
display it in some sort of chart or graph.

(a) The scores of 35 golfers competing
in a tournament were

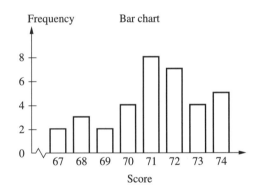

68	74	71	72	71	68	70
74	69	71	70	67	73	71
70	74	69	72	73	74	71
72	74	71	72	72	70	73
67	68	72	73	72	71	71

(b) A tally chart/frequency table is
made for the scores.

score	tally	frequency
67	||	2
68	|||	3
69	||	2
70	||||	4
71	卌 |||	8
72	卌 ||	7
73	||||	4
74	卌	5

(c) This data can be displayed on either a bar chart or on a bar-line
graph. The '⌇' shows that a section on the horizontal axis
has been cut out.

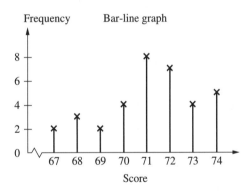

Exercise 2

1. In a survey children were asked to name their
favourite sport.
   (a) What was the most popular sport?
   (b) How many children chose Athletics?
   (c) How many children took part in the survey?

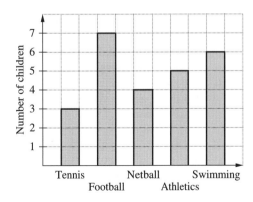

2. This chart shows the number of packets of different flavours of crisps sold by a shop.

(a) How many packets of crisps were sold on Wednesday?

(b) Each packet of Ready Salted crisps costs 15p. How much was spent on Ready Salted crisps in the whole week?

	M	Tu	W	Th	F
Ready Salted	3	1	2	4	0
Salt 'n Vinegar	4	2	5	3	1
Cheese 'n Onion	5	1	3	1	4
Roast Beef	3	2	6	4	1
Prawn	1	1	2	4	4

(c) This is a graph of one flavour of crisps.
Which flavour is it?

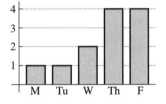

3. The number of people staying in two different hotels in each month of the year is shown below.

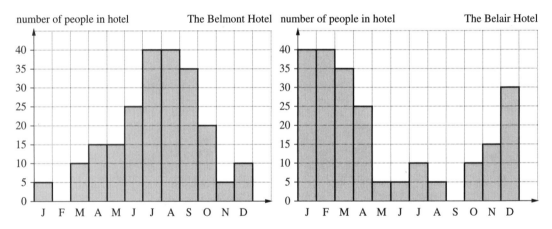

(a) How many people stayed in the 'Belmont' in July?
(b) How many people stayed in the 'Belair' in July?
(c) What was the total number of people staying in the two hotels in April?
(d) One hotel is in a ski resort and the other is by the seaside. Which hotel is in the ski resort?

4. The bar charts show the sale of different things over a year but the labels on the charts have been lost. Decide which of the charts A, B, C or D shows sales of:

(a) Christmas trees
(b) Crisps
(c) Flower seeds
(d) Greetings cards [including Christmas, Valentine's Day, etc.]

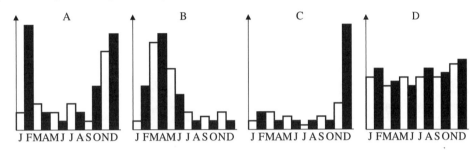

5. This bar line graph shows the number of bedrooms in the houses in one road.
   (a) How many houses had 4 bedrooms?
   (b) How many houses are in the road?
   (c) Why would it not be sensible to join the tops of the bars to make a line graph?

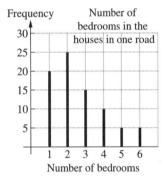

6. The bar chart shows the results of a survey in which 2000 people in each of 20 countries were asked if they had reported that their car had been stolen in the previous 12 months.
   (a) In which country or countries was the reported rate of theft worst?
   (b) Of the 2000 people questioned in the United States, how many had reported a car stolen?
   (c) What does the chart show for Switzerland?
   (d) Roughly how many times more likely were people in England and Wales to report a car theft compared to people in Germany?
   (e) Why do you think Scotland's rate of theft is so much lower than that in England?

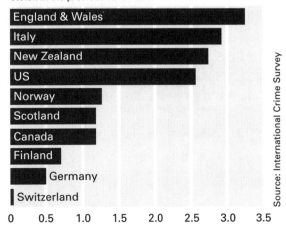

Car theft around the world

Percentage of motorists who reported that their car had been stolen in the previous 12 months

Source: International Crime Survey

Data in groups

When a large number of results are to be displayed it is often more convenient to put the data into groups. Suppose we wanted to draw a frequency diagram to show the heights of 25 children given below.

130·2, 145·4, 132·2, 140·9, 150·0, 152·7, 132·1, 141·8, 144·9,
142·0, 137·2, 146·0, 134·6, 143·3, 138·9, 144·5, 137·0, 136·2,
139·0, 142·7, 148·1, 147·2, 136·6, 143·9, 153·8. [In cm]

The heights are put into groups as shown and the number of people in each group is found. A frequency diagram can then be drawn.

class interval	frequency
130 ≤ h < 135	4
135 ≤ h < 140	6
140 ≤ h < 145	8
145 ≤ h < 150	4
150 ≤ h < 155	3
h = height (cm)	

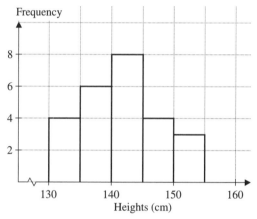

- The group 150 ≤ h < 155 means 'heights greater than or equal to 150 and less than 155.
  So a height of 150 goes into this group.
- A height of 149·5 goes into the group 145 ≤ h < 150.
- All heights are possible (not just certain values) so there are no gaps between the bars on the frequency diagram.

Exercise 3

1. At a medical inspection the 11/12 year-olds in a school have their heights measured. The results are shown.

   136·8, 146·2, 141·2, 147·2, 151·3, 145·0, 155·0,
   149·9, 138·0, 146·8, 157·4, 143·1, 143·5, 147·2,
   147·5, 158·6, 154·7, 144·6, 152·4, 144·0, 151·0.

   (a) Put the heights into groups

class interval	frequency
135 ≤ h < 140	
140 ≤ h < 145	
145 ≤ h < 150	

   (b) Draw a frequency diagram

   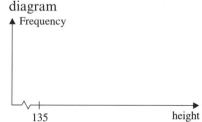

2. A group of 7 year-olds were each accompanied by one of their parents on a coach trip to a zoo. Each person on the coach was weighed in kg. Here are the weights:

21·1, 45·7, 22·3, 26·3, 50·1, 24·3, 44·2,
54·3, 53·2, 46·0, 51·0, 24·2, 56·4, 20·6,
25·5, 22·8, 52·0, 26·5, 41·8, 27·5, 29·7,
55·1, 30·7, 47·4, 23·5, 59·8, 49·3, 23·4,
21·7, 57·6, 22·6, 58·7, 28·6, 54·1.

(a) Put the weights into groups.

class interval	frequency
20 ⩽ w < 25	
25 ⩽ w < 30	
30 ⩽ w < 35	
⋮	

(b) Draw a frequency diagram.
(c) Why is the shape of the frequency diagram different to the diagram you drew in Question 1?
(d) What shape of frequency diagram would you expect to obtain if you drew a diagram to show the heights of pupils in your class?

3. A drug company claims that its new nutrient pill helps people to improve their memory.

As an experiment two randomly selected groups of people were given the same memory test. Group A took the new pills for a month while group B took no pills. Here are the results of the tests: (A high score indicates a good memory).

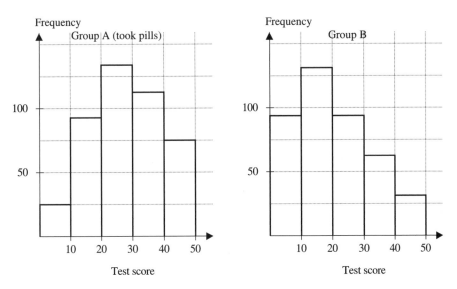

Does it appear that the new pills did in fact help to improve memory?

4. Farmer Gray rears pigs. As an experiment, he decided to feed half of his pigs with their normal diet and the other half on a new high fibre diet. The diagrams shows the weight of the pigs in the two groups.

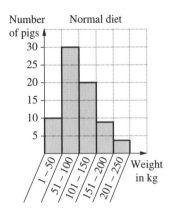 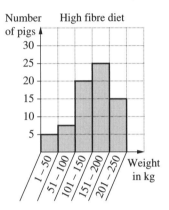

In one sentence describe what effect the new diet had.

5. A teacher has a theory that pupils' test results are affected by the amount of T.V. watched at home.

With the willing cooperation of the children's parents, the pupils were split into two groups:

    Group X watched at least two hours of T.V. per day.
    Group Y watched a maximum of half an hour per day.

The pupils were given two tests: one at the start of the experiment and another test six months later. Here are the results:

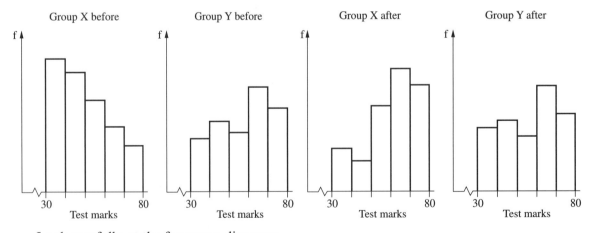

Look carefully at the frequency diagrams.
What conclusions can you draw? Was the teacher's theory correct?
Give details of how the pupils in group X and in group Y performed in the two tests.

6. Here is an age distribution pyramid for the children at a Center Parcs resort.

(a) How many girls were there aged 5–9?

(b) How many children were there altogether in the 0–4 age range?

(c) How many girls were at the resort?

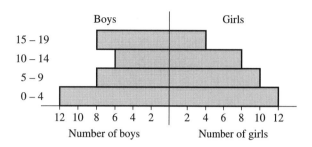

7. Here are age distribution pyramids for the U.K., Kenya and Saudi Arabia. The bars represent the percentage of the population in the age group shown.

(a) For the U.K. about what percentage of the population are *male aged 20–24*?

(b) For Kenya about what percentage are *female aged 0–4*?

(c) What percentage of the population are *female aged 75+*

   (i) for the U.K.?

   (ii) for Kenya?

(d) Look carefully at the charts for the U.K. and Kenya. Write a sentence to describe the main differences in the age distribution for the two countries. Write a possible explanation for the differences you observed.

(e) Look carefully at the charts for Kenya and Saudi Arabia. Do both countries have about half male and half female populations? Explain your answer using information in the charts.

Problems answered using statistics

Many problems in mathematics and other subjects, like science or geography can be solved by statistical methods.

The data relevant to such problems might be obtained from:

- a survey of a sample of people;

- an experiment;

- published material, such as tables or charts, from reference books.

Here are two examples of problems which can be answered using statistical methods.

1. Do different newspapers use words of different length or sentences of different length? Why would they do this?

   In this case you could conduct an experiment by choosing a similar page from different newspapers.

   Record your results in a table.

Number of words in a sentence	1–5	6–10	11–15	16–20	21 or more
Times					
Sun					
Mail					

2. What factors are most important to the customers of supermarkets?

   In this case you could conduct a survey asking about price of food, quality of food, speed of checkouts, ease of car parking and so on.
   You would need questions designed so that shoppers could state the importance, or otherwise, of the factors you include.

Reporting on results

Most work of this nature is easier to understand if data is presented in the form of graphs and charts. You should *justify* the choice of the data you present. You might find it helpful to include calculations of mean or range depending on the context.
Your report should highlight the main findings of your work and you shold write a clear *summary* which relates back to the original problem.

Collecting your own data

- For many people the most interesting data is the data *they* decide to find because it is what interests *them*. Below is a simple questionnaire and record sheet.
  Use some of the questions given and add others about topics which interest *you*.

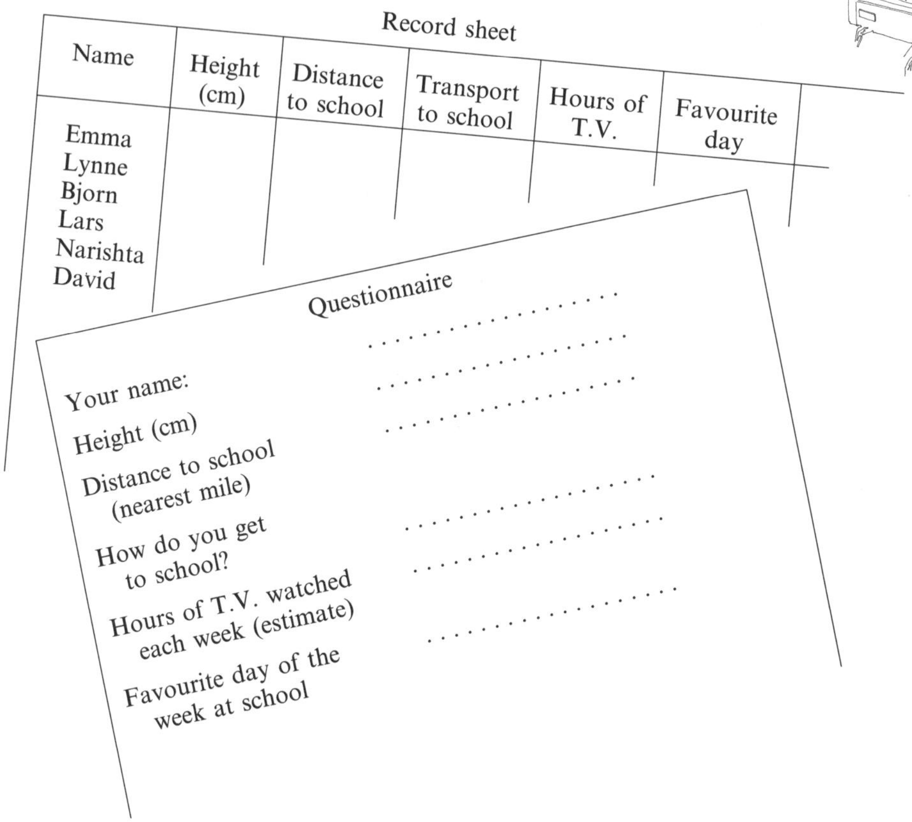

-

Record sheet

Name	Height (cm)	Distance to school	Transport to school	Hours of T.V.	Favourite day
Emma Lynne Bjorn Lars Narishta David					

Questionnaire

Your name: ....

Height (cm) ....

Distance to school
(nearest mile) ....

How do you get
to school? ....

Hours of T.V. watched
each week (estimate) ....

Favourite day of the
week at school

- Suppose you get 20 different answers to the question: 'What is your favourite T.V. program?'
  A bar chart with a bar for each program will look very dull! You could try putting the programs into groups like 'comedy', 'soaps', 'sports', 'drama' etc. The choice is yours.

Exercise 4

1. Write a questionnaire and ask as many people as possible to answer it. Complete a record sheet, like the one shown above, to summarise the results.

2. Choose three of the questions from the list or question of your choice and draw a chart to illustrate the results. Make at least one of the charts for data which has to be put in *groups* (like height, distance to school, hours of T.V.) Write a *short* report about the results you found.

3.6 Mid-book review

Exercise 1

1. Copy and complete these number machines

   (a) $5 \to \boxed{\times 3} \to \boxed{+12} \to \boxed{\div 9} \to ?$ (b) $? \to \boxed{\times 2} \to \boxed{+20} \to 50$

2. Work out the missing digits in each division.

   (a) $\dfrac{\boxed{}\,\boxed{}\,2}{4)\,7\ \ 2\ \boxed{}}$ (b) $\dfrac{2\ \ 9}{3)\,\boxed{}\ 7}$

3. A teacher marked 2000 questions. There were 25 pupils in the class. If each pupil did the same number of questions, how many questions did each pupil do?

4. How many hundreds make a million?

5. Find the number of hours and minutes between:
   (a) 15.30 and 18.00
   (b) 05.35 and 09.10
   (c) 9.30 a.m. and 1.40 p.m.

In Questions **6** to **14** answer 'true' or 'false'.
[$>$ means 'is greater than', $<$ means ' is less than']

6. $0.2 = \frac{1}{5}$ 7. $6.2 < 6.02$ 8. $6 = 6.00$
9. $£3.40 = £3.4$ 10. $0.88 > 0.088$ 11. $0.001 < 0.0001$
12. $0.6 > 0.59$ 13. $10p = £0.1$ 14. $0.75 = \frac{3}{5}$

15. Which list is arranged in ascending order?

    A   0·14, 0·05, 0·062, 0·09
    B   0·14, 0·09, 0·062, 0·05
    C   0·050, 0·062, 0·09, 0·14
    D   0·050, 0·090, 0·14, 0·062

16. Write down the next term in each sequence.

    (a) 71, 80, 89, 98,   (b) 3·6, 3·7, 3·8, 3·9,
    (c) 2·3, 2·2, 2·1, 2,   (d) $\frac{1}{4}, \frac{2}{5}, \frac{3}{6}, \frac{4}{7},$

17. The rule for the sequences here is '*multiply by 3 and add 1*'. Find the missing numbers

(a) $1 \rightarrow 4 \rightarrow 13 \rightarrow \square$

(b) $\square \rightarrow 7 \rightarrow 22 \rightarrow \square$

(c) $\square \rightarrow 2 \rightarrow \square \rightarrow 22$

18. Write down the next number in each sequence.

(a) $\frac{1}{3}$, 1, 3, 9   (b) 500, 50, 5,   (c) 10, 9, 11, 8, 12,

19. (a) Sort the shapes below into two groups and label them Group A and Group B.

    Shape 1   Shape 2   Shape 3   Shape 4   Shape 5   Shape 6

(b) Give a reason why you put your shapes into groups 'A' and 'B'.

(c) Write down the correct mathematical name for each of the six shapes.

20. Name the triangle with three equal sides and angles.

21. What is the name of the triangle with two equal angles?

22. A triangle has sides of three different lengths. What type of triangle is it?

23. What four sided shape has all sides the same length and all angles equal?

24. Any quadrilateral can be cut into two triangles. True or false?

25. What is the mathematical name for a snooker ball that has been cut in half.

26. A sphere is a prism. True or false?

27. Here is the net for a cube.
    (a) When the net is folded up, which edge will be stuck to the edge JI?
    (b) Which edge will be stuck to the edge AB?
    (c) Which corner will meet corner D?

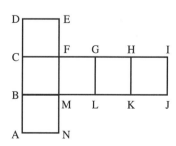

28. Round off to the nearest 100.
(a) 55627   (b) 258   (c) 674·2   (d) 44444

29. Round off correct to 1 decimal place.
(a) 3·628   (b) 0·764   (c) 11·25   (d) 8·041

30. Choose the correct answer: The number of seconds in a day is *about*:

     A   9000   **B**   90 000   **C**   30 000   **D**   300 000

31. At the end of year 7 Mark said 'I have now lived for over one million hours'. Work out if Mark was right.

32. The diagram opposite shows a room which is to be carpeted.
(a) Find the area of carpet required to cover the floor.
(b) What is the perimeter of the room?

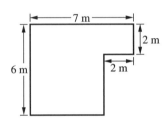

33. Work out the shaded area. All the lengths are in cm.

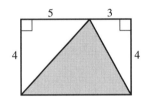

Exercise 2 [Topics in part 2]

1. Work out
(a) $\frac{3}{7} + \frac{1}{7}$ (b) $\frac{3}{8} - \frac{1}{4}$ (c) $\frac{5}{6} - \frac{1}{12}$ (d) $\frac{3}{5} - \frac{1}{15}$

2. Consider the fraction $\frac{2}{3}$. When both the numerator and the denominator are increased by 1, is the new fraction larger or smaller than $\frac{2}{3}$?

3. Work out
(a) $\frac{3}{8}$ of £24   (b) 10% of £36   (c) 25% of £48

(d) $\frac{1}{20}$ of £80   (e) 1% of £96   (f) 75% of £1000

4. The price of a playstation game was £30 but it is increased by 5%. What is the new price?

5. Write down the coordinates of the
   points which will produce this picture.

   Start at (3, 1) and follow the arrows.

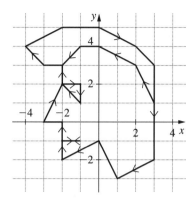

6. (a) Points A, D and E are three vertices of a
         square. Write down the coordinates of the
         other vertex.
   (b) A, B and C are three vertices of a square.
       Write down the coordinates of the other
       vertex.

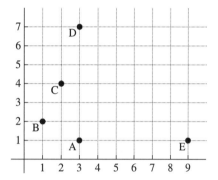

7. Draw a pair of axes with values of *x* and *y* from −6 to +6.
   Plot the points given and join them up to make a shape. Write
   down the name of the shape you have drawn.
   (a) (−6, −5) (−5, −3) (−2, −3) (−3, −5) [Join them up *in order!*]
   (b) (2, 0) (3, 2) (4, 2) (6, 0)
   (c) (2, −2) (5, −4) (2, −6) (1, −4)
   (d) (−4, 0) (−6, 6) (−2, 6)
   (e) (1, 5) (4, 6) (5, 3) (2, 2)

8. Find the expression I am left with.
   (a) I start with *x*, double it and then add 5.
   (b) I start with *n*, treble it and then subtract 7.
   (c) t ⇢ ×4 ⇢ +1 ⇢ ÷2 ⇢ ?

9. Find an expression for the
   perimeter of each shape

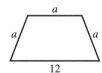 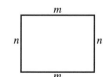

10. (a) Draw a shape with a *perimeter* of $2a + b$.
  (b) Draw a shape with *area* $6n$.

11. Simplify the following.
  (a) $3a + a + 2b + 2a$ (b) $5n + m - n + 3m$ (c) $4a + 7 - a - 6$

12. Here are five algebra cards.   **A** $\boxed{2n}$ **B** $\boxed{n+1}$ **C** $\boxed{3n-3}$
  (a) Add the expressions on card A
    and card C.
  (b) Which two cards always have the   **D** $\boxed{n+n}$ **E** $\boxed{5-n}$
    same value?
  (c) Which card has the largest value
    when $n = 4$?
  (d) Add the expressions on all five cards.

13. Use mental strategies to work out the following *in your head*.
  (a) $44 + 16 + 37$ (b) $99 + 47$ (c) double 74
  (d) 24×50 (e) double 128   (f) $95 - 29$

Exercise 3 [Topics in part 3]

1. Copy and continue this pattern for multiples of 7.
  7, 14, 21, $\underline{?}$, $\underline{?}$, $\underline{?}$ ...

2. List all the factors of each of these numbers
  (a) 18   (b) 27

3. Copy these numbers and circle the numbers that are not prime.
  (a) 7, 19, 13, 27.   (b) 31, 37, 39, 41.

4. Write down the first five multiples of:
  (a) 6   (b) 8

5. There is just one prime number between the numbers given.
  Copy each question and write the prime number in the box.
  (a) 20, $\square$, 26   (b) 44, $\square$, 52.

6. (a) List the numbers which are factors of both 18 and 30.
  (b) Write down the H.C.F. of 18 and 30.

7. Find a number which has 8 factors.

8. Write the number 2940 as the product of its prime factors.
Is 2940 a square number?

9. The number in a square is the product of the two numbers on either side of it. Copy and complete the two triangles.

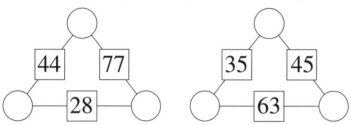

10. Work out
(a) $12 - 6 \div 3$ (b) $18 \div (1 + 5 \times 1)$ (c) $25 + 24 \div 24$
(d) $15 + 2^2$ (e) $5 \times 6 - 3 \times 4$ (f) $10 \times (2^2 - 1) + 4$

11. Use a calculator to work out the following. Give your answers correct to 1 d.p.

(a) $9 \cdot 23 + \dfrac{1 \cdot 7}{0 \cdot 92}$ (b) $\dfrac{3 \cdot 6^2 - 1 \cdot 74}{2 \cdot 2}$ (c) $\sqrt{\dfrac{98 \cdot 2}{1 \cdot 6}}$

(d) $9 \cdot 7 \times (11 \cdot 2 - 8 \cdot 714)$ (e) $\dfrac{9 \cdot 63 - 7 \cdot 291}{1 \cdot 73}$ (f) $\dfrac{32 \cdot 4}{8 \cdot 54 + 1 \cdot 69}$

12. Write the following with the correct signs inside the circles.
(a) $4 \times 3 \times 2 \bigcirc 1 = 25$
(b) $5 \times 2 \times 4 \bigcirc 3 = 37$
(c) $6 + 5 \bigcirc 4 \bigcirc 1 = 8$

13 A man's heart beats at 70 beats/min. How many times will his heart beat between 03.30 and 23.30 on the same day?

14. In one million seconds which of these would you be able to do?
(a) Take a term off school.
(b) Go without sleep for two whole days.
(c) Spend ten days on the beach in France.
(d) Go to Africa for a year.

Explain your working.

Operator squares

Each empty square contains either a number or an operation (+, −, ×, ÷). Copy each square and fill in the missing details. The arrows are equals signs.

1.

15	÷	3	→	
+		×		
		5	→	110
↓		↓		
37	−		→	

2.

14	+		→	31
×		+		
4		23	→	92
↓		↓		
	−		→	

3.

13	×		→	52
−		+		
	÷		→	
↓		↓		
8	÷		→	1

4.

17	×		→	170
−		÷		
	×		→	
↓		↓		
8	−	0.1	→	

5.

38	×	8	→	
÷		×		
2	×		→	
↓		↓		
	+	112	→	

6.

		574	→	1532
÷		+		
9	×	25	→	
↓		↓		
234	+		→	

7.

10	×		→	1
÷		×		
	×		→	
↓		↓		
2.5	+	0.02	→	

8.

19.6	÷	7	→	
×		−		
0.1	÷		→	1
↓		↓		
	+		→	

9.

8.42	×	0.2	→	
×		×		
100	×	0.3	→	
↓		↓		
	+		→	

10.

	−	0.1	→	
×		−		
	×	0.01	→	0.2
↓		↓		
400	×		→	

11.

1.22	×	3	→	
+		−		
	+		→	
↓		↓		
5	+		→	7.8

12.

	+		→	906
÷		−		
20	×	52	→	
↓		↓		
	+	526	→	

13.

	+	5.3	→	9.9
+		×		
0.4	×		→	400
↓		↓		
	+		→	

14.

	÷		→	
+		+		
40	÷		→	0.04
↓		↓		
2002	−		→	984

15.

	÷	13	→	50
÷		÷		
	÷		→	0.1
↓		↓		
32.5	+		→	

Designing squares

- Make up your own operator squares starting from a blank grid like the one shown. Try to make your square difficult to solve, but give enough information so that it can be done.

			→	
			→	
↓		↓		
			→	

- The grid shown opposite is much more difficult to fill (as you will discover!)
  Try to make up one of these 'super operator' squares.

			→	
			→	
↓		↓		↓
			→	

Here is one that works.

10	×	8	→	80
÷		÷		÷
2	×	2	→	4
↓		↓		↓
5	×	4	→	20

Part 4

4.1 Calculating angles

Angles on a straight line

The angles on a straight line add up to 180°

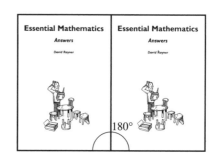

Find the angles marked with letters.

(a)

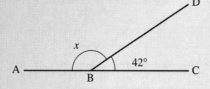

ABC is a straight line

$\therefore \quad x + 42 = 180$

$x = 138°$

(b)

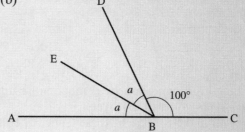

ABC is a straight line

$\therefore \quad a + a + 100 = 180$

$a = 40°$

Exercise 1

Find the angles marked with letters.

1.

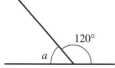

120°

a

2.

c 70°

3.

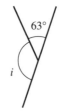

63°

i

4.

132°

j

5.

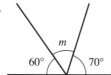

m

60° 70°

6.

n 50°

7.

18°

p

8.

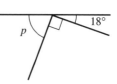

q 51°

42° 47°

9.

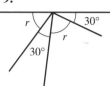

10.

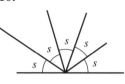

11.

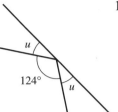

12.

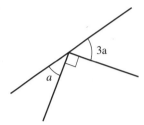

13.

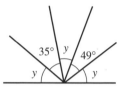

14.

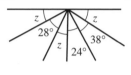

15.

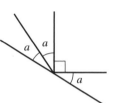

16.

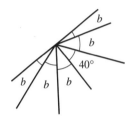

Angles at a point

The angles at a point add up to 360°

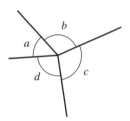

$$a + b + c + d = 360°$$

Exercise 2

Find the angles marked with letters.

1.

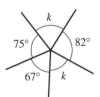

2.

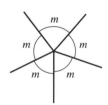

3.

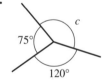

4.

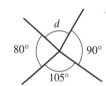

5.

6.

7.

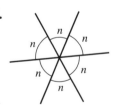

8.

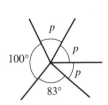

9.

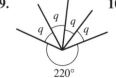

10.

11.

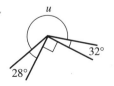

12.

Angles in triangles

Draw a triangle of any shape on a piece of card and cut it out accurately. Now tear off the three corners as shown.

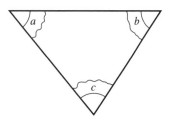

When the angles a, b and c are placed together they form a straight line.

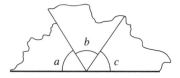

We see that:

> The angles in a triangle add up to 180°

Isosceles and equilateral triangles

An *isosceles* triangle has two equal sides and two equal angles.

The sides AB and AC are equal (marked with a dash) so angles $\widehat{B}$ and $\widehat{C}$ are also equal.

An *equilateral* triangle has three equal sides and three equal angles (all 60°).

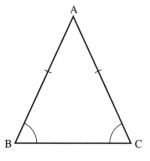

Intersecting lines

When two lines intersect, the opposite angles are equal.
In the diagram, $a = 36°$ and $b = 144°$

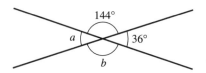

Find the angles marked with letters

(a)

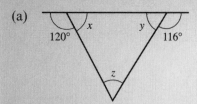

(b)

$x = 60°$ (angles on a straight line)
$y = 64°$ (angles on a straight line)
$z + 60 + 64 = 180$
$\quad z = 56°.$

$a = 71°$ (isosceles triangle)
$b + 71 + 71 = 180°$
$\quad\quad\quad b = 38°$

Exercise 3

Find the angles marked with letters.

1.
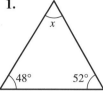

2.
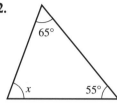

3.
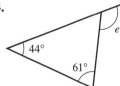

4.

5.
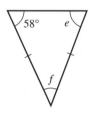

6.
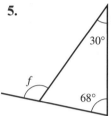

7.
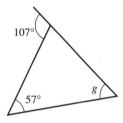

8.
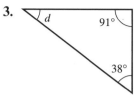

9.
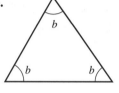

10.
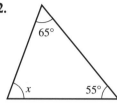

11.
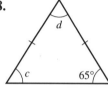

12.
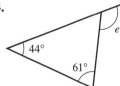

13.
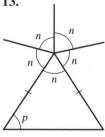

14.
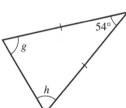

15.
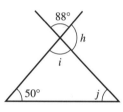

16.
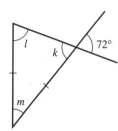

17.
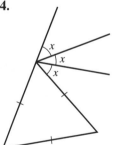

18.
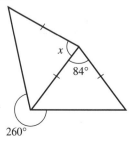

19.
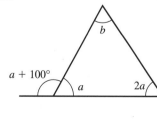

20.
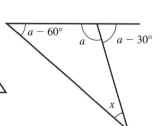

Angles and parallel lines

Two straight lines are *parallel* if they never meet.
They are always the same distance apart.

In the diagram, lines AB and CD are parallel.
Lines which are parallel are marked with arrows.
The line XY cuts AB and CD.

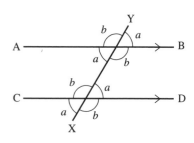

All the angles marked *a* are equal.
All the angles marked *b* are equal.
Remember:

All the acute angles are equal and all the obtuse angles are equal.

All the acute angles are equal and all the obtuse angles are equal

Many people prefer to think about 'Z' angles,   and 'F' angles

Find the angles marked with letters.

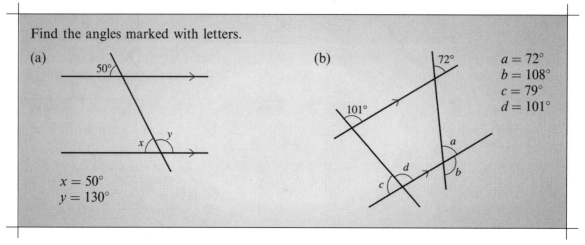

(a)

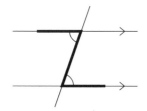

$x = 50°$
$y = 130°$

(b)

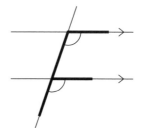

$a = 72°$
$b = 108°$
$c = 79°$
$d = 101°$

Exercise 4

Find the angles marked with letters.

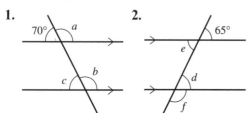

1.

2.

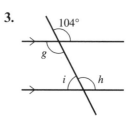

3.

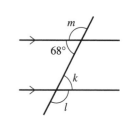

4.

5.
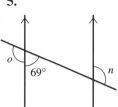

6.
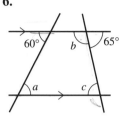

7.
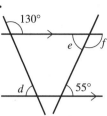

8.
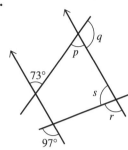

9.
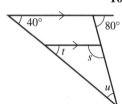

10.
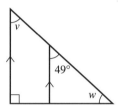

11.
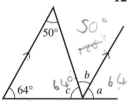

12.
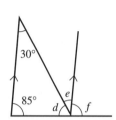

Angles in quadrilaterals

Draw a quadrilateral of any shape on a piece of paper or card and cut it out. Mark the four angles *a*, *b*, *c* and *d* and tear them off.

Arrange the four angles about a point.

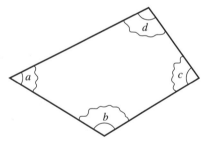

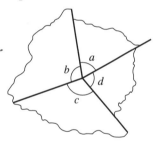

We see that: The angles in a quadrilateral add up to 360°

Mixed questions

Exercise 5

This exercise contains a mixture of questions which require a knowledge of all parts of this section. Find the angles marked with letters.

1.
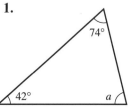

2.
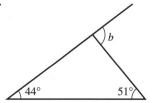

3.
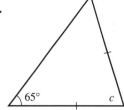

4.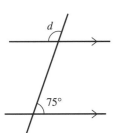

5.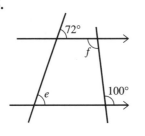

6.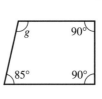

7.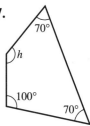

8.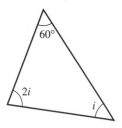

9.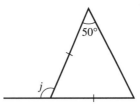

10.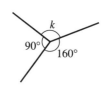

11.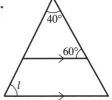

12.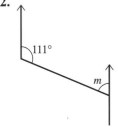

13.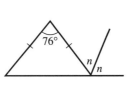

14.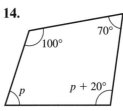

15.

16.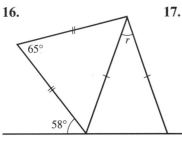

17.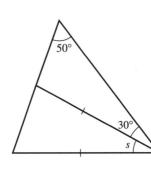

18.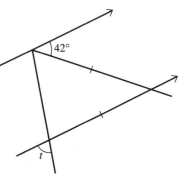

19.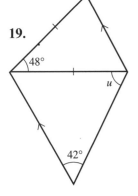

20.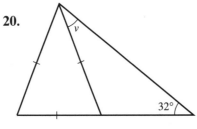

21.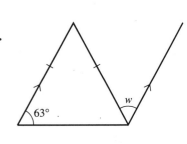

4.2 Ratio and proportion

Proportion

- We use proportion to compare part of something to the whole.
  We usually express a proportion as a fraction, decimal or
  percentage.
  For example:

  (a) In a class of 17 children, there are 7 boys and 10 girls. The
      proportion of boys in the class is $\frac{7}{17}$.
  (b) Clothes may be made from material in which the proportion
      which is cotton is 90%.

Exercise 1

1. The chart shows how people in a survey travel to work.
   (a) What proportion travel by train?
   (b) What proportion travel by car?

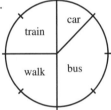

2. In a class of 30 children, 7 are left-handed. What proportion of
   the class is left-handed?

3. A soup contains 200 g of water and 50 g of vegetables. What
   proportion of the soup is vegetables?

4. The diagram shows how the government spends
   money on transport. Estimate, as a percentage,
   what proportion is spent on roads.

5. The proportion of lemon juice in a fruit drink is 250 ml in every
   litre. How much lemon juice is there in 3 litres of fruit drink?

6. Count the children in your class. What proportion of the class
   went to the same junior school as you?

● If 8 litres of petrol costs £7·20, find the cost of 10 litres. The cost of petrol is *directly proportional* to the quantity bought.

　　　8 litres costs £7·20

∴　　1 litre costs £7·20 ÷ 8 = £0·90

∴　　10 litres costs £0·90 × 10 = £9·00

Exercise 2

1. If 5 hammers cost £20, find the cost of 7.

2. Magazines cost £16 for 8. Find the cost of 3 magazines.

3. Find the cost of 2 cakes if 7 cakes cost £10·50.

4. A machine fills 1000 bottles in 5 minutes. How many bottles will it fill in 2 minutes?

5. A train travels 100 km in 20 minutes. How long will it take to travel 50 km?

6. 11 discs cost £13·20. Find the cost of 4 discs.

7. Fishing line costs £1·40 for 50 m. Find the cost of 3000 m.

8. If 7 cartons of milk hold 14 litres, find how much milk there is in 6 cartons.

9. A worker takes 8 minutes to make 2 circuit boards. How long would it take to make 7 circuit boards?

10. The total weight of 8 tiles is 1720 g. How much do 17 tiles weigh?

11. A machine can fill 3000 bottles in 15 minutes. How many bottles will it fill in 2 minutes?

12. A train travels 40 km in 120 minutes. How long will it take to travel 55 km at the same speed?

13. If 4 grapefruit can be bought for £2·96, how many can be bought for £8·14?

14. £15 can be exchanged for 126 francs. How many francs can be exchanged for £37·50?

15. Usually it takes 10 hours for 4 men to build a wall. How many men are needed to build a wall twice as big in 10 hours?

16. A car travels 280 km on 35 litres of petrol. How much petrol is needed for a journey of 440 km?

Ratio

● We use ratio to compare parts of a whole.

   For example:
   In an office of 18 people there are 12 men and 6 women.
   The ratio of men:women is 12:6.
   This is the same as 2:1.   [divide both numbers by 6]

● Ratios can often be written in a simpler form.

   For example:
   The ratios 4:16 and 1:4 are equivalent.   [divide by 4]
   The ratio 3:6:15 and 1:2:5 are equivalent.
   The ratios 0·5:3 and 1:6 are equivalent.   [multiply by 2]

● Split up £25 in the ratio 3:2

   We divide £25 into 3 + 2 'parts'.
   So there are 5 'parts'.
   Each part is £5.
   So 3 parts is £15 and 2 parts is £10.

Exercise 3

1. In a mixed class of 18 children, 11 are girls. Write down the ratio girls:boys.

2. In a cupboard there are 4 rulers and 20 pens. Find the ratio of pens:rulers.

3. In an evening, a vet sees 12 dogs and 8 cats. Find the ratio of dogs:cats.

4. Write these ratios in a more simple form.
   (a) 5:15   (b) 6:10   (c) 3:33
   (d) 4:6:8   (e) 14:35   (f) 0·5:4

5. On a farm, the ratio of cows to sheep is 5:8. If there are 25 cows, how many sheep are there?

6. In a crowd, the ratio of men to women is 3:5. If there are 12 men, how many women are there?

7. In a wood, the ratio of yew trees to ash trees is 2:3. If there are 30 ash trees, how many yew trees are there?

8. In a hall, the ratio of chairs to tables is 7:2. If there are 10 tables, how many chairs are there?

9. In a kitchen drawer, the ratio of knives to forks to spoons is 4:3:5. If there are 9 forks, how many knives are there and how many spoons are there?

10. Share these quantities in the ratios given.

   (a) 12 apples between Sam and Joe, ratio 2:1
   (b) 15 bananas between Emi and Maya, ratio 3:2
   (c) 35 chocolates between Rahul and Joel, ratio 1:6

11. Split up the quantity given in the ratio given.

   (a) split 35 kg in the ratio 2:3
   (b) split £99 in the ratio 4:7
   (c) split £39 in the ratio 4:9
   (d) split 44 kg in the ratio 6:2:3
   (e) split £80 in the ratio 4:1:5
   (f) split 56 m in the ratio 4:3:1

12. Andy, Ben and Chris did some work on a farm. They were paid in the ratio 4:2:1. Andy got £28, which was the most. What did Ben and Chris get paid?

13. Will says 'A ratio of 1 to 4 means the same as a proportion of 1 in 4.' Explain why Will is wrong.

14. On a bus, the ratio of children to adults is 4:1. What proportion of the people are adults?

4.3 Construction

Labelling angles

- The angle shown is AB̂C (or CB̂A).

- This angle is PÔR (or RÔP).

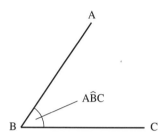

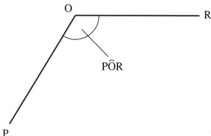

The 'B' must be in the middle.   The 'O' must be in the middle.

- Angles are labelled with capital letters and the middle letter wears a 'hat' to indicate an angle.

Exercise 1

Copy each diagram and write down the size of each angle requested.

1.

(a) DÊG   (b) FÊG

2.

(a) RQ̂S   (b) SQ̂P

3.

(a) MN̂L   (b) NL̂M   (c) LM̂N

4.

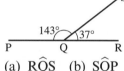

(a) KĴL   (b) JL̂K
(c) JK̂L

5.

(a) ZŴX   (b) XŴY

6.

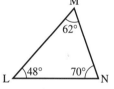

(a) DĈB   (b) DÂB
(c) CD̂A   (d) AB̂C

Using a protractor

A *protractor* is an instrument used to measure angles accurately.

Remember: When measuring an acute angle the answer must be less than 90°.
                      When measuring an obtuse angle the answer must be more than 90°.

Exercise 2

Give the measurement of each angle listed below.
Remember to read the correct scale. Some questions are done for you, to remind you of this.

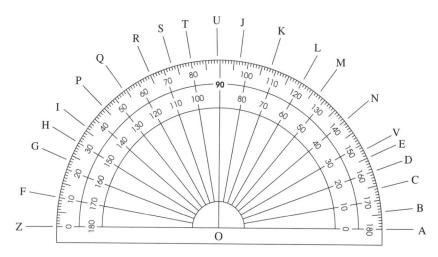

1. A$\hat{O}$D = 20°	**2.** A$\hat{O}$N =	**3.** A$\hat{O}$L = 60°	**4.** A$\hat{O}$K =
5. Z$\hat{O}$F =	**6.** Z$\hat{O}$P = 45°	**7.** Z$\hat{O}$R =	**8.** Z$\hat{O}$T = 80°
9. Z$\hat{O}$I =	**10.** Z$\hat{O}$G =	**11.** A$\hat{O}$C =	**12.** A$\hat{O}$V =
13. A$\hat{O}$Q = 126°	**14.** A$\hat{O}$P =	**15.** A$\hat{O}$F =	**16.** A$\hat{O}$B =
17. Z$\hat{O}$H =	**18.** Z$\hat{O}$B =	**19.** Z$\hat{O}$C =	**20.** Z$\hat{O}$D =
21. A$\hat{O}$G =	**22.** A$\hat{O}$H =	**23.** A$\hat{O}$I =	**24.** A$\hat{O}$M =
25. A$\hat{O}$R =	**26.** Z$\hat{O}$E =	**27.** Z$\hat{O}$J =	**28.** Z$\hat{O}$K =
29. Z$\hat{O}$L =	**30.** Z$\hat{O}$M =	**31.** A$\hat{O}$E =	**32.** A$\hat{O}$J =
33. A$\hat{O}$U =	**34.** A$\hat{O}$S =	**35.** Z$\hat{O}$N =	**36.** Z$\hat{O}$Q =
37. Z$\hat{O}$S =	**38.** Z$\hat{O}$U =	**39.** Z$\hat{O}$V =	**40.** A$\hat{O}$T =

Exercise 3

Measure these angles.

1.

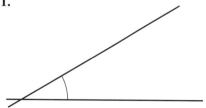

2.

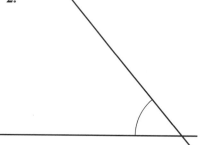

3.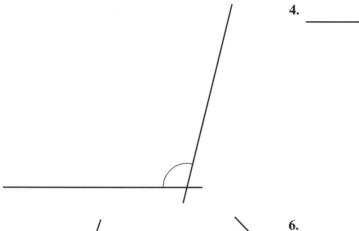

4.

5.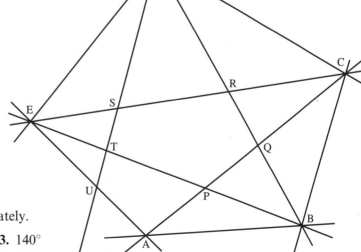

6.

Exercise 4 (More difficult)

Measure the following angles.

1. BÂC   2. RĈD
3. DÊR   4. EÂB
5. DR̂C   6. BÊA
7. SR̂B   8. AĈB
9. DT̂B   10. CP̂E
11. CD̂E   12. DŜC
13. DĈB   14. ED̂S
15. UD̂Q   16. EĈB

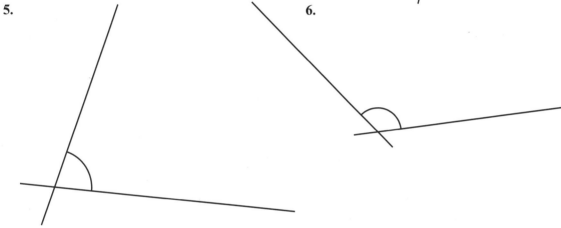

Exercise 5

Draw the following angles accurately.

1. 35°   2. 68°   3. 140°
4. 85°   5. 210°   6. 300°

Constructing triangles

A triangle is an extremely rigid structure. It is used extensively in the real world to support many objects. These objects can range from large structures, such as the roof on your house, to smaller structures, such as the brackets holding up your bookshelf.

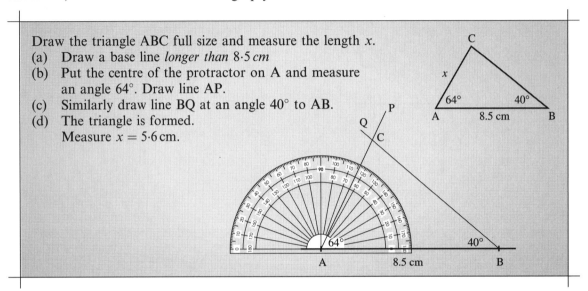

Draw the triangle ABC full size and measure the length x.
(a) Draw a base line *longer than* 8·5 cm
(b) Put the centre of the protractor on A and measure an angle 64°. Draw line AP.
(c) Similarly draw line BQ at an angle 40° to AB.
(d) The triangle is formed.
     Measure $x = 5·6$ cm.

Exercise 6

Construct the triangles and measure the lengths of the sides marked x.

1.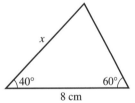

2.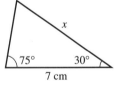

3.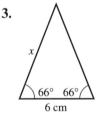

4.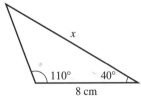

5.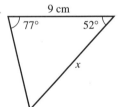

6.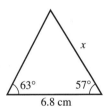

7.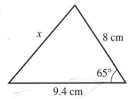

8.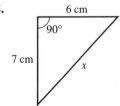

9.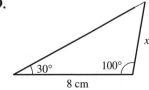

Questions **10**, **11**, **12** are more difficult.

10.

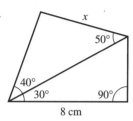

11.

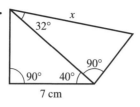

12.

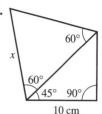

Constructing a triangle given three sides

Draw triangle XYZ and measure XẐY.

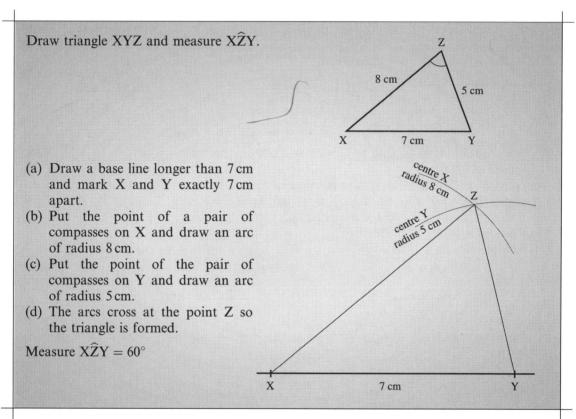

(a) Draw a base line longer than 7 cm and mark X and Y exactly 7 cm apart.
(b) Put the point of a pair of compasses on X and draw an arc of radius 8 cm.
(c) Put the point of the pair of compasses on Y and draw an arc of radius 5 cm.
(d) The arcs cross at the point Z so the triangle is formed.

Measure XẐY = 60°

Exercise 7

In Questions **1** to **6** use a pair of compasses and measure the angle *x*.

1.

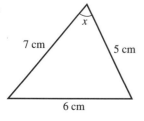

2.

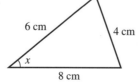

3.

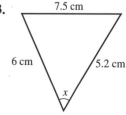

4.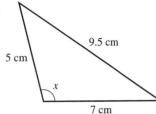

5.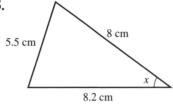

6.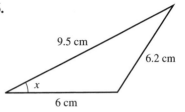

Questions **7**, **8**, and **9** are more difficult.

7.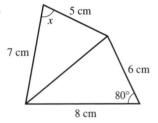

8.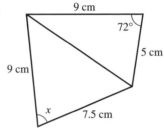

9.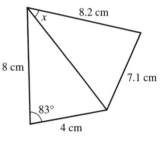

10. A disused airfield is to be sold at a price of £5500 per hectare.
(1 hectare $= 10\,000\,\text{m}^2$).
The outline of the airfield is a quadrilateral but it is not a
rectangle. The area can be found by splitting it into two
triangles and then finding the area of each part.
Find the selling price of the airfield.
[Use a scale of 1 cm to 100 m]

> You need to use the formula
> 'area $= \frac{1}{2}$ base × height' to find the area
> of a triangle.

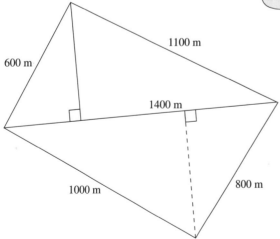

Keep the price down

A road is to be built between two towns: Brocket and Newton. The River Lea runs across the land between the towns. The land south of the river is very marshy and road building is more expensive than on the dry land north of the river. Building costs are as follows:

On dry land 1 km of road costs £100 000;
On marshy land 1 km of road costs £170 000;
A bridge over the river costs £400 000.

One possible 'scenic route' for the road is shown by the broken line.
(a) Find the total cost of building the road along the scenic route.
(b) Find the cheapest possible route for the road. Give the total cost by this route correct to the nearest £1000.

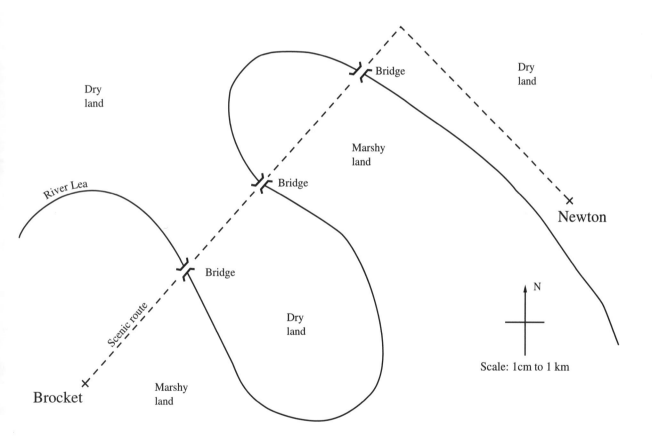

Teacher's note: The publisher has given permission for this page to be photocopied.

4.4 Decimals 2

Multiplying decimals by whole numbers

Method 1

- $7.93 \times 4 \approx 8 \times 4 = 32$
  (Estimate first)
  $7.93 \times 4 \quad 7.00 \times 4 = 28.00$
  $ 0.90 \times 4 = 3.60$
  $ 0.03 \times 4 = \underline{0.12} \ +$
  $ 31.72$

- $3.16 \times 6 \approx 3 \times 6 = 18$
  (Estimate first)
  $3.16 \times 6 \quad 3.00 \times 6 = 18.00$
  $ 0.10 \times 6 = 0.60$
  $ 0.06 \times 6 = \underline{0.36} \ +$
  $ 18.96$

Method 2

- $7.24 \times 4 \approx 7 \times 4 = 28$
  (Estimate first)
  7.24
  $\underline{\times 4}$
  28.96
  ${\scriptstyle 1}$

- $0.096 \times 9 \approx 0.1 \times 9 = 0.9$
  (Estimate first)
  0.096
  $\underline{\times 9}$
  0.864
  ${\scriptstyle 8\,5}$

> The answer has the same number of figures after the point as there are in the numbers being multiplied.

Exercise 1

Work out

1. 5.1
$\underline{\times 2}$

2. 2.3
$\underline{\times 3}$

3. 3.7
$\underline{\times 4}$

4. 5.6
$\underline{\times 5}$

5. 6.13
$\underline{\times 6}$

6. 10.22
$\underline{\times 7}$

7. 5.34
$\underline{\times 8}$

8. 1.29
$\underline{\times 9}$

9. 7×0.63 **10.** 1.452×6 **11.** 9×0.074 **12.** 11.3×5

13. 13.6×5 **14.** 0.074×5 **15.** 6×2.22 **16.** 8.4×11

17. Copy and complete with the missing numbers.

    (a) $0.3 \times 4 = \boxed{}$

    (b) $0.6 \times \boxed{} = 4.2$

    (c) $\boxed{} \times 5 = 2.0$

    (d) $1.5 = 6 \times \boxed{} + 0.3$

    (e) $\boxed{} \times 7 - 2 = 1.5$

    (f) $8 \times \boxed{} = 0.16$

18. Find the cost of 4 calculators at £6.95 each.

19. What is the cost of 2 CDs at £10.95 each?

20. If one brick weighs $1.35\,\text{kg}$, how much do 5 weigh?

Top Banana! The Banana man of Tesco's.

The following article is a true story. Read the article (which deliberately contains blanks) and then answer the questions below.

He is called the Banana man of Tesco. In a special offer Phil Calcott bought almost half a ton of bananas. He then gave it all away and still made a profit on the deal. In a way Mr Calcott made his local store pay him to take away its own fruit.

The offer said that if you bought a 3 lb bunch of bananas at £1.17, you would gain 25 Tesco 'Club Card' points. These points could be used to buy goods worth £1.25.

Mr Calcott asked the store to load up his Peugeot 205 with bananas.

'I took a car load at a time because even with the back seat down and the boot full I could only fit in 460 lbs of bananas,' he said.

He returned for another load the next day and altogether spent £ ____ buying 942 lbs of the fruit. This earned him almost ____ ,000 Tesco 'Club Card' points.

1. How much would it cost to buy ten 3 lb bunches of bananas?

2. How many Tesco Club Card points would you get?

3. How much would the points be worth?

4. How much profit would you make on this deal?

5. Do you like bananas?

6. Write down the paragraph, which starts 'He returned ...' and fill in the missing numbers.

Division of decimals by whole numbers

(a) $9.6 \div 3$

$$3.2$$
$$3 \overline{) 9.6}$$

(b) $22.48 \div 4$

$$5.62$$
$$4 \overline{) 22.^248}$$

(c) $7.3 \div 4$

$$1.825$$
$$4 \overline{) 7.^33^10^20}$$
$$\uparrow \; \uparrow$$
Note the extra zeros

(d) $21.28 \div 7$

$$3.04$$
$$7 \overline{) 21.2^28}$$

(e) $3.12 \div 4$

$$0.78$$
$$4 \overline{) 3.^31^32}$$

Exercise 2

1. $8.42 \div 2$
2. $205.2 \div 6$
3. $18.52 \div 4$
4. $4.984 \div 7$
5. $236.0 \div 5$
6. $18.93 \div 3$
7. $49.92 \div 8$
8. $487.26 \div 9$
9. $6.7 \div 5$

10. A father shares £4·56 between his three children. How much does each receive?

11. A length of wood measuring 39·41 cm has to be cut into seven equal lengths. How long is each piece?

12. The total bill for a meal for nine people is £76·23. How much does each person pay if they each paid the same?

13. Work out

    (a) $11·2 \div 5$ (b) $9·01 \div 4$ (c) $12·1 \div 8$
    (d) $0·82 \div 4$ (e) $17 \div 5$ (f) $22 \div 8$

Multiplying and dividing by 10, 100, 1000 etc

Look at these results:

$3·24 \times 10 = 32·4$ $8·5 \div 10 = 0·85$
$16·17 \times 100 = 1617$ $57·1 \div 100 = 0·571$
$0·53 \times 1000 = 530$ $265 \div 1000 = 0·265$

Some people think about moving the *digits* and other people prefer to think about moving the *decimal point*. Choose the method which is clearest to *you*.

Exercise 3

Do the following calculations.

1. $4·23 \times 10$ **2.** $5·63 \times 10$ **3.** $0·427 \times 100$ **4.** $46·3 \times 100$
5. $0·075 \times 10$ **6.** $0·0063 \times 100$ **7.** $1·147 \times 1000$ **8.** $10·7 \times 1000$
9. $6·33 \times 100$ **10.** $0·00714 \times 10\,000$ **11.** $6·36 \times 100$ **12.** $8·142 \times 10$
13. $0·71 \times 10\,000$ **14.** $8·9 \times 1000$ **15.** 12×100 **16.** 13×10

17. $2400 \div 10\,000$ **18.** $89 \div 100$ **19.** $63 \div 100$ **20.** $7 \div 1000$
21. $0·86 \div 10$ **22.** $516 \div 10\,000$ **23.** $0·077 \div 100$ **24.** $21·9 \div 1000$
25. $500 \div 10\,000$ **26.** $260 \div 100\,000$ **27.** $0·051 \div 100$ **28.** $890·4 \div 10$
29. $4007 \div 100$ **30.** $20 \div 1000$ **31.** $5·14 \times 10$ **32.** $6·26 \times 100$

33. $0·414 \times 100$ **34.** $0·0631 \times 1000$ **35.** $0·005 \times 100$ **36.** $0·0063 \times 10\,000$
37. $47·4 \div 10$ **38.** $8·97 \div 100$ **39.** $54·2 \div 1000$ **40.** 63×100
41. 47×10 **42.** $0·84 \times 10\,000$ **43.** $0·7 \div 100$ **44.** $6·2 \div 10$
45. $4·73 \times 10$ **46.** $0·001 \times 1000$ **47.** $47 \div 100$ **48.** 47×100

Multiplying decimal numbers

- 5×0.3 is the same as $5 \times \frac{3}{10}$. Work out $(5 \times 3) \div 10 = 15 \div 10 = 1.5$

  4.2×0.2 is the same as $4.2 \times \frac{2}{10}$. Work out $(4.2 \times 2) \div 10 = 8.4 \div 10 = 0.84$

  21.4×0.05 is the same as $21.4 \times \frac{5}{100}$. Work out $(21.4 \times 5) \div 100 = 1907 \div 100 = 19.07$

- Quick method:

  When we multiply two decimal numbers together, the answer has the same number of figures to the right of the decimal point as the total number of figures to the right of the decimal point in the question.

  (a) 0.3×0.4
     $(3 \times 4 = 12)$
  So $0.3 \times 0.4 = 0.12$

  (b) 0.7×0.05
     $(7 \times 5 = 35)$
  So $0.7 \times 0.05 = 0.035$

Exercise 4

1. 0.4×0.2
2. 0.6×0.3
3. 0.8×0.2
4. 0.4×0.03
5. 0.7×3
6. 0.7×0.02
7. 0.9×0.5
8. 6×0.04
9. 0.04×0.05
10. 0.7×0.7
11. 8×0.1
12. 14×0.3
13. 15×0.03
14. 0.4×0.04
15. 0.001×0.6
16. 33×0.02
17. 1.2×0.3
18. 3.2×0.2
19. 1.4×0.4
20. 2.1×0.5
21. 3.61×0.3
22. 2.1×0.6
23. 0.31×0.7
24. 0.42×0.02
25. 0.33×0.02
26. 3.24×0.1
27. 8.11×0.07
28. 16.2×0.8
29. 5.06×0.05
30. 30.9×0.3
31. 0.2^2
32. 0.4^2

33. Copy and complete the multiplication square.

$\times$	0·1	0·02		
		0·06		24
0·2			0·1	
2·1				
				80

Hidden words

(a) Start in the top left box.
(b) Work out the answer to the calculation in the box.
(c) Find the answer in the top corner of another box.
(d) Write down the letter in that box.
(e) Repeat steps (b), (c) and (d) until you arrive back at the top left box. What is the message.

1.

6·4	66	274	985	12
L	N	E	S	S
5 × 15	$2^3 + 3^3$	20% of 50	15 × 100	756 ÷ 9
422	75	1·68	10	2·4
N	S	R	C	I
10^3	150 − 67	8 × 22	8·7 ÷ 10	37 + 385
3·85	176	0·87	1000	83
U	E	H	F	O
0·16 × 10	421 − 147	5 + 1·4	8·4 ÷ 5	385 ÷ 7
55	1500	1·6	35	84
L	I	N	I	S
1000 − 15	$\frac{2}{3}$ of 99	0·4 × 6	25% of 48	5·32 − 1·47

2.

612	0·8	0·77	0·2	0·62
T	W	V	T	T
1·8 + 8·2	5% of 400	$2^3 × 6$	5 × 69	20% of 65
32	10	13	18	250
C	B	R	E	U
50 000 ÷ 200	$\frac{2}{5}$ of 450	0·6 × 2·6	80% of 80	$0·9^2 − 0·1^2$
1·56	0·6	180	0·15	64
E	R	E	S	S
$\frac{3}{8}$ of 48	$\frac{1}{2}$ of 0·3	$(0·2)^2$	$0·32 ÷ 10^2$	806 − 194
0·04	0·27	20	48	345
A	O	D	N	E
10% of 2	770 ÷ 1000	0·3 − 0·03	3·1 × 0·2	4·2 ÷ 7

3.

1·1	100·9	1·55	5·14	1
	Y	D	O	I
$5·2 + 52$	0·1% of 40 000	$0·5 \times 11$	$\frac{1}{3}$ of 19·5	$0 \div 0·07$
1000	84	6·5	57·2	5100
E	E	R	C	D
$26·6 \div 7$	$\frac{1}{100}$ of 170	$999 + 998$	$77 \div 100$	$2·1 \times 40$
0·2	3·5	6·4	0·08	3·8
U	H	D	S	H
half of 199	$10 \times 10 \times 10$	$5·1 \times 1000$	$100 \times 0·011$	$0·6 \times 0·7$
0·77	14·7	1997	5·5	40
A	W	D	T	O
$2·1 \times 9$	$46·26 \div 9$	$0·4 \times 0·2$	$4·2 - 0·7$	$100 \times 0·002$
0·42	0	99·5	1·7	18·9
I	N	F	N	N
$25·1 - 18·7$	$0·15 + 1·4$	$81 \div 81$	$6 + 8·7$	$111 - 10·1$

4.

45	4	371	21	0·51
	H	C	A	S
$\frac{1}{2} + \frac{1}{4}$	2^4	$10 \div 1000$	$5 \div 8$	$21 - 5 \times 4$
896	0·06	0·05	0·01	34
M	E	L	E	Y
$1^2 + 2^2 + 3^3$	$51 \div 100$	1% of 250	$5 \times (5 - 2)^2$	$5·1 \times 100$
0·625	1	$\frac{3}{4}$	$\frac{3}{8}$	32
T	O	M	S	I
$\frac{2}{3} \times \frac{1}{5}$	$6000 \div 20$	$4 + 5 \times 6$	$0·3 \times 0·2$	53×7
510	16	2·5	300	$\frac{2}{15}$
C	A	Y	N	C
$\frac{3}{5}$ of 35	$\frac{1}{2} - \frac{1}{8}$	$8 + 888$	$\frac{1}{4} - 0·2$	$20 \div (12 - 7)$

4.5 Solving equations

- Annie is thinking of a
  mystery number

We could write ⟦ ? ⟧ for the

mystery number.

If I double the number and then add seven, the answer is fifteen.

So Annie said $2 \times$ ⟦ ? ⟧ $+ 7 = 15$

This is an *equation*. There is
one unknown number shown
by the question mark.

- Mathematicians all over the world prefer to use *letters* to stand
  for unknowns when they write equations.

  For Annie's problem a mathematician might write
  $2 \times n + 7 = 15$, where *n* is the mystery number.
  or $2n + 7 = 15$
  What *is* Annie's mystery number?

- Equations are like weighing scales which are balanced. The scales
  remain balanced if the same weight is added or taken away from
  both sides.

  On the left pan is an unknown
  weight x plus a 2 kg weight. On the
  right pan there is a 2 kg weight and a
  3 kg weight

  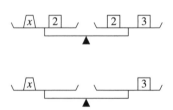

  If the two 2 kg weights are taken
  from each pan the scales are still
  balanced. So the weight x is 3 kg.

Exercise 1

Find the weight x by removing weights from both pans.
Weights are in kg.

1.

2.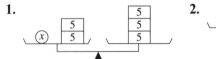

3.

4.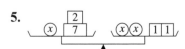

5.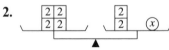

6.

7.

8.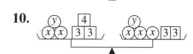

9.

10.

11.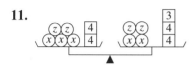

12.

Rules for solving equations

Equations are solved in the same way as we solve the weighing scale problems.

The main rule when solving equations is

'Do the same thing to both sides'

You may *add* the same thing to both sides.
You may *subtract* the same thing from both sides.
You may *multiply* both sides by the same thing.
You may *divide* both sides by the same thing.

Solve the equations. The operations circled are performed on both sides

(a) $x + 7 = 12$
$$\bigcirc{-7} \quad \bigcirc{-7}$$
$$x = 5$$

(b) $x - 3 = 11$
$$\bigcirc{+3} \quad \bigcirc{+3}$$
$$x = 14$$

(c) $2x = 12$
$$\bigcirc{\div 2} \quad \bigcirc{\div 2}$$
$$x = 6$$

(d) $\dfrac{x}{5} = 7$
$$\bigcirc{\times 5} \quad \bigcirc{\times 5}$$
$$x = 35$$

Exercise 2

Solve the equations.

1. $x + 7 = 10$ **2.** $x + 3 = 20$ **3.** $x - 7 = 7$

4. $x - 5 = 11$ **5.** $6 + x = 13$ **6.** $8 + x = 15$

7. $7 = x + 4$ **8.** $7 = x - 6$ **9.** $1 = x - 3$

10. $7 + x = 7$ **11.** $x - 11 = 20$ **12.** $14 = 6 + x$

$7 = x + 4$
is the same as
$x + 4 = 7$

Questions **13** to **24** involve different operations.

13. $3x = 15$ **14.** $2x = 30$ **15.** $5x = 35$

16. $8 = 2x$ **17.** $6 = 6x$ **18.** $2x = 1$

19. $3x = 2$ **20.** $4x = 1000$ **21.** $7x = 0$

22. $\dfrac{x}{3} = 5$ **23.** $\dfrac{x}{6} = 1$ **24.** $\dfrac{x}{16} = 10$

In Questions **25** to **42** find a.

25. $7 + a = 100$ **26.** $a - 13 = 13$ **27.** $5a = 1000$

28. $\dfrac{a}{4} = 20$ **29.** $1 = \dfrac{a}{5}$ **30.** $\frac{1}{2} = \dfrac{a}{10}$

31. $a - \frac{1}{2} = \frac{1}{2}$ **32.** $11a = 1$ **33.** $a + 58 = 110$

34. $3a = \frac{1}{3}$ **35.** $25 = \dfrac{a}{100}$ **36.** $12\frac{1}{2} = a - 1\frac{1}{2}$

37. $206 = a - 205$ **38.** $7a = 2$ **39.** $\frac{1}{2}a = 10$

40. $\frac{1}{4}a = 100$ **41.** $0 = 17a$ **42.** $a + \frac{1}{8} = \frac{1}{2}$

Equations with two operations

Solve the equations

(a) $\quad 4x - 1 = 8$

$\quad\quad (+1)\quad (+1)$

$\quad\quad\quad 4x = 9$

$\quad\quad (\div 4)\quad (\div 4)$

$\quad\quad\quad x = 2\frac{1}{4}$

(b) $\quad 7x + 3 = 9$

$\quad\quad (-3)\quad (-3)$

$\quad\quad\quad 7x = 6$

$\quad\quad (\div 7)\quad (\div 7)$

$\quad\quad\quad x = \dfrac{6}{7}$

Exercise 3

Solve the equations for x.

1. $2x - 3 = 1$ **2.** $3x + 4 = 16$ **3.** $5x - 4 = 6$

4. $2x + 1 = 2$ **5.** $3x + 5 = 32$ **6.** $6x - 11 = 1$

7. $6x = 5$ **8.** $9x = 2$ **9.** $4 + 3x = 5$

10. $3 + 7x = 31$ **11.** $10 + 20x = 11$ **12.** $8 + x = 19$

In Questions **13** to **24** solve the equations to find a.

13. $3a + 1 = 2$ **14.** $5a + 7 = 9$ **15.** $8a + 5 = 53$

16. $25a - 7 = 118$ **17.** $3 + 6a = 4$ **18.** $8 + 5a = 10$

19. $13a - 7 = 32$ **20.** $3 + 5a = 3$ **21.** $5a - 11 = 7$

22. $9a - 20 = 16$ **23.** $8a + 9 = 9$ **24.** $7a - 2 = 1$

Solve the equations where the 'x' terms are on the right hand side.

(a) $25 = 7x - 10$ (b) $8 = 6 + 3x$

$(+10)$ $(+10)$ (-6) (-6)

$35 = 7x$ $2 = 3x$

$(\div 7)$ $(\div 7)$ $(\div 3)$ $(\div 3)$

$5 = x$ $\frac{2}{3} = x$

Notice that x is written on the right hand side throughout.

In Questions **25** to **36** solve the equations to find x.

25. $4 = 3x + 1$ **26.** $9 = 5x - 1$ **27.** $15 = 6x - 3$

28. $20 = 4x - 8$ **29.** $0 = 5x - 6$ **30.** $17 = 13 + 3x$

31. $8 = 5 + 2x$ **32.** $3 = 2 + 4x$ **33.** $4 + 9x = 4$

34. $35 = 25 + 40x$ **35.** $11x + 11 = 12$ **36.** $71 = 3x + 69$

In Questions **37** to **48** find the value of the letter in each question.

37. $3y - 7 = 1$ **38.** $20 = 4c + 10$ **39.** $4 = 4 + 5t$

40. $6p - 7 = 17$ **41.** $8 + 5m = 908$ **42.** $2x - 3 = 0$

43. $7 = 5u - 73$ **44.** $8 = 100b + 7$ **45.** $66 = 6 + 6n$

46. $2x + \frac{1}{2} = 1$ **47.** $3x - \frac{1}{2} = 1\frac{1}{2}$ **48.** $2t + \frac{1}{4} = \frac{1}{2}$

Using equations to solve problems

Philip is thinking of a number. He tells us that when he doubles it and adds 7, the answer is 18. What number is Philip thinking of?

Suppose that Philip is thinking of the number x

He tells us that $2x + 7 = 18$

Subtract 7 from both sides: $2x = 11$

Divide both sides by 2 $x = \frac{11}{2}$

$x = 5\frac{1}{2}$

So Philip is thinking of the number $5\frac{1}{2}$

Exercise 4

In each question I am thinking of a number. Use the information to form an equation and then solve it to find the number.

1. If we multiply the number by 3 and then add 2, the answer is 13.

2. If we multiply the number by 5 and then subtract 3, the answer is 9.

3. If we multiply the number by 6 and then add 11, the answer is 16.

4. If we multiply the number by 11 and then subtract 4, the answer is 7.

5. If we double the number and add 10, the answer is 30.

6. If we multiply the number by 9 and then subtract $\frac{1}{2}$ the answer is 22.

7. If we treble the number and then add 1000 the answer is 4000.

8. If we multiply the number by 20 and then subtract 2, the answer is 3.

● A common difficulty with problem solving is knowing how to get started. If the problem does not include a letter 'x' (or any other letter) then a general rule is to let x be the quantity you are asked to find, not forgetting to state the units.

The total mass of three coins A, B and C is 33 grams. Coin B is twice as heavy as coin A and coin C is 3 grams heavier than coin B. Find the mass of coin A.

Let the mass of coin A be x grams.
Draw and label a simple diagram to help visualise the problem.

B is twice as heavy as A. So the mass of coin B is $2x$ grams.
C is 3 grams heavier than B. So the mass of coin C is $2x + 3$ grams.

The total mass of the three coins is 33 grams.

$$\therefore \quad x + 2x + 2x + 3 = 33$$
$$5x + 3 = 33$$
$$5x = 30$$
$$x = 6$$

The mass of coin A is 6 grams.

Exercise 5

1. Form equations to find x.

(a)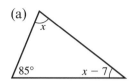

(b)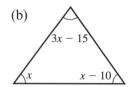

(c)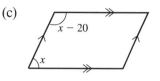

2. The angles of a triangle are A, B and C. Angle B is twice as big as angle A and angle C is 10° bigger than angle A. Find the size of angle A.

3. The sum of three *consecutive* whole numbers is 192. Let the first number be x. Write an equation and solve it to find the three numbers.

4. The length of a rectangle is twice its width. If the perimeter is 54 cm, find its width.

5. The length of a rectangle is three times its width. If the perimeter of the rectangle is 20 cm, find its width.

6. The length of a rectangle is 3 cm more than its width. If the perimeter of the rectangle is 30 cm, find its width.

7. Number walls are formed by adding adjacent numbers to get the number above. Find n in these walls

(a)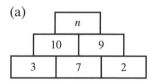

(b)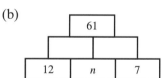

8. In a quadrilateral ABCD, BC is twice as long as AB and AD is three times as long as AB. Side DC is 10 cm long. The perimeter of ABCD is 31 cm. Write an equation and solve it to find the length of AB.

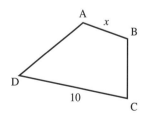

9. The diagram shows a rectangle of area 40 square units. Form an equation and solve it to find x.

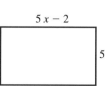

10. The total distance from P to T is 181 km. The
distance from Q to R is twice the distance from
S to T.
R is mid-way between Q and S.
The distance from P to Q is 5 km less than the
distance from S to T.
Find the distance from S to T.

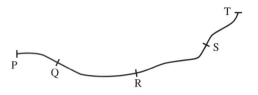

11. The total mass of four parcels A, B, C and D is 94 kg. Parcel C
is twice as heavy as parcel B and parcel D is 25 kg heavier than
parcel C.
Parcel A is 3 kg lighter than parcel B.
Find the mass of each parcel. [Let mass of B be x kg].

12. An equilateral triangle has sides of length $(3x - 2)$, $(2x + 3)$ and
13. Find x.

13. The width of a rectangle is $2x + 3$ and its perimeter is $12x + 6$.
(a) Find the length of the rectangle (in terms of x)
(b) Find x if the length of the rectangle is 7 cm.

4.6 Straight line graphs

- The points P, Q, R and S have coordinates
  (4, 4), (4, 3), (4, 2) and (4, 1) and they all lie
  on a straight line. Since the x-coordinate of all
  the points is 4, we say the *equation* of the line
  is $x = 4$.

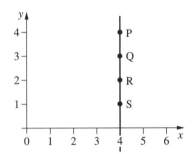

- The points A, B, C and D have coordinates
  (1, 3), (2, 3), (3, 3) and (4, 3) and they all lie
  on a straight line. Since the y-coordinate of all
  the points is 3, we say the *equation* of the line is
  $y = 3$.

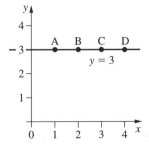

Exercise 1

1. Write down the equations for the lines marked A, B and C.

2. Write down the equations for the lines marked P, Q and R.

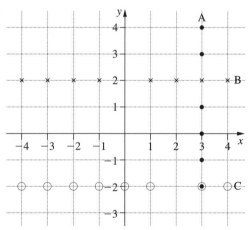

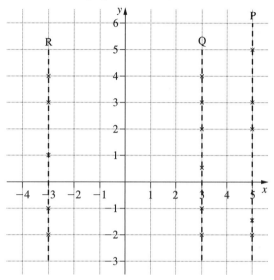

In Questions **3** and **4** there is a line of dots A, a line of crosses B and a line of circles C.
Write down the equations of the lines in each question.

3.

4.

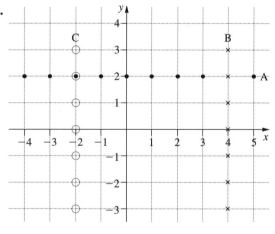

5. On squared paper
   (a) Draw the lines $y = 2$ and $x = 3$. Where do they meet?
   (b) Draw the lines $y = 5$ and $x = 1$. Where do they meet?
   (c) Draw the lines $x = 7$ and $y = 3$. Where do they meet?

6. Name two lines which pass through the following points.
   (a) (5, 2)   (b) (3, 7)   (c) (8, 0)   (d) (8, 8)   (e) (5, 21)

7. In the diagram, E and N lie on the line with
equation $y = 1$. B and K lie on the line $x = 5$.
In parts (a) to (h) find the equation of the line
passing through the points given:

(a) A and D   (e) L and E
(b) A, B and I   (f) D, K and G
(c) M and P   (g) C, M, L and H
(d) I and H   (h) P and F

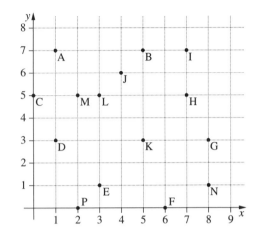

Relating *x* and *y*

● The sloping line passes through the following points:
(1, 1), (2, 2), (3, 3), (4, 4), (5, 5).

For each point, the *y*-coordinate is equal to the
x-coordinate.

The equation of the line is $y = x$ (or $x = y$).

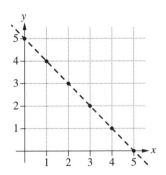

● This line passes through:
(0, 1), (1, 2), (2, 3), (3, 4), (4, 5).

For each point the *y*-coordinate is one more than the
x-coordinate. The equation of the line is $y = x + 1$.

We could also say that the *x* coordinate is always one less
than the *y* coordinate. The equation of the line could then
be written as $x = y - 1$.
[Most mathematicians use the equation beginning '*y* ='].

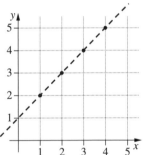

● This line slopes the other way and passes through:
(0, 5), (1, 4), (2, 3), (3, 2), (4, 1), (5, 0).

The sum of the *x* coordinate and the *y* coordinate is always 5.
The equation of the line is $x + y = 5$.

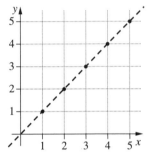

Exercise 2

For each question write down the coordinates of the points marked.
Find the equation of the line through the points.

1.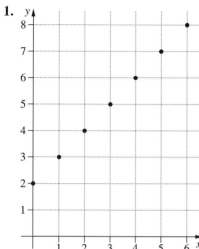

2.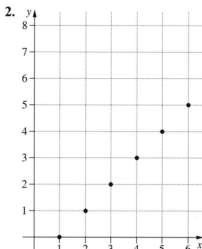

3.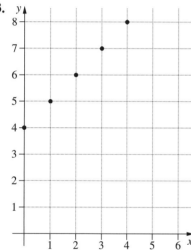

4.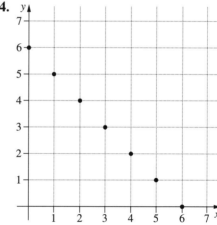

5.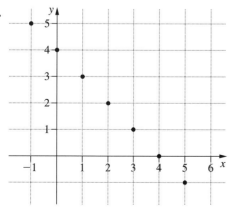

6.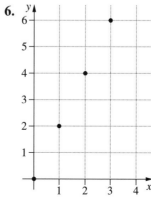

Drawing graphs

- The equation of a line is $y = x + 2$. Here is a list of five points on the line: (0, 2), (1, 3), (2, 4), (3, 5), (4, 6)
  The points are plotted on a graph and the line $y = x + 2$ is drawn. Notice that the line extends beyond (0, 2) and (4, 6).

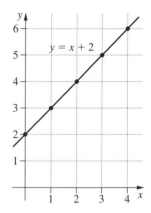

Exercise 3

1. The equation of a line is $y = x + 3$. Copy and complete a list of points on the line:

   (0, 3) (1, 4) (2, ☐) (3, ☐) (4, ☐)

   Draw the graph of $y = x + 3$

2. The equation of a line is $y = x + 5$. Copy and complete a list of points on the line:

   (0, 5) (1, 6) (2, ☐) (3, ☐) (4, ☐)

In Questions **3** to **10** you are given the equation of a line and a list of points on the line. Fill in the missing numbers and then draw the graph.

3. $y = x - 2$; (0, −2), (1, −1), (2, ☐), (3, ☐), (4, ☐)

4. $y = x - 4$; (0, −4), (1, −3), (2, ☐), (3, ☐), (4, ☐)

5. $y = 2x$; (0, 0), (1, 2), (2, ☐), (3, ☐), (4, ☐)

6. $y = 2x + 1$; (0, ☐), (2, ☐), (4, ☐)

7. $y = 2x - 2$; (0, ☐), (2, ☐), (4, ☐)

8. $y = 6 - x$; (1, ☐), (3, ☐), (5, ☐), (6, ☐)

9. $y = 4 - x$; (0, ☐), (2, ☐), (4, ☐)

10. $y = 3x + 2$; (0, ☐), (1, ☐), (2, ☐)

11. Draw the lines $y = 5 - x$ and $y = 2x - 1$ on the same graph. Write down the co-ordinates of the point where the lines meet.

4.7 Solving problems (no calculators)

Exercise 1

1. Work out
   (a) 4×808 (b) $370 - 25$ (c) 8×0
   (d) $348 \div 6$ (e) $8279 + 182$ (f) $2314 - 276$

2. Write the number 'three thousand and fourteen' in figures.

3. (a) Copy and shade one quarter
      of this shape:
   (b) What percentage of the shape
      is left unshaded?

4. Steve has read 97 of the 448 pages in his book. How many more pages must be read to reach the middle?

5. There are 15 piles of magazines. Eight piles have 20 magazines each, of the other piles each have 25 magazines. How many magazines are there altogether?

6. There are 127 youngsters playing football.
   How many teams of five can be formed?
   How many will be left over?

7. It cost 6 children a total of £12.90 to watch a film. What did it cost each child?

8. Copy and complete this multiplication square

$\times$	2	5		
		40		72
			18	
7	14			
			24	36

9. Write 10 million pence in pounds and pence.

10. The area of the 'Z' shape is $20\,cm^2$.
    (a) Write down the area of each small square.
    (b) Work out the length of the perimeter of the shape.

Exercise 2

1. In a 'magic square' all rows (←→) columns

   $\left(\updownarrow\right)$ and main diagonals $\left(\times\right)$ add up

   to the same 'magic number'. Copy and
   complete this magic square.

6		12	7
	4		
	16	13	2
10			11

2. (a) What is the length of this line in millimetres?
   (b) What is this length in centimetres?

   ├──────────────────────────────┤

3. In a new airport terminal, 25 new doors are
   required.
   (a) If each door is fastened by 3 hinges, how
       many hinges are needed altogether?
   (b) If each hinge requires 6 screws, what is
       the total number of screws required to fit
       all the doors?

4. A multi-storey office block has 104 offices altogether. If there
   are 8 offices on each floor, how many storeys does the building
   have?

5. Numbers are missing on four of these calculator buttons. Copy
   the diagram and write in numbers to make the answer 25.

   $\boxed{2}\,\boxed{8}\,\boxed{+}\,\boxed{}\,\boxed{}\,\boxed{-}\,\boxed{}\,\boxed{}\,\boxed{=}\,\boxed{2}\,\boxed{5}$

6. Here are some number cards. $\boxed{3}$ $\boxed{4}$ $\boxed{7}$ $\boxed{2}$ $\boxed{9}$

   (a) Use two cards to make a
       fraction which is equal to $\frac{1}{2}$. $\dfrac{\square}{\square}$

   (b) Use three of the cards to make
       the smallest possible fraction. $\dfrac{\square}{\square\square}$

7. (a) How many 12 centimetre pieces of string can be cut from a
       piece of string which is 1 metre in length?
   (b) How much string is left over?

8. Look at this group of numbers …

   $$15,\ 9,\ 27,\ 24,\ 7$$

   (a) Which of the numbers is a multiple of both 3 and 4?
   (b) Which of the numbers is a prime number?
   (c) Which of the numbers is a square number?

9. Write down these calculations and find the missing digits.

(a)   3 ☐ 4   (b)   5 ☐ 9   (c)   ☐ 2 ☐
    + 2 6 ☐   + 3 8 ☐   + 3 ☐ 4
    ―――――――   ―――――――   ―――――――
      6 3 9   ☐ 2 5   8 0 0

10. The rule for the number sequences below is *'double and add 2'*.
    Write down each sequence and fill in the missing numbers.

    (a) 1 → 4 → 10 → 22 → ☐

    (b) ☐ → 6 → 14 → 30

    (c) ☐ → 8 → ☐ → ☐

Exercise 3

1. How many grams of sugar must be added to 1·3 kg to make 3 kg altogether?

2. Serena bought a packet of 100 raspberries.
    She ate a quarter of them on Monday.
    She ate a fifth of the remaining
    raspberries on Tuesday.
    How many raspberries
    did she have left?

3. For sports day a school has 40 litres of drink. One cup of drink is 200 ml. How many cups of drink can be provided?

4. Change this cake recipe for 4 people to a recipe for 6 people.

        320 g   mixed fruit
         90 g   butter
        200 ml   milk
          4   eggs

5. Stainless steel contains Iron, Chromium and Nickel. 74·2% of stainless steel is Iron, 8·3% is Nickel. What percentage is Chromium?

6. Work out
    (a) 114×0.4 (b) $18 - 5.7$ (c) $211 + 57.3 + 5.42$

7. Write the number 'two and a half million' in figures.

8. How many minutes are there from 07·20 to 09·15?

9. Measure the sides of the rectangle
and work out
(a) the area
(b) the perimeter

10. Work out the missing numbers

    (a) $310 + 560 = \boxed{}$ (b) $530 + \boxed{} = 700$ (c) $734 + \boxed{} = 780$

    (d) $\boxed{} + 210 = 500$ (e) $338 + \boxed{} = 558$ (f) $\boxed{} - 420 = 535$

11. Work out the missing numbers

    (a) $5{\cdot}6 + \boxed{} = 6$ (b) $3{\cdot}7 - \boxed{} = 2$ (c) $0{\cdot}54 + \boxed{} = 0{\cdot}74$

    (d) $0{\cdot}4 - \boxed{} = 0{\cdot}15$ (e) $\boxed{} - 0{\cdot}7 = 1{\cdot}4$ (f) $0{\cdot}86 - \boxed{} = 0{\cdot}5$

12. Jesper has the same number of 20p and 50p coins. The total
value is £7. How many of each coin does he have?

Exercise 4

1. There are 35 rows of chairs and there are 20 chairs in each row.
(a) How many chairs are there altogether?
(b) How many rows of chairs are needed for 300 people?

2. I think of a number, add 2·3 and then multiply by 4. The answer
is 23·4. What is the number I am thinking of?

3. How many roses, costing 42p each, can
be bought for £20? How much change will
there be?

4. Use each of the digits 1 to 6.
Put one digit in each box to
make the statement true.
  $\boxed{5}\,\boxed{} \times \boxed{} = \boxed{1}\,\boxed{}\,\boxed{}$

5. A restaurant has 5000 litres of milk. It sells
350 litres per day on average. How many days
will the milk last?

6. Julie runs across the playground, which is
90 m wide, in 15 seconds. What was her
average speed in metres per second?

7. This is a number triangle. The numbers along each edge add up to 9.

Copy and complete the triangle.

The six numbers are 1, 2, 3, 4, 5, 6.

8. A box has a mass of 230 g when empty.
When it is full of sugar the total mass is 650 g.
What is its mass when it is half full?

9. This is a number ring.
Start with any number and multiply the units digit by 4 and then add the tens digit.

For example $(15) \rightarrow 5 \times 4 + 1 \rightarrow (21)$

The rule is then repeated on 21 and so on.

Use the same rule to complete this number ring.

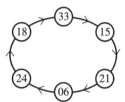

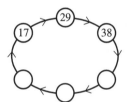

10. A piece of A4 size paper measures 297 mm by 210 mm.
    (a) A money spider starts at a corner and decides to walk around all sides of the paper.
    How far will the spider walk in millimetres?
    (b) Change your answer in part (a) into centimetres.
    (c) Has the spider travelled more or less than one metre?

11. A birthday card rests on a horizontal table.
Copy these sentences and fill the space with one of the words:

'vertical; horizontal; parallel; perpendicular'

(a) The edge BC is _____ .

(b) The edge AB is _____ to edge AD.

(c) Edges DE and DC are _____ .

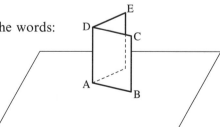

Part 5

5.1 Rotation

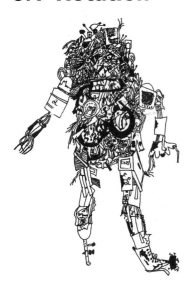

Professor M. Adman has designed a robot called 'The Rubbish Man' entirely from waste materials.

The robot is still in the early stages of development and is only able to move in four directions.

The 'Rubbish Man's' options are:-

1. Turn left (causing a change in direction of 90°).
2. Turn right (causing a change in direction of 90°).
3. Go straight on (meaning no change in direction).
4. About turn (causing a change in direction of 180°).

A *quarter turn* is a turn of **90°**, called *1 right angle*.
A *half turn* is a turn of **180°**, called *2 right angles*.
A *three-quarter* turn is a turn of **270°**, called *3 right angles*.
A *full turn* is a turn of **360°**, called *4 right angles*.

- When turning through right angles we have two options, we can turn clockwise (⁀) or anti-clockwise (⁀).

- Here are two example of rotations.

(a)

(b)

90° turn, clockwise

90° turn, anti-clockwise

Exercise 1

1. These pictures have been hung incorrectly. Give instructions to turn them the right way round. Remember to give both the angle and the direction.

(a)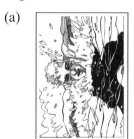

(b)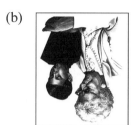

(c)

(d)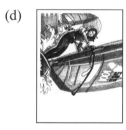

(e)

(f)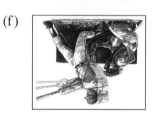

In Questions **2** to **10** copy each diagram and then draw its new position after it has been turned. You can use tracing paper if you wish.

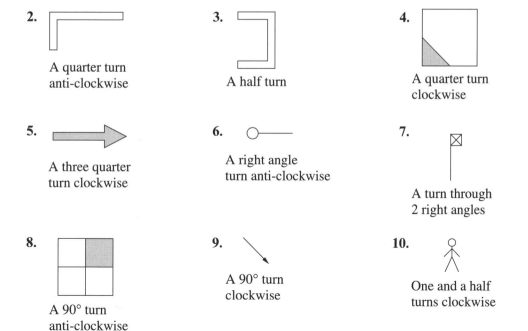

2. A quarter turn anti-clockwise

3. A half turn

4. A quarter turn clockwise

5. A three quarter turn clockwise

6. A right angle turn anti-clockwise

7. A turn through 2 right angles

8. A 90° turn anti-clockwise

9. A 90° turn clockwise

10. One and a half turns clockwise

In Questions **11** to **16** describe the turn.

11.

12.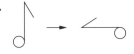

13.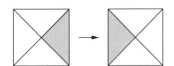

14.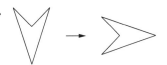

15.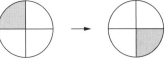

16.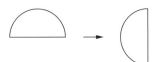

17. (a) This shape is going
    to be turned 90°
    clockwise around
    the point A

    Here is
    the result.

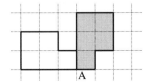

   (b) Turn this shape
    90° clockwise around
    the point B

    Shade in the new
    position of the shape

In Questions **18** to **20** copy the shape on squared paper and then
draw and shade its new position.

18.

Half turn around
the point C

19.

Quarter turn clockwise
around the point D

20.

Turn 90° anti-clockwise
around the point E

LOGO

LOGO is used to give commands to move a turtle on a computer.
Here is a list of the main commands.

FD 20   Go **F**orwar**D** 20 spaces
BK 30   Go **B**ac**K** 30 spaces

RT 90   **R**ight **T**urn 90 degrees
RT 45   **R**ight **T**urn 45 degrees
LT 90   **L**eft **T**urn 90 degrees

PU   **P**en **U**p   ⎫ These are used to move across the
PD   **P**en **D**own   ⎭ screen without drawing a line.

Here are two examples in which the turtle goes from A to B.

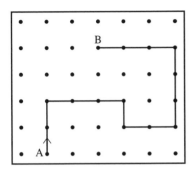

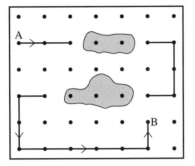

FD 20, RT 90, FD 30, RT 90,
FD 10, LT 90, FD 20, LT 90,
FD 30, LT 90, FD 30

In this one the turtle has to
'fly over' the obstacles shown.
FD 20, PU, FD 30, PD, FD 10,
RT 90, FD 20, RT 90, FD 10,
PU, FD 40, PD, FD 10, LT 90,
FD 20, LT 90, FD 50, LT 90,
FD 10

Exercise 2

1. Write down the commands that would move the turtle from A
   to B. The dots are 10 spaces apart

(a)

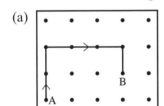

(b)

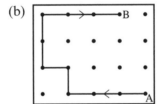

2. Write the commands that
   would move the turtle from A
   to B. In this question the
   turtle has to 'jump over' the
   obstacles shown by shaded
   areas.

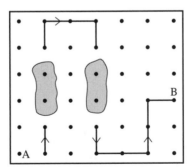

3. Write the commands that
   would move the turtle along
   the route given.
   (a) A → E → D → C → F → A
   (b) A → B → D → H → G → I → J → A
   (c) A → B → A → F → C

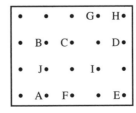

4. Leslie Smith wants to write her initials. Write down the LOGO commands.
   Start at the top of the 'L'.

5. Write down the LOGO commands for *your* own initials.

6. Draw the patterns given by the commands below.
   (a) FD 50, RT 90, FD 50, RT 90, FD 40, RT 90, FD 40, RT 90,
       FD 30, RT 90, FD 30, RT 90, FD 20, RT 90, FD 20, RT 90,
       FD 10, RT 90, FD 10.
   (b) FD 40, RT 90, FD 20, RT 90, FD 20, RT 90, FD 20, LT 90,
       FD 20, LT 90, PU, FD 30, PD, FD 20, LT 90, FD 20, LT 90,
       FD 20, BK 20, RT 90, FD 20, LT 90, FD 20.

7. Design your own pattern and write down the LOGO commands
   for it. Ask a friend to test your commands.

8. Investigate the patterns you can obtain using the 'Repeat'
   command.

Compass directions

Another way of describing a direction is provided by the *points* of
the *compass*.

There are four major directions (called cardinal points) on a
compass:

N represents north.
E represents east.
S represents south.
W represents west.

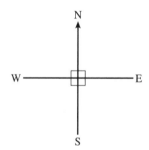

The directions between the four cardinal points are:

NE representing North-East.
SE representing South-East.
SW representing South-West.
NW representing North-West.

Exercise 3

Copy and complete this table.

	You are facing	Movement (Angle and Direction)	Direction you are now facing
1.	N	180°	?
2.	E	360°	?
3.	S	90° clockwise	?
4.	W	90° clockwise	?
5.	NW	180°	?
6.	SE	90° anti-clockwise	?
7.	NE	270° clockwise	?
8.	SW	270° anti-clockwise	?
9.	S	90° anti-clockwise	?
10.	E	?	W
11.	NW	?	SW
12.	NE	?	E
13.	W	?	S
14.	?	90° clockwise	W
15.	?	90° anti-clockwise	S
16.	?	180°	NE
17.	?	90° clockwise	E
18.	SW	?	S
19.	N	?	SW
20.	S	?	NE

21. The points A, B, C, D, E, F, G, H, I are places on a map.
    Work out where I am in the following:

    (a) I am North of G and West of C
    (b) I am South of A and West of E
    (c) I am West of D and North of F
    (d) I am East of H and South of B
    (e) I am South-East of G and South of I
    (f) I am East of A and South of C
    (g) I am South-West of C and East of H
    (h) I am North-West of G and South-West of B.

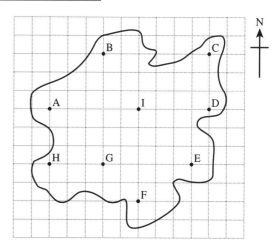

Rotational symmetry

The shape B fits onto itself three times when rotated through a complete turn. It has *rotational symmetry of order three*.

The shape C fits onto itself six times when rotated through a complete turn. It has rotational symmetry of order six.

Exercise 4

For each diagram decide whether or not the shape has rotational symmetry. For those diagrams that do have rotational symmetry state the order.

1.

2.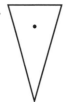

3.

4.

5.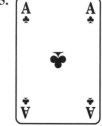

6.

7.

8.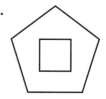

9.

10.

11.

12.

13.

14.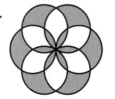

15.

16.

5.2 Reflection

Paper folding activities

1. Take a piece of paper, fold it once and then cut out a shape across the fold. This will produce a shape with one line of symmetry, which is a mirror line.

cut along the broken line →

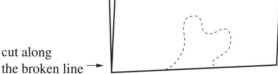

2. Fold another piece of paper twice so that the second fold is at right angles to the first fold. Again cut along the fold to see what shapes you can make.
This will produce a shape with two lines of symmetry. [i.e. two mirror lines]

3. Fold the paper three times and cut.

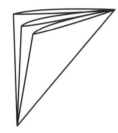 

This will produce a shape with four lines of symmetry.

Below are three shapes obtained by folding and cutting as above.
Try to make similar shapes yourself.
Stick the best shapes into your exercise book.

1.

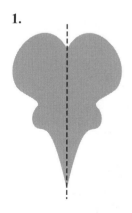

2.

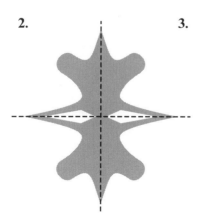

3.

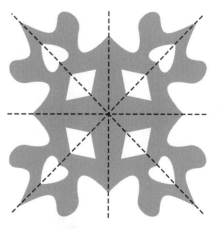

one line of symmetry
(or one mirror line)

two lines of symmetry
(or two mirror lines)

four lines of symmetry
(or four mirror lines)

4. More interesting shapes can be obtained as follows:
   (a) Cut out a circle and fold it in half.

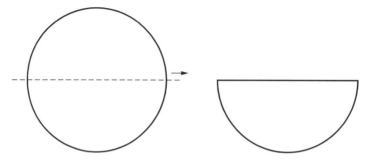

   (b) Fold about the broken line so
       that sectors A and B are equal.

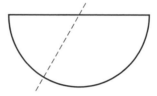
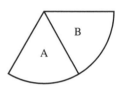

   (c) Fold sector B behind sector A. Now cut
       out a section and see what you obtain.

   (d) Even more complicated shapes can be
       obtained by folding once again down the
       middle of the sector.

Here are two shapes obtained by this method of folding.

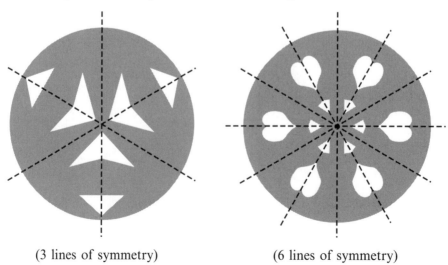

(3 lines of symmetry)   (6 lines of symmetry)

Reflection

A reflection is a transformation in which points are mapped to images by folding along a mirror line.

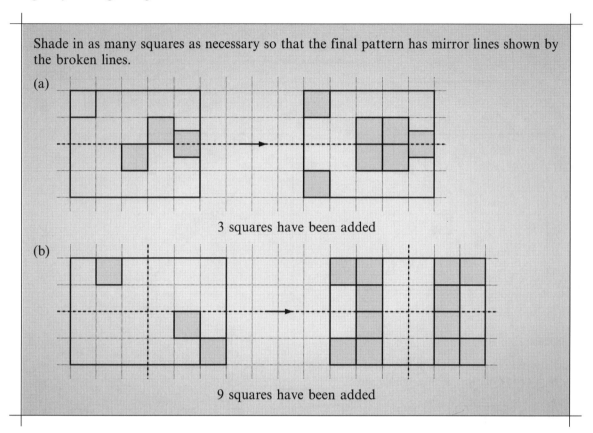

Shade in as many squares as necessary so that the final pattern has mirror lines shown by the broken lines.

(a)

3 squares have been added

(b)

9 squares have been added

Exercise 2

Copy each diagram and, using a different colour, shade in as many squares as necessary so that the final pattern has mirror lines shown by the broken lines. For each question write down how many new squares were shaded in.

1. 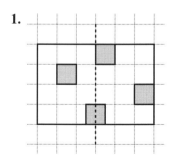   **2.** 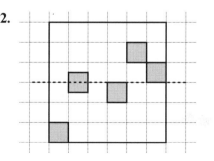   **3.**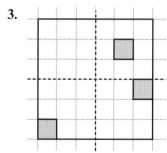

4. 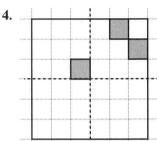   **5.** 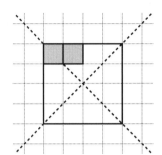   **6.**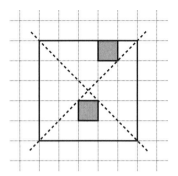

7. 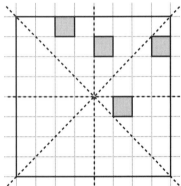   **8.**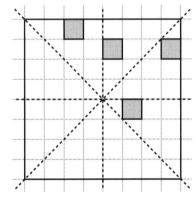

Exercise 3

1. You have 3 square black tiles and 2 square white tiles, which can be joined together along whole sides.

So this [tile] is allowed but this [tile] is *not* allowed.

Draw as many diagrams as possible with the 5 tiles joined together so that the diagram has line symmetry.

For example fig. 1 and fig. 2 have line symmetry but fig. 3 does not have line symmetry so fig. 3 is not acceptable.

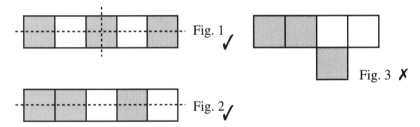

2. Now you have 2 black tiles and 2 white tiles. Draw as many diagrams as possible with these tiles joined together so that the diagram has line symmetry.

3. Finally with 3 black tiles and 3 white tiles draw as many diagrams as possible which have line symmetry.

Here is one diagram which has line symmetry

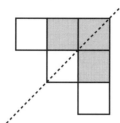

4. Shape A is a single square. A Shape B consists of four squares. 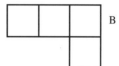 B

Draw three diagrams in which shapes A and B are joined together along a whole edge so that the final shape has line symmetry.

5. Shape C is a single square. C Shape D consists of five squares. 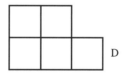 D

Draw four diagrams in which shapes C and D are joined together along a whole edge so that the final shape has line symmetry.

6. Copy the diagram and shade in all the new squares so that the final shape has four lines of symmetry.

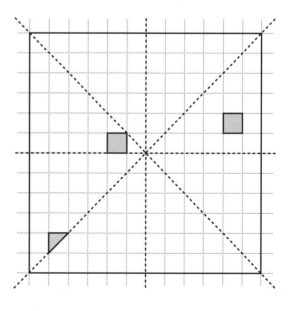

Triangles and quadrilaterals

1. On a square grid of 9 dots it is possible to draw several different triangles with vertices on dots.

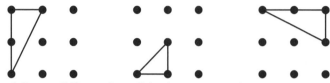

A and B are different but C is the same as A.

(a) Copy A and B above and then draw as many different triangles as you can. Check carefully that you have not repeated the same triangle.

If a triangle could be cut out and placed exactly over another triangle then the two triangles are the same.

[We say the two triangles are *congruent*].

(b) Go through your triangles and draw a line of symmetry with a broken line in those triangles with line symmetry.

2. On a grid of 9 dots it is also possible to draw several different quadrilaterals. Here are three:

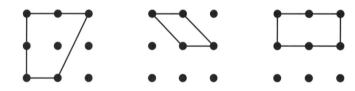

(a) Copy the three shapes above and then draw as many other different quadrilaterals as possible. You are doing well if you can find 12 shapes but there are a few more!

(b) Draw a line (or lines) of symmetry on all the quadrilaterals which have line symmetry.

5.3 Translation

A translation is a transformation in which every point of the object moves the same distance in a parallel direction.

A translation can be described by two instructions, the move parallel to the *x*-axis and the move parallel to the *y*-axis.

In the example shown, the translation is 5 units to the right and 1 unit up.

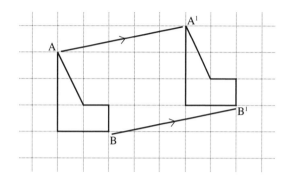

Exercise 1   Use squared paper

1. (a) Draw the object triangle A on squared paper.
   (b) Draw the image of A after a translation of 4 units to the right and 1 unit up. Label the image B.
   (c) Draw the image of A after a translation of 2 units to the right and 2 units down. Label the image C.

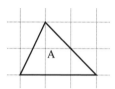

2.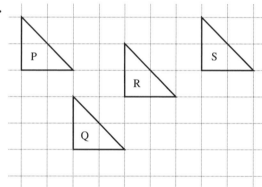

   Describe the following translations.
   (a) P → Q
   (b) Q → S
   (c) R → P
   (d) S → P

3. (a) Draw shape A as shown.
   (b) Translate shape A 5 units right and label the image B.
   (c) Translate shape B 3 units down and label the image C.
   (d) Translate shape C 3 units left and 1 unit down and label the image D.
   (e) What is the single translation which would move shape A onto shape D?

4.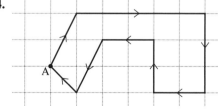

   A computer controls a pen which starts at A. Describe the 8 translations required to draw the shape given.

5.4   Long multiplication and division

Long multiplication

- Seventeen 23s is the same as ten 23s plus seven 23s
  17×23 is the same as $10 \times 23 + 7 \times 23$

  (a)   23   (b)   23   (c)   230   Quick method   23
       $\times 10$ $\times\ 7$ $+161$ $\times 17$
       $\overline{230}$ $\overline{161}$ $\overline{391}$ $\overline{230}$ $\longleftarrow 10 \times 23$
                                                                          161 $\longleftarrow 7 \times 23$
                                                                          $\overline{391}$

- $16 \times 35 = 10 \times 35 + 6 \times 35$

  (a)   35   (b)   35   (c)   350   Quick method   35
       $\times 10$ $\times\ 6$ $+210$ $\times 16$
       $\overline{350}$ $\overline{210}$ $\overline{560}$ $\overline{350}$ $\longleftarrow 10 \times 35$
                                      3 210 $\longleftarrow 6 \times 35$
                                                                          $\overline{560}$

- 2.5×1.3

  Ignore the decimals.

  Work out   25   There are two figures after the decimal
                $\times 13$ points in the members being multiplied.
                $\overline{250}$ So there are two figures after the point
                  75 in the answer.
                $\overline{325}$ $2.5 \times 1.3 = 3.25$

Exercise 1

Do the following, after working out an approximate answer first.

1. 15×23	**2.** 14×31	**3.** 16×32	**4.** 17×14
5. 18×33	**6.** 19×24	**7.** 17×31	**8.** 13×52
9. 21×24	**10.** 27×32	**11.** 26×28	**12.** 27×21
13. 32×25	**14.** 33×27	**15.** 36×14	**16.** 35×27
17. 234×41	**18.** 142×61	**19.** 331×47	**20.** 453×21
21. 123×32	**22.** 291×42	**23.** 804×61	**24.** 74×243

Questions **25** to **32** contain decimals

25. 4.5×6.2	**26.** 8.4×0.13	**27.** 6.9×4.2	**28.** 1.51×0.22
29. 4.6×82	**30.** 0.73×37	**31.** 0.44×1.1	**32.** 3.14×1.3

Long division

A Use the method for 'short division' with working at the side.

24 remainder 1

17)40⁶9

check:
$409 \div 17 \approx 400 \div 20$
≈ 20

17
×2
34

17
×4
68

B In this method we set it out so that the remainders are easier to find

24

17)409
$-34 \downarrow$
69
-68
1

- 17 into 40 goes 2 times
- $2 \times 17 = 34$
- $40 - 34 = 6$
- 'bring down' 9
- 17 into 69 goes 4 times
- $4 \times 17 = 68$
- $69 - 68 = 1$
- Answer is 24 remainder 1

Exercise 2

Do the following after working out an approximate answer first.

1. 13)275
2. 14)311
3. 16)498
4. 17)544

5. 14)452
6. 15)634
7. 19)669
8. 21)698

9. 17)459
10. 15)516
11. 14)672
12. 17)550

13. $451 \div 22$
14. $276 \div 24$
15. $517 \div 23$
16. $558 \div 26$

17. $317 \div 31$
18. $547 \div 25$
19. $886 \div 42$
20. $963 \div 33$

21. $557 \div 26$
22. $528 \div 45$
23. $118 \div 52$
24. $785 \div 63$

25. 32)715
26. 18)924
27. 25)776
28. 53)781

29. 64)696
30. 27)583
31. 15)667
32. 98)694

Exercise 3

To do these questions you have to multiply or divide. Do not use a calculator. Begin by finding an approximate answer.

1. Work out the total cost of 45 pens at 22p each. Give your answer in pounds.

2. A box of 15 golf balls costs 975 pence. How much does each ball cost?

3. There are 23 rooms in a school and each room has 33 chairs. How many chairs are there altogether?

4. A shop owner buys 52 tins of paint at 84p each. How much does he spend altogether?

5. Eggs are packed twelve to a box. How many boxes are needed for 444 eggs?

6. Figaro the cat eats one tin of cat food every day. How much will it cost to feed Figaro for 31 days if each tin costs 45p?

7. How many 23-seater coaches will be needed for a school trip for a party of 278?

8. Steve wants to buy as many 24p stamps as possible. He has £5 to spend. How many can he buy and how much change is left?

9. It costs £972 to hire a boat for a day. A trip is organised for 36 people. How much does each person pay?

10. Tins of spaghetti are packed 24 to a box. How many boxes are needed for 868 tins?

11. On average a school needs 87 exercise books a week. How many books are needed for 38 weeks?

12. A prize of 470 chocolate bars is shared equally between 18 winners. How many bars does each winner get and how many are left over?

13. Each class of a school has 31 pupils plus one teacher and there are 15 classes in the school.
The school hall can take 26 rows of chairs with 18 chairs in a row. Is that enough chairs for all the pupils and teachers?

14. When Philip was digging a hole in his garden he struck oil! The oil came out at a rate of £17 for every minute of the day and night. How much does Philip receive in a 24-hour day?

5.5 Averages and range

If you have a set of data, like exam marks or heights, and are asked to find the 'average', just what are you trying to find? The answer is: a single number which can be used to represent the entire set of data. This could be done in three different ways.

- **The mean**
  All the data is added and the total is divided by the number of items. In everyday language the word 'average' usually stands for the mean.

- **The median**
  When the data is arranged in order of size, the median is the one in the middle. If there are two 'middle' numbers, the median is in the middle of these two numbers.

- **The mode** is the number which occurs most often. The mode is the most popular value and comes from the french 'a la mode' meaning 'fashionable'. A set of data may have more than one mode.

- **Range**
  The range is not an average but is the difference between the largest value and the smallest value. The range is a measure of how spread out the data is.

The marks achieved by 10 pupils in a test were:

8, 5, 7, 4, 5, 6, 9, 7, 5, 10.

(a) Mean mark $= \dfrac{8+5+7+4+5+6+9+7+5+10}{10} = \dfrac{66}{10} = 6 \cdot 6$

(b) Arrange the marks in order: 4   5   5   5   6   7   7   8   9   10

   the median is here

   Median $= \dfrac{6+7}{2} = 65$

(c) Mode $= 5$, since there are more fives than any other number.
(d) Range $= 10 - 4 = 6$

Exercise 1

1. A fisherman caught five fish. Their masses were 200g, 300g, 220g, 190g and 90g. What is the mean mass of the fish?

2. In four different shops the price of one litre of lemonade is 43p, 37p, 41p, 35p. What is the mean price of the lemonade?

3. In a test the marks were 9, 3, 4, 7, 7. Calculate the mean mark.

4. For each set of numbers find (i) the mean
   (ii) the median
   (a) 8, 5, 9, 8, 7
   (b) 1, 5, 6, 11, 3, 4, 5
   (c) 4, 9, 2, 5.

5. The marks awarded to a skater were
   58, 60, 57, 59, 56.
   Find the mean mark.

6. The shoe sizes of the children in a Year 6 class were
   3, 2, 3, 4, 3, 2, 3, 4, 3, 2, 3, 3
   3, 3, 4, 5, 3, 4, 3, 3, 3, 5, 2, 3.
   What shoe size is the mode?

7. The temperature in a garden was measured at midnight every day for a week. The results (in °C) were
   −3, 0, 1, 7, −5, 3, 0.
   What was the range of the temperatures?

8. There were 9 people in the Oxford rowing boat.
   The mean age of the people was 22 and the range of their ages was 6.
   Write each sentence below and write next to it whether it is *True*, *Possible* or *Impossible*.
   (a) Every person was 22 years old.
   (b) All the people were at least 20 years old.
   (c) The oldest person was 6 years older than the youngest person.
   (d) The youngest person on the boat was 14 years old.

9. The total mass of seven cows is 3570 kg.
   Calculate the mean mass of the cows.

10. The total height of 6 children is 930 cm.
    Calculate the mean height of the children.

11. There were 5 people living in a house. The *median* age of the
people was 21 and the range of their ages was 3.
Write each sentence below and write next to it whether it is
True, Possible or *False*.
(a) Every person was either 20 or 21 years old.
(b) The oldest person in the house was 24 years old.
(c) The mean age of the people was less than 21 years.

12. Think of five numbers which have a mean of 6 and a median of
4. Ask a friend to check your answer.

Exercise 2

1. The temperature was recorded at 0400 in seven towns across the
U.K. The readings were 0°, 1°, −4°, 1°, −2°, −5°, −4°.
What was the median temperature.

2. The number of occupants in the 33 houses in a street is as
follows:

    2 4 3 4 1 4 2 4 1 5 2
    3 0 5 3 4 3 6 7 3 3 6
    4 1 4 2 0 1 4 3 2 5 0

What is the modal number of occupants in the houses?

3. The test results for a class of 30 pupils were as follows:

Mark	3	4	5	6	7	8
Frequency	2	5	4	7	6	6

What was the modal mark?

4. (a) Calculate the mean of the numbers 3, 2, 5, 11, 9, 6
(b) Calculate the new mean when the lowest number is removed.

5. In a maths test the marks for the boys were 9, 3, 5, 7, 4, 8 and
the marks for the girls were 10, 6, 7, 3.
(a) Find the mean mark for the boys.
(b) Find the mean mark for the girls.
(c) Find the mean mark for the whole class.

6. (a) Copy and complete: 'For the set of numbers
5, 5, 6, 8, 9, 10, 10, 11, there are ☐ modes. The modes
are ☐ and ☐.'
(b) Find the mode or modes for this set of numbers
1, 2, 2, 2, 3, 3, 5, 6, 7, 7, 7, 9.

7. The range for nine numbers on a card is 60. One number is covered by a piece of blu-tac. What could that number be?

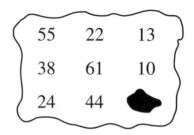

8. The total weight of seven cars on a transporter is 3360 kg. What is the mean weight of the cars.

9. Sally throws a dice eight times and wins 20p if the median score is more than 3. The dice shows 6, 1, 2, 6, 4, 1, 3, 6. Find the median score. Does she win 20p?

10. Lynn has 3 cards.
She takes another card and the mean goes up by 3. What number is on the new card?

| 6 | 2 | 7 |

| 6 | 2 | 7 | ? |

11. Make a list of 9 numbers (not all the same!) so that the mode, the median and the mean are all the same value.
For example: The set of numbers 5, 6, 7, 7, 10 have mode, median and mean equal to 7.
Ask a friend to check your list.

12. Serena has 5 cards.
The mean of the five cards is 8.
The range of the five cards is 6.
What numbers are on the two other cards?

| 8 | 8 | 8 | | |

13. I can dial a computer helpline at either AOL or COMPI. For my last five calls to each company, this is how long I had to wait.

| AOL | 7 min | 8 min | 5 min | 7 min | 8 min |
| COMPI | 2 min | 14 min | 8 min | 1 min | 5 min |

Calculate the mean and the range for the waiting time for each company. Using the mean and the range, decide which company gives the better service. Explain why.

14. A dice was thrown 20 times. Here are the results.

Score on dice	1	2	3	4	5	6
Number of throws	2	4	5	1	5	3

Copy and complete: mean score $= \dfrac{(1 \times 2) + (2 \times 4) + (3 \times 5) + \ldots}{20}$

$= \boxed{}$

15. Work out the mean score in these two dice rolling experiments.

(a)

Score on dice	1	2	3	4	5	6
Number of throws	4	5	3	2	6	5

(b)

Score on dice	1	2	3	4	5	6
Number of throws	7	6	9	5	6	7

5.6 Negative numbers

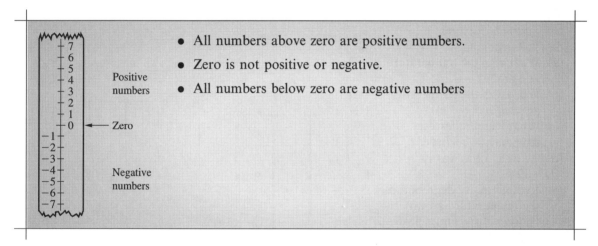

- All numbers above zero are positive numbers.
- Zero is not positive or negative.
- All numbers below zero are negative numbers

- The most common application of negative numbers is in illustrating temperature.

  This is a weather map showing temperatures across the United Kingdom and Ireland on a day in Winter.

  The temperatures are given in degrees Celsius (°C).

  Water freezes at 0°C.

  The weather map shows lower temperatures in the north than in the south.

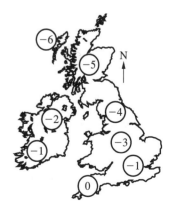

Exercise 1

1. What temperature is shown at each arrow?

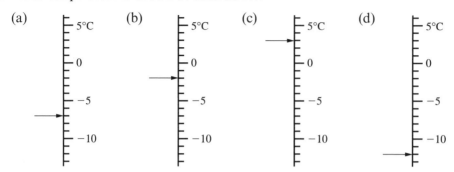

(a)   (b)   (c)   (d)

2.

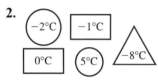

(a) Which of these temperatures is the coldest?
(b) Which of these temperatures is the hottest?
(c) Which temperatures are below freezing?

3. The graph shows the temperatures for one day in Greenland.
   (a) What was the temperature at 6 pm?
   (b) What was the temperature at 9 am?
   (c) What was the lowest temperature recorded?
   (d) At what time was it −12°C?
   (e) By how many degrees did the temperature go up between 6 am and 6 pm?

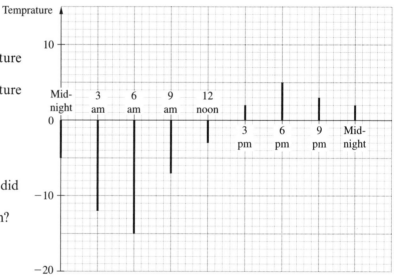

4. Find the new temperature in the following problems.
   (a) The temperature is 5°C and falls by 9°C.
   (b) The temperature is −7°C and falls by 4°C.
   (c) The temperature is −6°C and rises by 13°C.
   (d) The temperature is −9°C and rises by 11°C.
   (e) The temperature is 13°C and falls 17°C.

5. State in the following questions whether the temperature has risen or fallen and by how many degrees.
   (a) It was −3°C and it is now −7°C.
   (b) It was 6°C and is now −2°C.
   (c) It was −11°C and is now −5°C.
   (d) It was −9°C and is now 1°C.
   (e) It was 12°C and is now −23°C.

Exercise 2

1. The *range* is the difference between the highest and the lowest.
The scale shows the highest and lowest temperatures one day in Paris.

The range of the temperatures is 10°C.

Find the range in these temperatures

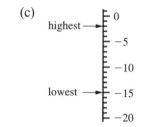

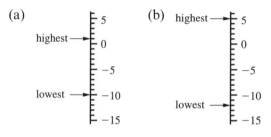

(d) 5°C and −3°C   (e) 0°C and −11°C   (f) 12°C and −10°C.

2. Write down each statement with either > or < in place of the box.

(a) −3 ☐ −2   (b) −1·5 ☐ −5   (c) 0 ☐ −3

3. Give a possible value for *x* and *y*.

(a) −10·5 < *x* < −9   (b) −2·5 < *y* < 0

4. In a test there are +2 marks for a correct answer and −1 marks for an incorrect answer. Find the total marks in the tests below:

Test A   ✓, ✓, ✗, ✗, ✗, ✓, ✓, ✗, ✓, ✗.

Test B   ✗, ✗, ✓, ✓, ✗, ✓, ✗, ✗, ✗, ✗.

5. Here is a number line from −10 to +10

Find the difference between
(a) −7 and 2   (b) −6 and −1   (c) 8 and −3
(d) −5 and 0   (e) −8 and 8   (f) −3 and −10.

6. Write down these temperatures in order, coldest first.
(a) 7°,   −2°,   −7°,   0°,   8°,   −5°
(b) −6°,   3°,   −15°,   21°,   −7°   2°
(c) −8°,   11°,   0°,   −5°,   −10°,   2°

7. Write down each sequence and fill in the missing number.

(a)   6   4   2   0   −2   ☐

(b)   10   6   2   −2   ☐

(c)   10   7   4   1   −2   ☐

(d)   9   5   1   ☐   −7

(e) −12   −9   −6   −3   ☐

(f)   ☐   −1   4   9   14

8. The heights of places on a map are always measured in relation to sea level. For example a hill marked 510 m is 510 m above sea level.
(a) Think of something which could be at a height of −20 m.
(b) Some places in Holland are at a height of −3 m. What problems does this cause and what do the people do about it?

9. A diver is below the surface of the water at −20 m. She dives a further 8 m, then rises 5 m. At what depth is she now?

Adding and subtracting

For adding and subtracting with negative numbers a number line is very useful.

go *right*
+ →

− ←
go *left*

−3   +   6   answer = 3

start here   go right   6 places

6   −   10   answer = −4

start here   go left   10 places

−1   −   4   answer = −5

start here   go left   4 places

Exercise 3

1. Use a number line to work out

2. Use a number line to work out

3. Use a number line to work out
   (a) $3 - 6$ (b) $-2 + 4$ (c) $-3 - 2$
   (d) $-6 + 9$ (e) $5 - 8$ (f) $-8 + 2$
   (g) $5 - 10$ (h) $-8 + 3$ (i) $-3 - 4$
   (j) $-3 + 7$ (k) $-10 + 10$ (l) $8 - 12$

4. Work out
   (a) $-7 + 4$ (b) $6 - 11$ (c) $-3 - 3$
   (d) $8 - 20$ (e) $-4 + 8$ (f) $9 - 2$
   (g) $-8 - 3$ (h) $-12 + 5$ (i) $-2 + 2$
   (j) $4 - 10$ (k) $-6 + 1$ (l) $-6 - 5$

5. Now work out these
   (a) $-5 + 5$ (b) $6 - 9$ (c) $-4 - 1$
   (d) $8 - 7$ (e) $-2 + 2$ (f) $-6 - 2$
   (g) $2 - 10$ (h) $-5 + 6$ (i) $8 - 13$
   (j) $-50 + 10$ (k) $-4 - 14$ (l) $20 - 100$

6. Work out the missing number.
   (a) $8 - ? = 6$ (b) $3 - ? = -1$ (c) $-8 + ? = -3$
   (d) $-2 - ? = -7$ (e) $? - 7 = -3$ (f) $? + 4 = -4$
   (g) $? + 8 = 3$ (h) $8 - ? = -4$ (i) $-5 - ? = -12$

Two signs together

The calculation $8 - (+3)$ can be read as
  '8 take away positive 3'.

Similarly $6 - (-4)$ can be read as
  '6 take away negative 4'.

In the sequence of subtractions on
the right the numbers in column A
go down by one each time.
The numbers in column B
increase by one each time.

$$
\begin{array}{ccc}
\text{A} & \text{B} \\
\downarrow & \downarrow \\
8 - (+3) & = & 5 \\
8 - (+2) & = & 6 \\
8 - (+1) & = & 7 \\
8 - \ (0) & = & 8 \\
\end{array}
$$

Continuing the sequence downwards:

$$
\begin{array}{ccc}
8 - (-1) & = & 9 \\
8 - (-2) & = & 10 \\
8 - (-3) & = & 11 \\
\end{array}
$$

We see that $8 - (-3)$ becomes $8 + 3$.

This always applies when subtracting negative numbers. It is possible to replace *two* signs next to each other by *one* sign as follows:

$$+ \ + \ = \ +$$
$$- \ - \ = \ +$$
$$- \ + \ = \ -$$
$$+ \ - \ = \ -$$

Remember: 'same signs: $+$'

'different signs: $-$'

When two adjacent signs have been replaced by one sign in this way, the calculation is completed using the number line as before.

Work out the following

(a) $\quad -7 + (-4)$
$\quad = -7 - 4$
$\quad = -11$

(b) $\quad 8 + (-14)$
$\quad = 8 - 14$
$\quad = -6$

(c) $\quad 5 - (+9)$
$\quad = 5 - 9$
$\quad = -4$

(d) $\quad 6 - (-2) + (-8)$
$\quad = 6 + 2 - 8$
$\quad = 0$

Exercise 4

1. Work out

(a) $6 + (-4)$

(b) $5 - (+7)$

(c) $8 - (-4)$

(d) $-3 + (+2)$

(e) $-3 + (-6)$

(f) $-9 + (-1)$

(g) $7 - (+10)$

(h) $8 - (-2)$

(i) $10 - (-3)$

(j) $-8 + (-2)$

(k) $-6 - (-6)$

(l) $-7 + (-2)$

2. Work out

(a) $-3 - (-2)$

(b) $7 + (-8)$

(c) $-6 + (-2)$

(d) $8 + (-11)$

(e) $-4 - (-4)$

(f) $7 - (+10)$

(g) $-6 - (-2)$

(h) $9 + (-9)$

(i) $-3 - (+4)$

(j) $5 + (-9)$

(k) $-3 - (-8)$

(l) $4 + (-8)$

3. Now do these

(a) $8 + (-6)$

(b) $-7 - (+3)$

(c) $16 - (-2)$

(d) $-9 - (-3)$

(e) $11 + (-20)$

(f) $-17 - (-3)$

(g) $12 + (-9)$

(h) $3 - (+8)$

(i) $100 + (-99)$

(j) $-17 - (+4)$

(k) $-5 - (-5)$

(l) $6 - (+11)$

4. Work out the missing number.

(a) $7 + (?) = -2$

(b) $5 - (?) = 8$

(c) $? - (-2) = 10$

(d) $? + (-8) = -10$

(e) $9 + (?) = -20$

(f) $7 - (?) = 12$

(g) $3 - (?) = 6$

(h) $7 - (?) = 0$

(i) $12 + (?) = -100$

5.7 Mathematical reasoning

This section contains a wide variety of activities. There is no standard method for most of these problems. You need to think logically and should avoid guessing.

Cross numbers without clues

Here are cross number puzzles with a difference. There are no clues, only answers, and you have to find where the answers go.
(a) Copy out the cross number pattern.
(b) Fit all the given numbers into the correct spaces. Work logically and tick off the numbers from lists as you write them in the squares.

1. Ask your teacher if you do not know how to start.

2 digits	3 digits	4 digits	5 digits	6 digits
18	375	1274	37 125	308 513
37	692	1625		
53	828	3742		
74		5181		
87				

2.

2 digits	3 digits	4 digits	5 digits	6 digits
13	382	2630	12 785	375 041
21	582	2725		
45	178	5104		
47		7963		
72				

3.

2 digits	3 digits	4 digits	6 digits
53	182	4483	375 615
63	324	4488	
64	327	6515	7 digits
	337		3 745 124
	436		4 253 464
	573		8 253 364
	683		8 764 364
	875		

4.

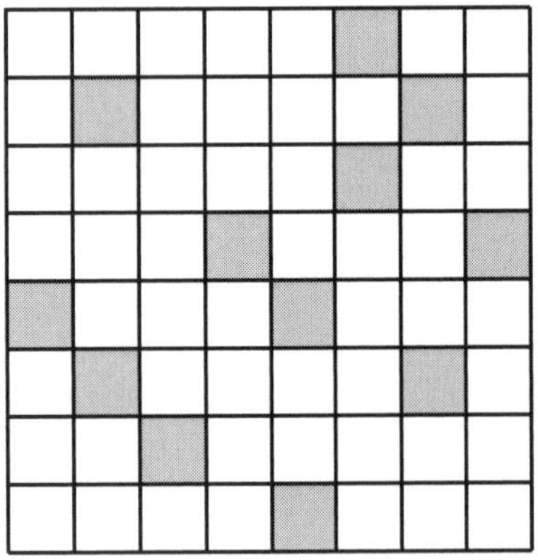

2 digits	3 digits	4 digits	5 digits	6 digits
27	161	1127	34 462	455 185
36	285	2024	74 562	
54	297	3473	81 072	
63	311	5304	84 762	
64	412	5360		
69	483	5370		
	535	5380		
	536			
	636			
	714			

5.

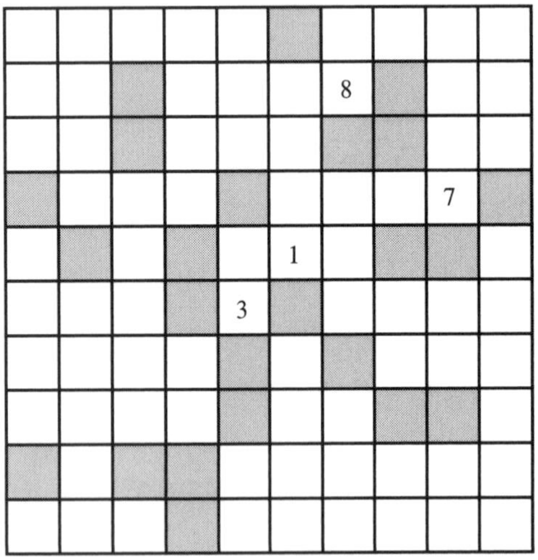

2 digits	3 digits	4 digits	5 digits	6 digits
21	121	1349	24 561	215 613
22	136	2457	24 681	246 391
22	146	2458	34 581	246 813
23	165	3864		
36	216	4351		
53	217	4462		
55	285	5321		
56	335	5351		
58	473	5557		
61	563	8241		
82	917	8251		
83		9512		
91				

6. *This one is more difficult.*

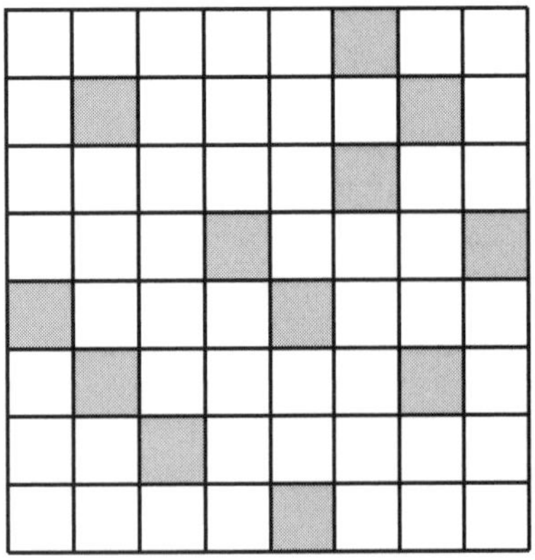

2 digits	3 digits	4 digits	5 digits	6 digits
16	288	2831	47 185	321 802
37	322	2846	52 314	
56	607	2856	56 324	
69	627	2873	56 337	
72	761	4359		
98	762	5647		
	768	7441		
	769			
	902			
	952			

General statements, counter examples

- Consider the statement: 'If n is a positive, integer (whole number), then n^2 is never equal to $2n + 8$.'

  For $n = 1$, 2 and 3 the statement is true.
  But when $n = 4$, the statement is not true because 4^2 does equal $2 \times 4 = 8$.

  This is a *counter example* which shows the statement is false.

- Consider the statement: 'The sum of any five consecutive numbers is five times the middle number.'

  This statement is always true. Here are two examples:

  $1 + 2 + ③ + 4 + 5 = 15$ and $5 \times 3 = 15$
  $6 + 7 + ⑧ + 9 + 10 = 40$ and $5 \times 8 = 40$.

Exercise 1

In each question there is a general statement. Some statements are true and some are not true.
If you think the statement is true, write 'true' and give two examples to illustrate it. Otherwise write down a counter example which shows the statement is not true.

1. The sum of three consecutive numbers is three times the middle number.

2. The product of two consecutive numbers is even.

3. All prime numbers are odd numbers.

4. The product of three consecutive numbers is a multiple of 6.

5. Except for 1, no square number is also a cube number.

6. The sum of four even numbers is always divisible by four.

7. For any two rectangles, the rectangle with the larger perimeter has the larger area.

8. If the product of two numbers is zero, then one of the numbers must be zero.

9. Dividing a number by 0·1 makes the answer ten times as big as the original number.

10. Every positive integer greater than 10 has an even number of factors.

Break the codes

1. The symbols γ, $\uparrow$, !, $\ominus$, $\perp$ each stand for one of the digits 1, 2, 3, 5 or 9 but not in that order. Use the clues below to work out what number each symbol stands for.

(a) $\uparrow \times \uparrow = \perp$
(b) $\ominus \times \uparrow = \uparrow$
(c) $\ominus + \ominus = \gamma$
(d) $\gamma + \uparrow = !$

2. The ten symbols below each stand for one of the digits 0, 1, 2, 3, 4, 5, 6, 7, 8 or 9 but not in that order.

♂ $\mathbb{W}$ □ ⊙ ↑ ✳ ▨ △ ① ⊠

Use the clues below to work out what number each symbol stands for.

(a) ♂ + ♂ + ♂ + ♂ + ♂ = $\mathbb{W}$
(b) $\mathbb{W}$ + ⊠ = $\mathbb{W}$
(c) $\mathbb{W}$ + ♂ = ⊙
(d) ① + ① + ① + ① = ↑
(e) ✳ × ✳ = ▨
(f) ⊙ − ① = △
(g) ✳ + △ = □

3. The ten symbols used in part 2 are used again but with different values.

(a) ⊠ × ⊙ = ⊙
(b) ⊠ + ⊠ + ⊠ = ✳
(c) ✳ − ⊠ = △
(d) △ × △ × △ = ⊙
(e) ⊙ − ⊠ = ↑
(f) ✳ + $\mathbb{W}$ = ✳
(g) ⊙ ÷ △ = ①
(h) ✳ + △ = □
(i) ↑ − ⊠ = ▨
(j) ♂ − △ = ↑

4. These clues are more difficult to work out.

(a) □ + ↑ = □
(b) ♂ × □ = ♂
(c) ▨ × ▨ × ▨ = ♂
(d) ♂ − ▨ = ①
(e) ① − ▨ = △
(f) ① − □ = ⊠
(g) ⊠ + ▨ = ⊙
(h) $\mathbb{W}$ × $\mathbb{W}$ = ✳

Part 6

6.1 Probability

In probability we ask questions like ...

'How likely is it?'
'What are the chances of ... ?'

Here are some questions where we do not know the answer ...

'Will my parachute open?'
'Will I live to be over 100 years old?'
'Who will win the F.A. cup?'

Some events are certain. Some events are impossible.

Some events are in between certain and impossible.

> The probability of an event is a measure of the chance of it happening.
>
> The probability (or chance) of an event occurring is measured on a scale like this ...
>
> |————————|————————|————————|————————|
> impossible   unlikely   evens   likely   certain

Exercise 1

Draw a probability scale like this ...

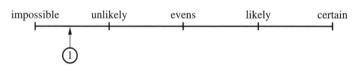

Draw an arrow to show the chance of the events below happening.

[The arrow for question ① has been done for you.]

1. When a card is selected from a pack it will be an 'ace'.

2. When a coin is tossed it will show a 'head'.

3. The letter 'a' appears somewhere on the next page of this book.

4. When a drawing pin is dropped it will land 'point up'.

5. There will be at least one baby born somewhere in Great Britain on the first day of next month.

6. Your local vicar will win the national lottery next week.

7. The day after Monday will be Tuesday.

8. There will be a burst pipe in the school heating system next week and the school will have to close for 3 days.

9. You will blink your eyes in the next minute.

10. You will be asked to tidy your room this week.

11. When a slice of toast is dropped, it will land on the floor buttered side down.

12. You will get maths homework this week.

13. England will win the next World Cup at football.

14. Your maths teacher has a black belt in Judo.

15. You will be captured by aliens tonight.

Probability as a number

Different countries have different words for saying how likely or unlikely any particular event is.
All over the world people use probability as a way of doing this, using numbers on a scale instead of words.
The scale looks like this ...

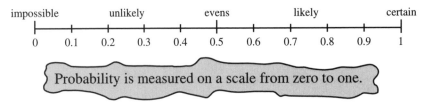

Probability is measured on a scale from zero to one.

Exercise 2

Look at the events in the last exercise and for each one estimate the probability of it occurring using a probability from 0 to 1.

As an example in question ① you might write 'about 0·1'. Copy each question and write your estimate of its probability at the end.

Experimental probability

The chance of certain events occurring can easily be predicted. For example the chance of tossing a head with an ordinary coin. Many events, however, cannot be so easily predicted.

Experiment: To find the experimental probability that the third word in the third line on any page in this book contains the letter 'a' (You could use a non-mathematical book if you prefer)

Step 1. We will do 50 *trials*. Write down at random 50 page numbers between 1 and 180 (say 3, 15, 16, 21, 27, etc.).

Step 2. For each page look at the third word in the third line. This is a *trial*.
If there is not a third word on the third line it still counts as a trial. (The third line might be all numbers.)

Step 3. If the word contains the letter 'a' this is a *success*.

Step 4. Make a tally chart like this ...

> **37**
>
> ## Angles in triangles
> Draw a triangle of any shape on a piece of card and cut it out accurately. Now tear off the three corners as shown.
>
> (third line, third word.)

Number of trials	Number of successes
ЖТ ЖТ ‖	ЖТ ‖

$$\text{Experimental probability} = \frac{\text{Number of trials in which a success occurs}}{\text{Total number of trials made}}$$

Exercise 3

Carry out experiments to work out the experimental probability of some of the following events.
Use a tally chart to record your results. Don't forget to record how many times you do the experiment (the number of 'trials').

1. Roll a dice. What is the chance of rolling a six? Perform 100 trials.

2. Toss two coins. What is the chance of tossing two tails? Perform 100 trials.

3. Pick a counter from a bag containing counters of different colours. What is the chance of picking a red counter? Perform 100 trials.

4. Roll a pair of dice. What is the chance of rolling a double? Perform 100 trials.

5. Butter a piece of toast and drop it on the floor. What is the chance of it landing buttered side down? Would you expect to get the same result with margarine? How about butter and jam? Suppose you don't toast the bread?
If you run into difficulties at home, blame your maths teacher, not the authors of this book.

Expected probability

For simple events, like throwing a dice or tossing a coin, we can
work out the expected probability of an event occurring.
For a fair dice the *expected probability* of throwing a '3' is $\frac{1}{6}$.
For a normal coin the expected probability of tossing a 'head' is $\frac{1}{2}$

$$\text{Expected probability} = \frac{\text{the number of ways the event can happen}}{\text{the number of possible outcomes}}$$

Random choice: If a card is chosen at random from a pack it
means that every card has an equal chance of
being chosen.

Nine identical discs numbered 1, 2, 3, 4, 5, 6, 7, 8, 9
are put into a bag. One disc is selected at random.

In this example there are 9 possible equally likely outcomes of a trial.

(a) The probability of selecting a '4' $= \frac{1}{9}$

This may be written p (selecting a '4') $= \frac{1}{9}$

(b) p (selecting an odd number) $= \frac{5}{9}$

(c) p (selecting a number greater than 5) $= \frac{4}{9}$

Exercise 4

1. A bag contains a red ball, a blue ball and a yellow ball. One ball
   is chosen at random. Copy and complete these sentences.

   (a) The probability that the red ball is chosen is ... $\dfrac{\square}{3}$

   (b) The probability that the blue ball is chosen is ... $\dfrac{\square}{\square}$

   (c) The probability that the yellow ball is chosen is ... $\dfrac{\square}{\square}$

2. One ball is chosen at random from a bag which contains a red
   ball, a blue ball, a yellow ball and a white ball. Write down the
   probability that the chosen ball will be

   (a) red   (b) blue   (c) yellow.

3. One ball is chosen at random from a box which contains 2 red balls and 2 blue balls. Write down the probability that the chosen ball will be
(a) red.
(b) blue.
(c) yellow.

4. A hat contains 2 white balls and 1 black ball. One ball is chosen at random. Find the probability that it is
(a) white.
(b) black.

5. A pencil case contains pencils of the following colours:- 6 red, 3 black, 1 green and 1 blue. One pencil is selected without looking. Find the probability that the pencil is
(a) red.
(b) black.
(c) green.

6. I roll an ordinary dice.
Find the probability that I score
(a) 3
(b) 1
(c) less than 5

7. Eight identical discs numbered 1, 2, 3, 4, 5, 6, 7, 8 are put into a bag. One disc is selected at random. Find the probability of selecting
(a) a '5'.   (b) an odd number.   (c) a number less than 6.

8. Nine identical discs numbered 1, 3, 4, 5, 7, 8, 10, 11, 15 are put into a bag. One disc is selected at random. Find the probability of selecting.
(a) a '10'.   (b) an even number.   (c) a number more than 6.

9. A bag contains 4 red balls and 7 white balls. One ball is selected at random. Find the probability that it is
(a) red.   (b) white.

10. One card is selected at random from the ten cards shown …
Find the probability of selecting
(a) the King of spades   (b) a heart
(c) a diamond   (d) a 3

11. A bag contains 2 red balls, 4 white balls and 5 blue balls. One ball is selected at random. Find the probability of selecting.
(a) a red ball   (b) a white ball   (c) a blue ball

12. I buy a fish at random from a pond containing 3 piranhas, 2 baby sharks and 7 goldfish. Find the probability that the fish I choose is
(a) a goldfish.   (b) a baby shark
(c) dangerous   (d) glad I rescued it!
(e) able to play the piano.

Probability Problems

A pack of playing cards, without Jokers, contains 52 cards.
There is Ace, King, Queen, Jack, 10, 9, 8, 7, 6, 5, 4, 3, 2 of four suits.
The suits are ...

spades   hearts   diamonds   clubs

A pack of cards is shuffled and then one card is chosen at random.
(a) The probability that it is a King of hearts is $\frac{1}{52}$
(b) The probability that it is an ace is $\frac{4}{52}\left(=\frac{1}{13}\right)$
(c) The probability that it is a spade is $\frac{13}{52}\left(=\frac{1}{4}\right)$

Exercise 5

1. One card is picked at random from a pack of 52.
   Find the probability that it is
   (a) a Queen
   (b) the King of diamonds
   (c) a spade

2. One card is selected at random from a full pack of 52 playing
   cards. Find the probability of selecting
   (a) a heart
   (b) a red card
   (c) a '2'
   (d) any King, Queen or Jack
   (e) the ace of spades

3. A small pack of twenty cards consists of the Ace, King, Queen,
   Jack and 10 of spades, hearts, diamonds and clubs. One card is
   selected at random. Find the probability of selecting
   (a) the ace of hearts
   (b) a King
   (c) a '10'
   (d) a black card
   (e) a heart

4. A bag contains 3 black balls, 2 green balls, 1 white ball and 5
   orange balls. Find the probability of selecting
   (a) a black ball
   (b) an orange ball
   (c) a white ball

5. A bag contains the balls shown. One ball is taken out at random. Find the probability that it is

Y = yellow
B = blue
R = Red

(a) yellow   (b) blue   (c) red

One more blue ball and one more red ball are added to the bag.

(d) Find the new probability of selecting a yellow ball from the bag.

6. If Jake throws a 1 or a 4 on his next throw of a dice when playing 'Snakes and Ladders' he will climb up a ladder on the board. What is the probability that he will *miss* a ladder on his next throw?

7. A box contains 11 balls: 3 green, 2 white, 4 red and 2 blue
   (a) Find the probability of selecting
      (i) a blue ball
      (ii) a green ball
   (b) The 3 green balls are replaced by 3 blue balls. Find the probability of selecting
      (i) a blue ball
      (ii) a white ball.

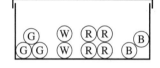

8. Here are two spinners.
Say whether the following statements are true or false. Explain why in each case.
   (a) 'Sarah is more likely to spin a 6 than Ben'.
   (b) 'Sarah and Ben are equally likely to spin an even number.'
   (c) 'If Sarah spins her spinner six times, she is bound to get at least one 6.'

Sarah's spinner   Ben's spinner

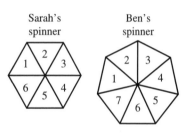

In Questions **9**, **10**, **11**, **12** a bag contains a certain number of red balls and a certain number of white balls. The tally charts show the number of times a ball was selected from the bag and then replaced. Look at the results and say what you think was in the bag each time.

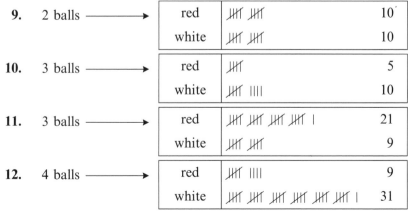

9.	2 balls	red	𝈾𝈾 𝈾𝈾	10
		white	𝈾𝈾 𝈾𝈾	10
10.	3 balls	red	𝈾𝈾	5
		white	𝈾𝈾 ||||	10
11.	3 balls	red	𝈾𝈾 𝈾𝈾 𝈾𝈾 𝈾𝈾 |	21
		white	𝈾𝈾 𝈾𝈾	9
12.	4 balls	red	𝈾𝈾 ||||	9
		white	𝈾𝈾 𝈾𝈾 𝈾𝈾 𝈾𝈾 𝈾𝈾 𝈾𝈾 |	31

13. A bag contains 9 balls, all of which are black or white. Jane selects a ball and then replaces it. She repeats this several times. Here are her results (B = black, W= white):

B W B W B B B W B B W B B W B
B B W W B B B B W B W B B W B

How many balls of each colour do you think there were in the bag?

14. Cards with numbers 1, 2, 3, 4, 5, 6, 7, 8, 9, 10 are shuffled and then placed face down in a line. The cards are then turned over one at a time from the left. In this example the first card is a '4'.

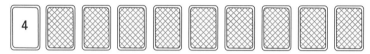

Find the probability that the next card turned over will be
(a) 7
(b) a number higher than 4.

15. Suppose the second card is a 1

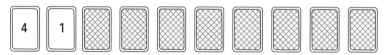

Find the probability that the next card will be
(a) the 6
(b) an even number
(c) higher than 1.

16. Suppose the first three cards are [4] [1] [8] ...

Find the probability that the next card will be
(a) less than 8
(b) the 4
(c) an odd number.

17. Melissa, who is 8 years old, plays two games with her mother, 'Snakes and Ladders' and then 'Monopoly'. Comment on the following statements:
(a) Melissa has an evens chance of winning at 'Snakes and Ladders'.
(b) Melissa has an evens chance of winning at 'Monopoly'.

18. Three friends Aljit, Ben and Curtis sit next to each other on a bench.
(a) Make a list of all the different ways in which they can sit.
(Use A = Aljit, B = Ben and C = Curtis).
Find the probability that
(b) Aljit sits in the middle.
(c) Aljit sits next to Curtis.
(d) Ben sits at one end of the bench.

19. A pack of cards is split into two piles. Pile P
contains all the picture cards and aces and
pile O contains all the other cards.
(a) Find the probability of selecting
    (i) the Jack of hearts from pile P
    (ii) a seven from pile O
(b) All the diamonds are now removed from both piles.
    Find the probability of selecting
    (i) the King of clubs from pile P
    (ii) a red card from pile O.

20. Each letter in the words of the sentence below is written on a
separate card.
'I have told you a million times, don't exaggerate!'
The cards are placed in a bag and one card is selected at
random. Find the probability of selecting
(a) an 'a'
(b) a 't'
(c) a 'b'

21. Helen played a game of cards with Michelle. The cards were
dealt so that both players received two cards. Helen's cards
were a seven and a four. Michelle's first card was a 10.

Find the probability that Michelle's second card was
(a) a picture card [a King, Queen or Jack]
(b) a seven.

22. One person is selected at random from the crowd of 14 750
watching a tennis match at Wimbledon. What is the probability
that the person chosen will have his or her birthday that year
on a Sunday?

23. One ball is selected at random from a bag containing x red balls
and y white balls. What is the probability of selecting a red ball?

18. Debbie, Alan and Nicky were asked to toss a fair coin 16 times.
Here are the results they wrote down.

Debbie   H T H T H T H T H T H T H T H T
Alan   H H T H T T H T T T H H T H H T
Nicky   H H H H H H H H T T T T T T T T

One of the three did the experiment properly while the other two
just made up results. Explain what you think each person did.

6.2 Fractions, decimals, percentages

Changing fractions to decimals

- Many fractions can be converted to decimals by using known
  equivalent fractions. You should *learn* the following:

  $\frac{1}{4} = 0.25$, $\frac{1}{2} = 0.5$, $\frac{3}{4} = 0.75$, $\frac{1}{10} = 0.1$, $\frac{2}{10} = 0.2$, $\frac{7}{100} = 0.07$ etc

- Here are some examples:

  $\frac{6}{8} = \frac{3}{4} = 0.75$ $\frac{1}{25} = \frac{4}{100} = 0.04$

  $\frac{1}{5} = \frac{2}{10} = 0.2$ $\frac{30}{120} = \frac{1}{4} = 0.25$

  $\frac{7}{20} = \frac{35}{100} = 0.35$ $\frac{11}{50} = \frac{22}{100} = 0.22$

Exercise 1

Convert the fractions to decimals. These are fractions where you
should *know* the decimal equivalent.

1. $\frac{1}{4}$ **2.** $\frac{7}{10}$ **3.** $\frac{99}{100}$ **4.** $\frac{1}{2}$

5. $\frac{9}{10}$ **6.** $\frac{8}{100}$ **7.** $\frac{3}{4}$ **8.** $\frac{1}{100}$

Copy and complete the working.

9. $\frac{2}{8} = \frac{1}{4} = 0.\square\square$ **10.** $\frac{3}{5} = \frac{6}{10} = 0.\square$

11. $\frac{3}{20} = \frac{15}{100} = 0.\square\square$ **12.** $\frac{11}{20} = \frac{\square}{100} = \square$

13. $\frac{4}{5} = \frac{\square}{10} = \square$ **14.** $\frac{2}{25} = \frac{\square}{100} = \square$

Use the method above to convert these fractions to decimals

15. $\frac{2}{5}$ **16.** $\frac{1}{20}$ **17.** $\frac{3}{20}$ **18.** $\frac{1}{25}$

19. $\frac{9}{20}$ **20.** $\frac{21}{25}$ **21.** $\frac{140}{200}$ **22.** $\frac{150}{200}$

Convert the fractions to decimals and then write the numbers in order of size, smallest first.

23. $\frac{3}{4}$, $\frac{3}{5}$, 0·7   **24.** $\frac{8}{20}$, 0·3, $\frac{9}{25}$

25. $\frac{1}{5}$, 0·15, $\frac{1}{20}$ **26.** $\frac{12}{16}$, 0·75, $\frac{4}{5}$

Changing decimals to fractions

- $0·8 = \frac{8}{10} = \frac{4}{5}$ $0·21 = \frac{21}{100}$

  $0·35 = \frac{35}{100} = \frac{7}{20}$ $0·08 = \frac{8}{100} = \frac{2}{25}$

Simplify the answer if possible

Exercise 2

Change the decimals to fractions in their most simple form.

1. 0·6   **2.** 0·9   **3.** 0·05   **4.** 0·55   **5.** 0·07

6. 0·11   **7.** 0·48   **8.** 0·25   **9.** 0·04   **10.** 0·95

11. 0·06   **12.** 0·44   **13.** 0·37   **14.** 1·1   **15.** 2·5

16. 4·01   **17.** 0·96   **18.** 3·75   **19.** 0·88   **20.** 3·05

Changing to a percentage and vice versa

- Fraction to percentage

  (a) $\frac{2}{5} = \frac{40}{100} = 40\%$

  $\frac{1}{20} = \frac{5}{100} = 5\%$

  $2\frac{1}{2} = \frac{250}{100} = 250\%$

- Percentage to fraction

  $40\% = \frac{40}{100} = \frac{2}{5}$

  $22\% = \frac{22}{100} = \frac{11}{50}$

  $8\% = \frac{8}{100} = \frac{2}{25}$

- You should learn the following:

  $\frac{1}{4} = 25\%$ $\frac{1}{8} = 12\frac{1}{2}\%$ $\frac{1}{3} = 33\frac{1}{3}\%$ $\frac{2}{3} = 66\frac{2}{3}\%$

Exercise 3

Convert these percentages to fractions. Cancel down where possible.

1. 60%   **2.** 75%   **3.** 80%   **4.** 44%

5. 10%   **6.** 99%   **7.** 2%   **8.** 9%

Copy and complete the following

9. $\frac{3}{5} = \frac{60}{100} = \boxed{}$ %

10. $\frac{11}{25} = \frac{44}{100} = \boxed{}$ %

11. $\frac{3}{20} = \frac{15}{100} = \boxed{}$ %

12. $\frac{7}{25} = \frac{\boxed{}}{100} = \boxed{}$ %

13. $\frac{7}{10} = \frac{\boxed{}}{100} = \boxed{}$ %

14. $\frac{7}{50} = \frac{\boxed{}}{100} = \boxed{}$ %

Write down each fraction with its equivalent percentage.

15. $\frac{3}{4}$ **16.** $\frac{1}{8}$ **17.** $\frac{1}{3}$ **18.** $\frac{2}{3}$

19. The chart shows the kinds of trees in a wood.
What percentage of the trees are:
(a) oak
(b) beech
(c) birch?

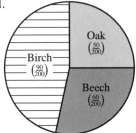

20. Here are some test results. Change them to percentages.
(a) $\frac{19}{25}$ (b) $\frac{13}{20}$ (c) $\frac{32}{40}$

21. Rewrite these sentences using percentages.
(a) One quarter of the meat sold in Britain is beef.
(b) One in five cars have at least one fault.
(c) Seven out of twenty people in a train were reading a paper.

22. Draw three lines 10 cm long and fill in the missing numbers.

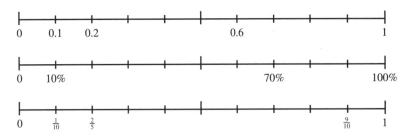

23. Change these decimals to percentages.
(a) 0·27   (b) 0·19   (c) 0·09   (d) 0·6

24. Change these percentages to decimals.

(a) 37%   (b) 42%   (c) 90%   (d) 8%

(e) 6%   (f) 11%   (g) 12·5%   (h) 120%

25. Copy and complete the table.

	fraction	decimal	percentage
(a)		0·4	
(b)			35%
(c)	$\frac{3}{5}$		

Exercise 4

Each fraction, decimal or percentage has an equivalent in the list with letters. Find the letters to make a sentence.

A. $\boxed{50\%, \frac{1}{4}, 10\%, 0\cdot2, 0\cdot11}$ $\boxed{17\%, 11\%}$ $\boxed{0\cdot75, 99\%, \frac{1}{10}}$ $\boxed{20\%, \frac{1}{4}, \frac{1}{8}, 0\cdot7}$

B. $\boxed{\frac{7}{10}, 0\cdot8, 45\%, \frac{17}{100}, 0\cdot5, \frac{1}{4}, \frac{10}{25}, 0\cdot11}$ $\boxed{\frac{3}{6}, \frac{4}{16}, 0\cdot05, 80\%}$ $\boxed{\frac{22}{200}, 0\cdot8, 75\%, 11\%, \frac{8}{10}}$

C. $\boxed{17\%}$ $\boxed{45\%, 0\cdot25, 75\%, 10\%}$ $\boxed{0\cdot11, \frac{99}{100}, \frac{4}{10}, \frac{41}{50}, \frac{400}{500}}$

$\boxed{0\cdot8, \frac{3}{20}, \frac{1}{3}, 0\cdot25, \frac{1}{10}, \frac{17}{100}, \frac{198}{200}, \frac{15}{20}, \frac{110}{1000}}$

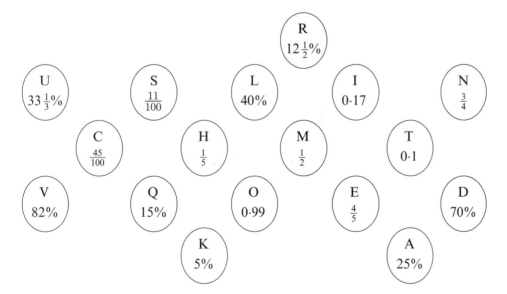

6.3 Formulas

Finding a rule

- Here is a sequence of shapes made from sticks

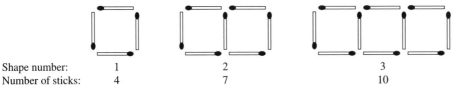

Shape number:	1	2	3
Number of sticks:	4	7	10

- There is a *rule* or *formula* which we can use to calculate the number of sticks for any shape number.

  'The number of sticks is three times the shape number add one'.

  Check that this rule works for all the shapes above and also for shape number 4 which you can draw.

- We could also write the rule using symbols. Let *n* stand for the diagram number and let *s* stand for the number of sticks.

  The rule (or formula) is '$s = 3n + 1$'.

Here is a sequence of boxes with three spaces.

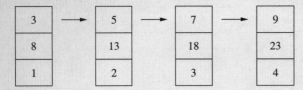

We can write letters in the spaces like this

In words the rule is: 'To find *n* you multiply *x* by 3 and then subtract *y*.'

Using algebra the rule is: $n = 3x - y$

Exercise 1

1. Here is a sequence of triangles made from sticks.

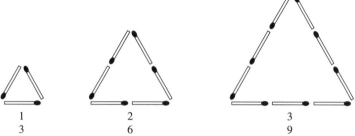

Shape number:	1	2	3
Number of sticks:	3	6	9

(a) Draw shape number 4 and count the number of sticks.

(b) Write down and complete the rule for the number of sticks in a shape: 'The number of sticks is ____ times the shape number'.

2. Here is a sequence of 'steps' made from sticks

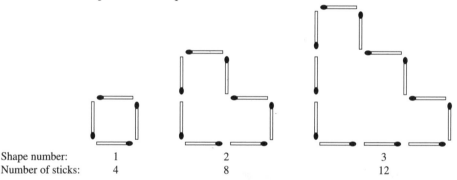

Shape number:	1	2	3
Number of sticks:	4	8	12

(a) Draw shape number 4 and count the number of sticks.

(b) Write down the rule for the number of sticks in a shape. 'The number of sticks is ____ times the shape number'.

3. Louise makes a pattern of triangles from sticks.

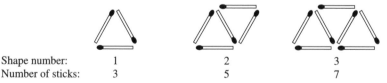

Shape number:	1	2	3
Number of sticks:	3	5	7

(a) Draw shape number 4 and shape number 5

(b) Make a table:

shape number	1	2	3	4	5
number of sticks	3	5	7		

(c) Write down the rule for the number of sticks in a shape. 'The number of sticks is ____ times the shape number and then add ____.'

4. Crosses are drawn on 'dotty' paper to make a sequence.

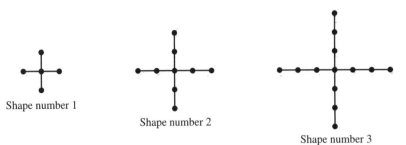

Shape number 1

Shape number 2

Shape number 3

(a) Draw shape number 4

(b) Make a table:

shape number	1	2	3	4
number of dots	5	9	13	

(c) Write down the rule.
   'The number of dots is _____ times the shape number and then add _____ .'

5. In these diagrams black squares are surrounded on three sides by white squares. Let the number of black squares be b and let the number of white squares be w.

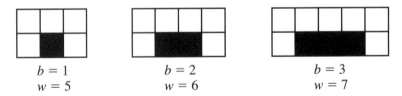

$b = 1$
$w = 5$

$b = 2$
$w = 6$

$b = 3$
$w = 7$

(a) Draw the next diagram which has 4 black squares.
(b) Write down the rule.
   'The number of white squares is . . . .'

6. Look again at Questions **1**, **2**, **3**, and **4**. Use n for the shape number and s for the number of sticks or dots. For each question write the rule connecting n and s without using words. In each question write '$s =$.'

Sequences

- Here is a sequence 5, 10, 15, 20, ...

  The first term is 5×1, the second term is 5×2, the third term is 5×3 ......
  the 30th term is 5×30.
  The *general term*, or the *n*th term, is $5 \times n$.

  We can use the *n*th term to write down any term of the sequence.
  E.g. 14th term $= 5 \times 14$, 100th term $= 5 \times 100$.

- In another sequence the nth term is $5n + 3$

  1st term $= 5 \times 1 + 3$ 2nd term $= 5 \times 2 + 3$ 3rd term $= 5 \times 3 + 3$
  $(n = 1)$ $= 8$ $(n = 2)$ $= 13$ $(n = 3)$ $= 18$

Exercise 2

1. The *n*th term of a sequence is $3n$. Write down:
   (a) the first term   (put $n = 1$)
   (b) the second term   (put $n = 2$)
   (c) the tenth term   (put $n = 10$)

2. The *n*th term of a sequence is $7n$. Write down:
   (a) the first term   (put $n = 1$)
   (a) the fifth term
   (a) the one hundredth term

In Questions **3** to **7** you are given the *n*th term of a sequence.
Write down the first four terms of each sequence.

   3. $5n$ **4.** $11n$ **5.** $n + 2$ **6.** $20 - n$ **7.** $2n + 10$

8. Write down each sequence and select the correct formula for the
   *n*th term from the list given.
   (a) 2, 4, 6, 8, ...
   (b) 10, 20, 30, 40, ...
   (c) 4, 8, 12, 16, 20, ...
   (d) 11, 22, 33, 44, ...
   (e) 100, 200, 300, 400, ...
   (f) 6, 12, 18, 24, ...
   (g) $1^2, 2^2, 3^2, 4^2, ...$
   (h) 3, 5, 7, 9, 11, ...

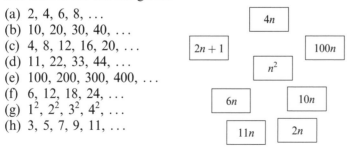

9.

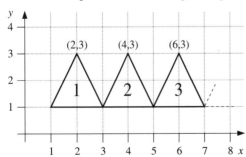

The numbers N1, N2, N3, N4 and M1, M2, M3, M4 form two
sequences.
(a) Find M5, M6, N5, N6.
(b) Think of rules and use them to find M15 and N20.

10. Here is a sequence of touching squares.
    Copy and complete the table.

Square number	Coordinates of centre
1	(2, 2)
2	(4, 4)
3	
5	
40	
45	

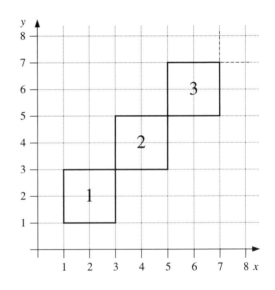

11. Here is a sequence of touching triangles.

Find the coordinates of:
(a) the top of triangle 5
(b) the top of triangle 50
(c) the bottom right corner of triangle 50
(d) the bottom right corner of triangle 100.

12.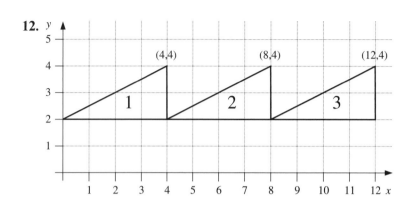

Find the coordinates of the top vertex of:
(a) triangle 4
(b) triangle 20
(c) triangle 2000.

13. Write down the coordinates of the centres of squares 1, 2 and 3.
Find the coordinates of:
(a) the centre of square 4
(b) the centre of square 10
(c) the top vertex of square 70.

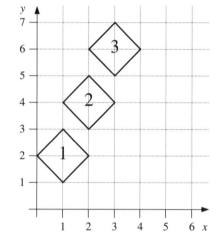

14. Write down the coordinates of the centres of the first six squares.
Find the coordinates of:
(a) the centre of square 60
(b) the centre of square 73
(c) the top left corner of square 90
(d) the top left corner of square 101.

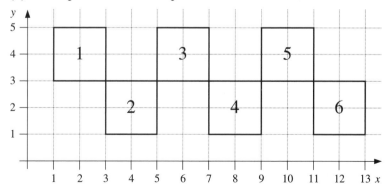

15. Now design some patterns of your own.

Count the crossovers: an investigation

Two straight lines have a maximum of one crossover

Three straight lines have a maximum of three crossovers.

Notice that you can have less than three crossovers if the lines all go through one point. Or the lines could be parallel.
In this work we are interested only in the *maximum* number of crossovers.

Four lines have a maximum of six crossovers.

▨ Draw five lines and find the maximum number of crossovers.

▨ Does there appear to be any sort of sequence in your results?
   If you can find a sequence, use it to *predict* the maximum number of crossovers with six lines.

▨ Now draw six lines and count the crossovers to see if your prediction was correct.
   (Remember not to draw three lines through one point.)

▨ Predict the number of crossovers for seven lines and then check if your prediction is correct by drawing a diagram.

▨ Write your results in a table:

Number of lines	Number of crossovers
2	1
3	3
4	6
5	
6	

(a) Predict the number of crossovers for 20 lines.

(b) (Harder) Predict the number of crossovers for 2000 lines.

Substituting into a formula

The perimeter, P, of the shape is given by the formula

$P = 5a + b$

Find P when $a = 4$ and $b = 3$.

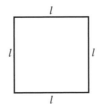

$P = 5a + b$
$P = 5 \times 4 + 3$
$P = 23$

Work *down* the page.

Exercise 3

1. A formula to give the perimeter P of a square is $P = 4l$.
Find P, when $l = 11$.

2. The cost in pounds, C, for hiring a car is given by the formula $C = 2m + 30$, where m is the number of miles travelled.
Find C, when $m = 200$.

3. For a rectangle with sides l and b the perimeter is given by the formula $P = 2(l + b)$.
Find P, when $l = 7$ and $b = 5$.

4. A formula for the perimeter of the trapezium shown is $P = 3a + b$.
Find P, when $a = 12$ and $b = 15$.

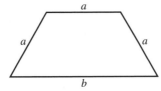

5. A formula for calculating the speed of an accelerating object is $v = u + at$.
Calculate the value of v when, $u = 3$, $a = 10$ and $t = 2$.

In Questions **6** to **24** you are given a formula. Find the value of the letter required in each case.

6. $p = 4a + 10$

Find p, when $a = 8$.

7. $t = 5m - 7$

Find t, when $m = 5$.

8. $x = \dfrac{a}{4} + 5$

Find x, when $a = 20$.

9. $y = \dfrac{b}{3} - 2$

Find y, when $b = 27$.

10. $h = 3(p + 4)$

Find h, when $p = 6$.

11. $h = 5(m - 7)$

Find h, when $m = 10$.

12. $r = \dfrac{s}{10} + 6$

Find r, when $s = 1000$.

13. $m = \dfrac{2n + 1}{3}$

Find m, when $n = 7$.

14. $e = ab + 5$

Find e, when $a = 3$, $b = 5$.

15. $B = ut - 6$

Find B, when $u = 9$, $t = 8$.

Remember:
'*ab*' means $a \times b$
'*ut*' means $u \times t$

16. $w = 2x + xy$

Find w, when $x = 4$, $y = 5$.

17. $k = 3(a + a^2)$

Find k, when $a = 5$.

18. $g = u^2 - v^2$

Find g, when $u = 9$, $v = 1$.

19. $f = x(y + 2)$

Find f, when $x = 2$, $y = 5$.

20. $y = ab + b^2$

Find y, when $a = 5$, $b = 3$.

21. $t = 3mp + 1$

Find t, when $m = 10$, $p = 5$.

22. $h = \dfrac{m}{n} + m^2$

Find h, when $m = 6$, $n = 2$.

23. $c = \dfrac{x + x^2}{6}$

Find c, when $x = 5$.

24. p and q are connected by the formula $p = 2(4q + q^2)$
Find p, when $q = 3$.

6.4 Interpreting graphs

On a travel graph the motion of a moving object is shown, with time usually plotted on the horizontal axis and distance from a point plotted on the vertical axis.

- The graph shows the journey of a car from Amble to Cabley via Boldon. The vertical axis shows the distance of the car from Amble between 1400 and 1700.

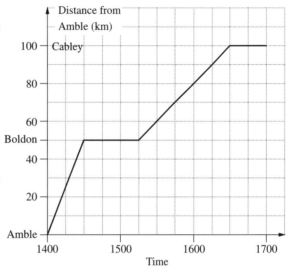

  (a) At 1530 the car is 60 km from Amble.

  (b) The car stopped at Boldon for 45 minutes. The graph is horizontal from 1430 until 1515 which shows that the car does not move.

  (c) The car takes $\frac{1}{2}$ hour to travel 50 km from Amble to Boldon. Thus the speed of the car is 100 km/h.

  (d) The speed of the car from Boldon to Cabley is 40 km/h.

$$\left[\text{Speed} = \frac{\text{distance travelled}}{\text{time taken}} = \frac{50}{1\frac{1}{4}} \right]$$

- This graph shows the details of a cycle ride that Jim took starting from his home.

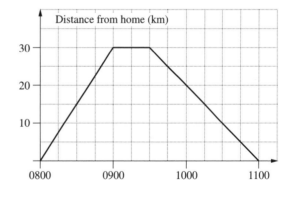

  (a) In the first hour Jim went 30 km so his speed was 30 km/h.

  (b) He stopped for $\frac{1}{2}$ hour at a place 30 km from his home.

  (c) From 0930 until 1100 he cycled back home. We know that he cycled back home because the distance from his home at 1100 is 0 km.

  (d) The speed at which he cycled home was 20 km/h.

Exercise 1

1. The graph shows a car journey from A to C via B.
   (a) How far is it from A to C?
   (b) For how long does the car stop at B?
   (c) When is the car half way between B and C?
   (d) What is the speed of the car
       (i) between A and B?
       (ii) between B and C?

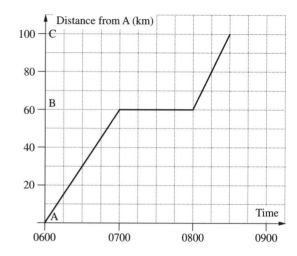

2. The graph shows the motion of a train as it accelerates away from Troon.
   (a) How far from Troon is the train at 0845?
   (b) When is the train half way between R and S?
   (c) Find the speed of the train
       (i) from R to S
       (ii) from Q to R
       (iii) (harder) from P to Q.

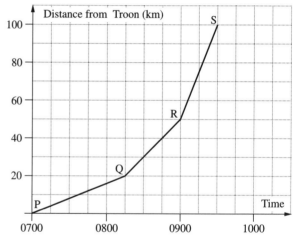

3. The graph shows a car journey from Lemsford.
   (a) For how long did the car stop at Mabley?
   (b) When did the car arrive back at Lemsford?
   (c) When did the car leave Mabley after stopping?
   (d) Find the speed of the car
       (i) from Lemsford to Mabley
       (ii) from Nixon back to Lemsford.

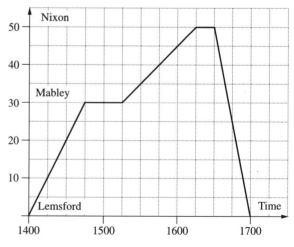

4. This graph shows a car journey from London to Stevenage and back.

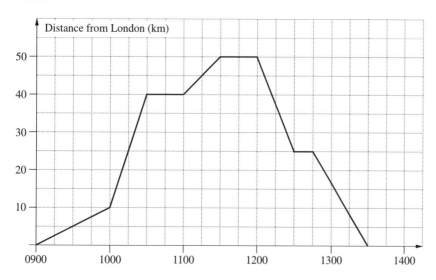

(a) For how long in the whole journey was the car at rest?

(b) At what time was the car half way to Stevenage on the outward journey?

(c) Between which two times was the car travelling at its highest speed?

5. The graph shows the journey of a coach and a lorry along the same road between Newcastle and Carlisle.

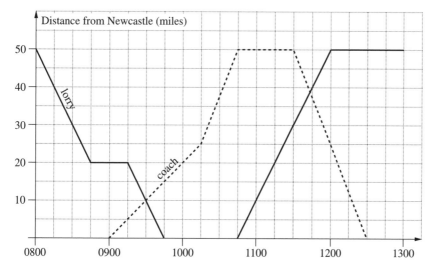

(a) How far apart were the two vehicles at 0915?

(b) At what time did the vehicles meet for the first time?

(c) At what speed did the coach return to Newcastle?

(d) What was the highest speed of the lorry during its journey?

6. The graph shows the motion of three cars A, B and C during a race of length 140 km.

(a) What was the order of the cars after 40 minutes?

(b) Which car won the race?

(c) At approximately what time did C overtake B?

(d) At what speed did car B finish the race?

(e) Describe what happened to car C during the race.

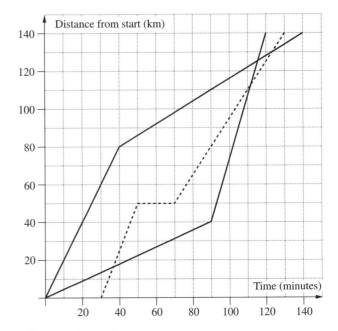

7. Explain why the two graphs below cannot be travel graphs.

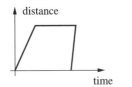

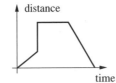

8. The diagram shows the travel graphs of five objects.

Which graph shows:

(a) A car ferry from Dover to Calais

(b) A hovercraft from Dover to Calais

(c) A car ferry from Calais to Dover

(d) A buoy outside Dover harbour

(e) A cross channel swimmer from Dover?

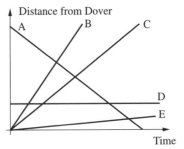

Solving problems with travel graphs

Exercise 2

In Questions **1** to **6** use the same scales as in question **5** of the last exercise.

1. At 17 00 Lisa leaves her home and cycles at 20 km/h for 1 hour. She stops for $\frac{1}{4}$ hour and then continues her journey at a speed of 40 km/h for the next $\frac{1}{2}$ hour. She then stops for $\frac{3}{4}$ hour. Finally she returns home at a speed of 40 km/h.

Draw a travel graph to show Lisa's journey. When did she arrive home?

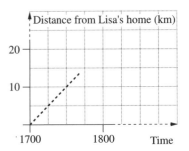

2. Suzy leaves home at 1300 on her horse and rides at a speed of 20 km/h for one hour. Suzy and her horse then rest for 45 minutes and afterwards continue their journey at a speed of 15 km/h for another one hour. At what time do they finish the journey?

3. As Mrs Sadler leaves home in her car at 13 00 she encounters heavy traffic and travels at only 20 km/h for the first $\frac{1}{2}$ hour. In the second half hour she increases her speed to 30 km/h and after that she travels along the main road at 40 km/h for $\frac{3}{4}$ h. She stops at her destination for $\frac{1}{2}$ hour and then returns home at a steady speed of 40 km/h.

Draw a graph to find when she returns home.

4. At 12 00 Mr Dean leaves home and drives at a speed of 30 km/h. At 12 30 he increases his speed to 50 km/h and continues to his destination which is 65 km from home. He stops for $\frac{1}{2}$ hour and then returns home at a speed of 65 km/h.

Use a graph to find the time at which he arrives home.

5. At 08 00 Chew Ling leaves home and cycles towards a railway station which is 65 km away. She cycles at a speed of 30 km/h until 09 30 at which time she stops to rest for $\frac{1}{2}$ hour. She then completes the journey at a speed of 20 km/h.
At 09 45 Chew Ling's father leaves their home in his car and drives towards the station at 60 km/h.
(a) At what time does Chew Ling arrive at the station?
(b) When is Chew Ling overtaken by her father?

6. Kate lives 80 km from Kevin. One day at 1200 Kate cycles towards Kevin's home at 25 km/h. At the same time Kevin cycles at 30 km/h towards Kate's home

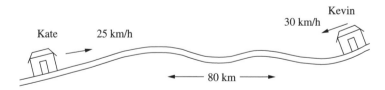

Draw a travel graph with 'Distance from Kate's home' on the vertical axis.
Approximately when and where do they meet?

In questions **7** and **8** use a scale of 2 squares to 15 minutes across the page and 1 square to 10 km up the page.

7. At 0100 a bank robber leaves a bank as the alarm sounds and sets off along a motorway at 80 km/h towards his hideout which is 150 km from the bank.

As soon as the alarm goes off a police car leaves the police station, which is 40 km from the bank, and drives at 80 km/h to the bank. After stopping at the bank for 15 minutes, the police car chases after the robber at a speed of 160 km/h.

Draw a travel graph with 'Distance from police station' on the vertical axis.
(a) Find out if the police caught the robber before the robber reached his hide out.
(b) If the robber was caught, say when. If he was not caught say how far behind him the police were when he reached his hideout.

8. The diagram shows three towns A, B and C. The distance from A to B is 50 km and the distance from B to C is 110 km.
At the same moment 3 cars leave A, B and C at the speeds shown and in the directions shown.

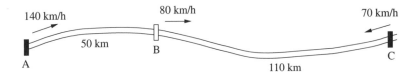

The cars from A and C are trying to intercept the car from B as quickly as possible.
(a) Which car intercepts the car from B first?
(b) After how many minutes does the car from A catch the car from B?

Line graphs

Information is sometimes given in the form of a *line graph*. Line graphs are particularly useful when quantities vary continuously over a period of time.

Exercise 3

1. The temperature in a centrally heated house is recorded every hour from 12.00 till 24.00; the results are shown below.

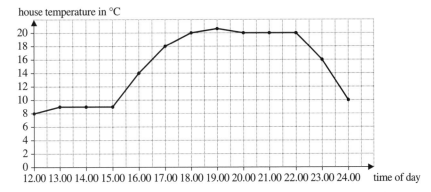

(a) What was the temperature at 20.00?

(b) Estimate the temperature at 16.30.

(c) Estimate the two times when the temperature was 18°C.

(d) When do you think the central heating was switched on?

(e) When do you think the central heating was switched off?

2. A man climbing a mountain measures his height above sea level after every 30 minutes; the results are shown below.

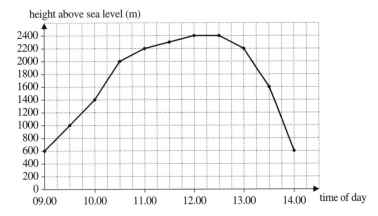

(a) At what height was he at 10.00?

(b) At what height was he at 13.30?

(c) Estimate his height above sea level at 09 45.

(d) At what two times was he 2200 m above sea level?

(e) How high was the mountain? (He got to the top!)

(f) How long did he rest at the summit?

(g) How long did he take to reach the summit?

3. The cost of making a telephone call depends on the duration of
the call as shown below.

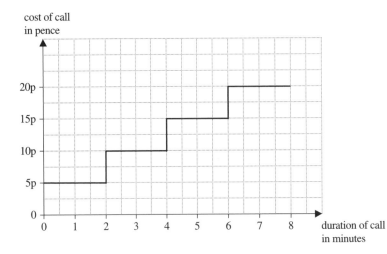

(a) How much is a call lasting 1 minute?
(b) How much is a call lasting 1 minute
     30 seconds?
(c) How much is a call lasting 6 minutes
     30 seconds?

(d) How much is a call lasting 4 minutes 27
(e) seconds?
     What is the minimum charge for a call?
(f) A call costing 15p is between ___ min-
     utes and ___ minutes in length. Fill in
     the spaces.

4. A car went on a five hour journey starting at 12.00 with a full
tank of petrol. The volume of petrol in the tank was measured
after every hour; the results are shown below.

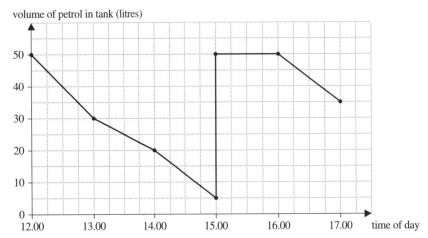

(a) How much petrol was in the tank at
     13.00?
(b) At what time was there 5 litres in the
     tank?
(c) How much petrol was used in the first
     hour of the journey?

(d) What happened at 15.00?
(e) What do you think happened between
     15.00 and 16.00?
(f) How much petrol was used between
     12.00 and 17.00?

5. This diagram shows the temperature and rainfall readings in one week.
The rainfall is shown as the bar chart. The temperature is shown as the line graph.

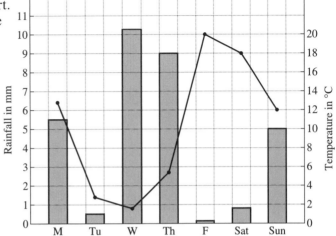

(a) Use *both* graphs to describe the weather on Wednesday.
(b) On which two days was the weather fairly wet and warm?
(c) Compare the weather on Tuesday and Saturday.

6. The graph shows the minimum distance between cars at different speeds in good or bad weather.

(a) Think carefully and decide which line is for good weather and which line is for bad weather.

(b) A car is travelling at 50 m.p.h in good weather. What is the minimum distance between cars?

(c) In bad weather John is driving 60 metres behind another car. What is the maximum speed at which John should drive?

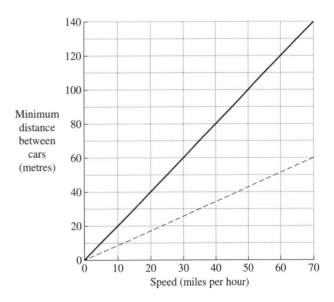

6.5 Mixed problems

Exercise 1

1. Mark is paid a basic weekly wage of £65 and then a further 30p for each item completed. How many items must be completed in a week when he earns a total of £171·50?

2. What number, when divided by 7 and then multiplied by 12, gives an answer of 144?

3. A 10p coin is 2 mm thick. Alex has a pile of 10p coins which is 16·6 cm tall. What is the value of the money in Alex's pile of coins?

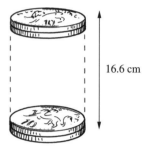

16.6 cm

2 mm

4. A British Airways Concorde leaves Paris at 07 00 and arrives in New York at 10 20.
   A 747 leaves Paris at 07 10 and flies at half the speed of the Concorde. When should it arrive in New York?

5. Percy's garden is 48 m long and 10 m wide and he wants to cover it with peat which comes in 60 kg sacks.
   10 kg of peat covers an area of 20 m². How many sacks of peat are needed for the whole garden?

6. Find two numbers which multiply together to give 60 and which add up to 19.

$\bigcirc \times \bigcirc = 60 \qquad \bigcirc + \bigcirc = 19$

7. A shopkeeper buys coffee beans at £4·20 per kg and sells them at 95p per 100 g. How much profit does he make per kg?

8. A Jaguar XJ6 uses 8 litres of petrol for every 50 km travelled. Petrol costs 90p per litre. Calculate the cost in £'s of travelling 600 km.

9. A school play was attended by 226 adults, each paying £1·50, and 188 children, each paying 80p. How much in £'s was paid altogether by the people attending the play?

10. The exchange rate in Germany is 2·85 Marks to the pound. In a German shop a television is priced at 598·50 Marks. What is the equivalent cost in £'s?

Exercise 2

1. A man smokes 50 cigarettes a day and a packet of 20 costs £4·20.
How much does he spend on cigarettes in six days?

2. As an incentive to tidy her bedroom, a girl is given 1p on the first day, 2p on the second day, 4p on the third day and so on, doubling the amount each day.

How much has she been given after 10 days?

3. A shopkeeper has a till containing a large number of the following coins:
   £1; 50p; 20p; 10p; 5p; 2p; 1p.
He needs to give a customer 57p in change. List all the different ways in which he can do this using no more than six coins.

4. Place the following numbers in order of size, smallest first:
   0·34; 0·334; 0·032; 0·04; 0·4.

5. A book has pages numbered 1 to 300 and the thickness of the book, without the covers, is 15 mm. How thick is each page?
[Hint: Most people get this question wrong!]

6. In an election 7144 votes were cast for the two candidates. Mr Dewey won by 424 votes. How many people voted for Dewey?

7. The tenth number in the sequence 1, 4, 16, 64 . . . . . . is 262 144.
What is (a) the ninth number,
       (b) the twelfth number?

8. Two fifths of the children in a swimming pool are boys. There are 72 girls in the pool. How many boys are there?

9. Two weights *m* and *n* are placed on scales and *m* is found to be more than 11 g and *n* is less than 7 g. Arrange the weights 8·5 g, *m* and *n* in order, lightest first.

10. A satellite link between Britain and Australia can be hired at a cost of £250 per minute from 06 00 to 14 00 and at £180 per minute after 14 00.
    The link is used to televise a football match which starts at 13 30 and ends at 15 22.
    How much does it cost?

Exercise 3

1. Lisa is 12 years old and her father is 37 years older than her. Lisa's mother is 3 years younger than her father. How old is Lisa's mother?

2. 36 small cubes are stuck together to make the block shown and the block is then painted on the outside. How many of the small cubes are painted on:
   (a) 1 face   (b) 2 faces
   (c) 3 faces   (d) 0 faces?

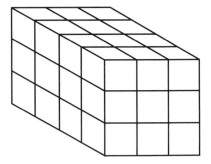

3. Find the letters in these additions.

   (a)   8 7 A   (b)   A 2 4 5
          3 B 5   5 B 8 4
       + C 4 2   + 1 4 C 6
       _____   _____
       D 8 4 1   E 0 5 2 D

4. Grass seed should be sown at the rate of $\frac{3}{4}$ of an ounce per square yard. One packet of seed contains 3 lb of seed. How many packets of seed are needed for a rectangular garden measuring 60 feet by 36 feet? [3 feet = 1 yard, 16 ounces = 1 lb]

5. Work out, without a calculator
   (a) 100 ÷ 10 000   (b) 0·1 × 0·4   (c) 0·94 + 5·6
   (d) 4·32 ÷ 0·3   (e) 246 × 32   (f) 4318 ÷ 17

6. Petrol costs 56·2p per litre. How many litres can be bought for £17? Give your answer to the nearest litre.

7. A flight on Concorde takes 2 h 36 min. How long would the same flight take on a plane travelling at half the speed of Concorde?

8. Seven oak trees were planted in Windsor when Queen Victoria was born. She died in 1901 aged 82. How old were the trees in 1993?

9. A mixed school has a total of 876 pupils.
There are 48 more boys than girls.
How many boys are there?

10. Four 4's can be used to make 12: $\dfrac{44 + 4}{4}$

(a) Use three 6's to make 2
(b) Use three 7's to make 7
(c) Use three 9's to make 11
(d) Use four 4's to make 9
(e) Use four 4's to make 3

11. A Rover 216XL travels 7·4 miles on a litre of petrol and petrol costs 53p per litre. In six months the car is driven a total of 4750 miles. Find the cost of the petrol to the nearest pound.

12. In a code the 25 letters from A to Y are obtained from the square using a 2 digit grid reference similar to coordinates.
So letter 'U' is 42 and 'L' is 54.
The missing letter 'Z' has code 10.

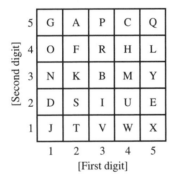

Decode the following messages:

(a) 41, 52
13, 52, 52, 12
43, 14, 34, 52
22, 42, 43, 22

(b) 44, 25, 31, 52
25
13, 32, 45, 52
12, 25, 53

(c) 22, 35, 42, 34, 22
25, 34, 52
34, 42, 33, 33, 32, 22, 44

In part (d) each pair of brackets gives one letter

(d) $\left(\frac{1}{4} \text{ of } 140\right)$, $(7^2 + 5)$, $(7 \times 8 - 4)$, $(4^2 + 3^2)$, $\left(\frac{1}{5} \text{ of } 110\right)$, $\left(26 \div \frac{1}{2}\right)$
$(3 \times 7 + 1)$, $(83 - 31)$, $(2 \times 2 \times 2 \times 2 + 5)$
$(100 - 57)$, $(4^2 - 2)$, (17×2), $(151 - 99)$
$(2 \times 2 \times 2 \times 5 + 1)$, $\left(\frac{1}{4} \text{ of } 56\right)$, $(2 \times 3 \times 2 \times 3 - 2)$, $(5^2 - 2)$.

(e) Write your own message in code and ask a friend to decode it.

Exercise 4

1. Unifix cubes can be joined together to make different sized cuboids.

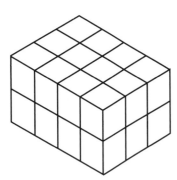 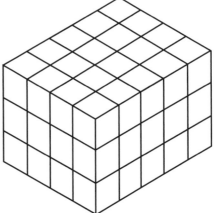

   If the smaller cuboid weighs 96 g, how much does the large cuboid weigh?

2. A lorry is travelling at a steady speed of 56 m.p.h. How far does the lorry travel between 10.50 a.m. and 11.05 a.m.?

3. A map has a scale of 1 to 100 000. Calculate the actual length of a lake which is 8 cm long on the map.

4. In a 'magic' square the sum of the numbers in any row, column or main diagonal is the same. Find x in each square

   (a)

3		
8		4
7	x	

   (b)

14		7	2
x		12	
	5	9	16
15			3

5. This table shows the approximate weights of coins

1p	2p	5p	10p	20p
3·6 g	7·2 g	3·2 g	6·5 g	5·0 g

   (a) What is the lightest weight with a value of 12p made from these coins?

   (b) A group of mixed coins weighs 228 g, of which 48 g is the silver coins.
   What is the value of the bronze coins?

6. The test results of 50 students are shown below.

Mark	5	6	7	8	9	10
Frequency	0	2	12	17	10	9

   What percentage of the students scored 8 marks or more?

7. On the 30th June 1994 the day was extended by 1 second to allow for the irregularity in the speed of rotation of the Earth. A newspaper carried an article stating that people in Britain eat 54 digestive biscuits every second. How many digestive biscuits are eaten in a normal day?

8. Which of the shapes below can be drawn without taking the pen from the paper and without going over any line twice?

(a)   (b)   (c)

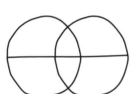
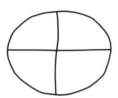
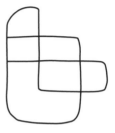

9. A corn field is a rectangle measuring 300 m by 600 m. One hectare is 10 000 m^2 and each hectare produces 3·2 tonnes of corn. How much corn is produced in this field?

10. Four and a half dozen eggs weigh 2970 g. How much would six dozen eggs weigh?

11. The numbers 1 to 12 are arranged on the star so that the sum of the numbers along each line is the same.

Copy and complete the star.

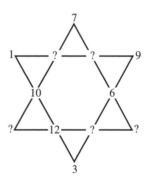

12. A jar with 8 chocolates in it weighs 160 g. The same jar with 20 chocolates in it weighs 304 g. How much does the jar weigh on its own?

Exercise 5

1. A floor measuring 5 m by 3·6 m is to be covered with square tiles of side 10 cm. A packet of 20 tiles costs £6·95. How much will it cost to tile the floor?

2. A small boat travels 350 km on 125 litres of fuel. How much fuel is needed for a journey of 630 km?

3. Work out   (a) $1^1 + 2^2 + 3^3 + 4^4$
                     (b) $\frac{1}{3} \times \frac{2}{4} \times \frac{3}{5} \times \ldots \ldots \times \frac{9}{11} \times \frac{10}{12}$.

4. A shop keeper bought 30 books at £3·40 each and a number of C.D.'s costing £8·40 each. In all he spent £312. How many C.D.'s did he buy?

5. It costs 18p per minute to hire a tool. How much will it cost to hire the tool from 0850 to 1115?

6. In a restaurant six glasses of wine cost £7·50. How many glasses of wine could be bought for £22?

7. When a car journey starts, the mileometer reads 23 715 miles. After half an hour the mileometer reads 23 747 miles. What is the average speed of the car?

8. A rectangular box, without a lid, is to be made from cardboard. The cardboard costs 2 pence per cm^2.
Find the cost of the cardboard for the box.

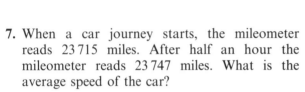

9. The numbers '7' and '3' multiply to give 21 and add up to 10.
Find two numbers which:
(a) multiply to give 48 and add up to 19.
(b) multiply to give 180 and add up to 27.

10. The words for the numbers from one to ten are written in a list in alphabetical order. What number will be third in the list?

11. The diagram shows a corner torn from a sheet of graph paper measuring 18 cm by 28 cm.
Calculate the total length of all the lines drawn on the whole sheet of graph paper.

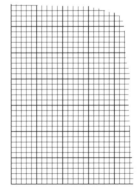

12. Sima has the same number of 10p and 50p coins. The total value is £9. How many of each coin does she have?

Exercise 6

1. How many 26p stamps can be bought for £10 and how much change will there be?

2. If £1 is equivalent to $1·42,
   (a) how many dollars are equivalent to £600,
   (b) how much British money is equivalent to $400?

3. A lorry starts a journey at 06 10 and goes 50 km at an average speed of 20 km/h. At what time will it finish?

4. A suitcase is packed with 24 books and 85 magazines. The total weight of the suitcase and its contents is 8·85 kg. The empty suitcase weighs 880 g and each book weighs 70 g. Find the weight of each magazine.

5. Cake mix is sold in two shops in different sized boxes. Which is the better value for money:
   a 1·2 kg box for £1·02   or a 2 kg box for £1·78?

6. I think of a number. If I add 5 and then multiply the result by 10 the answer is 82. What number was I thinking of?

7. A boat sails 2·4 km in 30 minutes. How long will it take to sail one km?

8. Show how the 3 by 8 rectangle can be cut into two identical pieces and joined together to make a 2 by 12 rectangle.

9. What is the smaller angle between the hands of a clock at
   (a) Half past two
   (b) (harder) Twenty past six.

10. The 31st of March 1993 is written 31–3–93. This a special date because $31 \times 3 = 93$.
    (a) How many such dates are there in 1995?
    (b) How many such dates are there in 1996?
    Give the actual dates in each case.

6.6 Mathematical games

Biggest number: a game for the whole class

(a) Draw a rectangle like this with 4 boxes

(b) Your teacher will throw a dice and call out the number which is showing. (eg 'four')

(c) Write this number in one of the boxes.

| | 4 | | |

(d) Your teacher will throw the dice again. (eg 'two')
Write the number in another box.

| | 4 | | 2 |

(e) Your teacher will throw the dice two more times (eg 'three' and then 'two') and again you write the numbers in the boxes.

| 2 | 4 | 3 | 2 |

(f) The object of the game is to get the biggest possible four figure number. The skill (or luck!) is in deciding which box to use for each number.
You score one point if you have written down the largest four digit number which can be made from the digits thrown on the dice. In the example above you score a point if you have 4322 and no points for any other number.
The game can also be played with 5 boxes or 6 boxes for variety.

Boxes: a game for two players

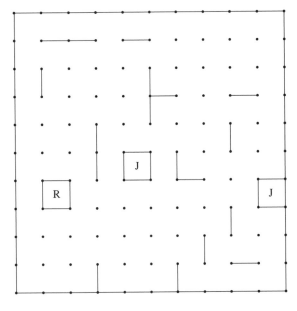

- Draw around the border of a 10×10 square on dotty paper (you can also use squared paper).
- Two players take turns to draw horizontal or vertical lines between any two dots on the grid.
- A player wins a square (and writes his initial inside the square) when he draws the fourth side of a square.
- After winning a square a player has one extra turn.
- The winner is the player who has most squares at the end.

In the game above J has
two squares so far and
R has one square.

Find the hidden treasure

This is a game for two players: one player hides the treasure and the other player tries to find it.

(a) Player A draws a grid with x and y from -6 to 6. He puts the treasure at any point with whole number coordinates. Say $(4, -2)$.

(b) Player B draws his own grid and makes his first guess. Say $(1, 1)$.

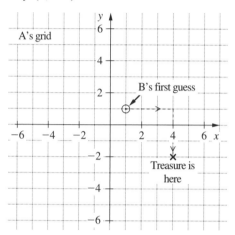

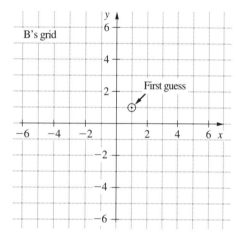

(c) Player A tells player B how far away he is by adding the *horizontal* and *vertical* distances from his guess to the treasure. So the point $(1, 1)$ is a distance 6 away.

(d) Player B has another guess and player A gives the distance from the new point to the treasure.

(e) Play continues until player B finds the treasure.

(f) Roles are then reversed so that B hides a new treasure and A tries to find it in as few goes as possible.

- After several games you may realise that you can improve your chances by using a 'mathematical strategy'.

'Lines': a game for two players

- Mark several points on a piece of paper (say 13 points).
- Players take turns to join two of the points with a straight line.
- It is not allowed to draw a line which crosses another line or to draw two lines from one point.
- The winner is the last player to draw a line.

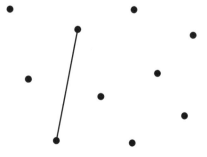

Curves from straight lines

- On a sheet of unlined paper draw a circle of radius 8·5 cm and mark 36 equally spaced points on the circle. Use a protractor inside the circle and move around 10° for each point.
- Mark an extra 36 points in between the original 36 so that finally you have 72 points equally spaced around the circle.
- Number the points 0, 1, 2, 3, ...72 and after one circuit continue from 73 to 144.

- You can obtain three different patterns as follows:

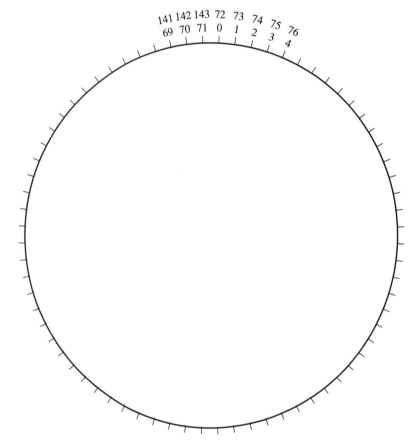

A (i),   Join 0 → 10, 1 → 11, 2 → 12 etc
   (ii),   Join 0 → 20, 1 → 21, 2 → 22 etc
   (iii), Join 0 → 30, 1 → 31, 2 → 32 etc.

B Join each number to double that number.
   ie. 1 → 2, 2 → 4, 3 → 6, ...

C Join each number to treble that number.
   ie. 1 → 3, 2 → 6, 3 → 9, ...
   For **C** you need to continue numbering points around the circle from 145 to 216.

Part 7

7.1 Multiple choice papers

Test 1

1. Solve the equation
$4x - 1 = 0$

A 4
B −4
C $\frac{1}{4}$
D $-\frac{1}{4}$

2. A pile of 250 cards is
1 m deep. How thick is
each card?

A 0·4 cm
B 0·4 m
C 2·5 cm
D 0·25 cm

3. Without using a
calculator, work out
2·5% of £220

A £8·80
B £88
C £5·50
D £55

4. Find the size of angle a

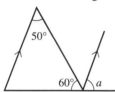

A 40°
B 50°
C 60°
D 70°

5. A train travels 20 km in
8 minutes. How long
will it take to travel
25 km at the same
speed?

A 6·4 min
B 9 min
C 10 min
D 12·4 min

6. The line $y = 3$ cuts the
line $y = -2$ at the point
with coordinates:

A (3, −2)
B (−2, 3)
C (0, 3)
D None of
the above

7. Find the value of x
$3 \times 5\frac{1}{2} - 4 = x - \frac{1}{2}$

A 5
B 6
C 13
D 14

8. Find the area
of triangle ABC.
All lengths are
in cm.

A 96 cm²
B 60 cm²
C 48 cm²
D None of
the above

9. $\frac{3}{5}$ of 14 =

A $\frac{3}{70}$
B 8·2
C 8·4
D 84

10. £1600 decreased by 4%
is

A £1596
B £64
C £1200
D £1536

11. In the triangle the size
of the largest angle is

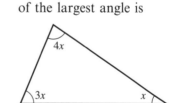

A 70°
B 80°
C 90°
D 100°

12. What is the value of
$1 - 0·15$ as a fraction?

A $\frac{3}{20}$
B $\frac{17}{20}$
C $\frac{15}{100}$
D Impossible
to find

13. A car travels for 20
minutes at a speed of
66 km/h. How far does
the car travel?

A 13·2 km
B 1320 km
C 33 km
D 22 km

14. Which of the statements is(are) true?

1. $a = b$
2. $c = a$
3. $c = d$

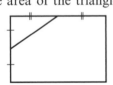

    A 1 only
    B 1 and 2
    C 1 and 3
    D 1, 2 and 3

15. Which point does *not* lie on the line $y = x$?
    A $\left(\frac{1}{2}, \frac{1}{2}\right)$
    B $(0, 0)$
    C $(-3, -3)$
    D $(-2, 2)$

16. A metal ingot weighing 64 kg is made into 20 000 buttons. What is the weight of one button?
    A 3·2 kg
    B 3·2 g
    C 312·5 g
    D 312·5 kg

17. The number of letters in the word ROUTE that have line symmetry is
    A 1
    B 2
    C 3
    D 4

18. What fraction of the area of the rectangle is the area of the triangle?
    A $\frac{1}{4}$
    B $\frac{1}{8}$
    C $\frac{1}{16}$
    D $\frac{1}{32}$

19. How many prime numbers are there between 10 and 20?
    A 2
    B 3
    C 9
    D None of the above

20. The probability of selecting an Ace at random from a pack of 52 cards is
    A $\frac{1}{52}$
    B $\frac{1}{13}$
    C $\frac{1}{4}$
    D $\frac{3}{52}$

21. What is the area, in m^2, of a square with sides of length 0·03 m?
    A 0·0009
    B 0·009
    C 0·06
    D 0·09

22. The number midway between 3·1 and 3·11 is
    A 3·105
    B 3·111
    C 3·15
    D 3·5

23. A quarter share of a fifth share of 10% of £8000 is
    A £40
    B £80
    C £400
    D £36

24. The number of seconds in a day is *about*
    A 9000
    B 90 000
    C 30 000
    D 300 000

25. A quarter of $(8·8 \div 0·01)$ is
Do not use a calculator.
    A 2·2
    B 22
    C 220
    D 88

Test 2

1. A floor measures 6 m by $4\frac{1}{2}$ m and is covered by square carpet tiles measuring 50 cm by 50 cm. How many carpet tiles are needed?
    A 54
    B 108
    C 120
    D 216

2. Work out $\frac{3}{4} + 0·15$
    A $\frac{18}{104}$
    B $\frac{45}{400}$
    C $\frac{9}{10}$
    D 0·09

3. Solve the equation $8 = 9 - 2x$
    A $\frac{1}{2}$
    B $-\frac{1}{2}$
    C $8\frac{1}{2}$
    D 1

4. Which of the following statements are true?
1. 1% of $10 = 0·1$
2. $12 \div 5 = 2·4$
3. $7 \div 8 = 0·875$
    A 1 and 2
    B 1 and 3
    C 2 and 3
    D 1, 2 and 3

5. At what point will the line $y = x$ cut the line $x = -3$?
    A $(-3, -3)$
    B $(3, 3)$
    C $(-3, 0)$
    D Impossible to say

6. A picture measuring 30 cm by 20 cm is surrounded by a border 5 cm wide. What is the area of the border?

    A 200 cm^2
    B 225 cm^2
    C 400 cm^2
    D 600 cm^2

7. Find the area of triangle OAB in square units

    A 7
    B 8
    C 9
    D 10

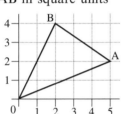

8. A man's heart beats at 70 beats/min. How many times will his heart beat between 0330 and 2330 on the same day?

    A 6000
    B 8400
    C 72 000
    D 84 000

9. Which is the best estimate when 20 yards is converted into metres.

    A 19 m
    B 21 m
    C 210 m
    D 1·9 m

10. The pie chart shows the nationalities of people on a ferry. What angle should be drawn for the UK sector?

    A 10·28°
    B 35°
    C 126°
    D 132°

11. In how many ways can you join the square X to shape Y along an edge so that the final shape has line symmetry?

    A 1
    B 2
    C 3
    D 4

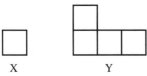

Use the graph below for questions **12** to **15**.

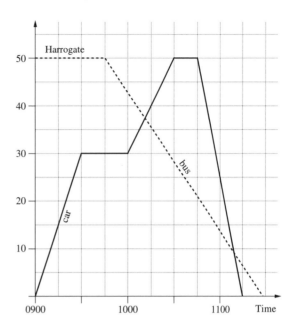

12. When does the car arrive in Harrogate?

    A 0900
    B 0930
    C 1030
    D 1115

13. When does the bus leave Harrogate?

    A 0900
    B 0945
    C 1000
    D 1126

14. At what speed does the car travel on the return journey to York?

    A 30 km/h
    B 40 km/h
    C 50 km/h
    D 100 km/h

15. How far apart are the car and the bus at 1015?

    A 2·5 km
    B 5 km
    C 10 km
    D 22·5 km

16. A roll of wallpaper is 10 m long and 50 cm wide. How many rolls of wallpaper are needed to cover a wall 2·5 m high and 8 m long?

    A 2
    B 3
    C 4
    D 5

17. What fraction of the area of triangle ABC is the area of triangle ADE?

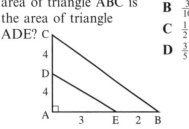

A $\frac{1}{4}$

B $\frac{3}{10}$

C $\frac{1}{2}$

D $\frac{3}{5}$

18. The value of $1^1 \times 2^2 \times 3^3$ is

A 30
B 36
C 72
D 108

19. What is the next number in the sequence 6, 13, 27, 55?

A 76
B 84
C 111
D None of the above

20. Which of the following statements are true?
1. 200 mm = 2 m
2. $\frac{4}{5}$ is greater than $\frac{3}{4}$
3. All rectangles have four lines of symmetry.

A 1 only
B 2 only
C 3 only
D 2 and 3

21. Draw triangle ABC in which AB = AC. If $A\hat{C}B = 53°$, calculate the size of $A\hat{B}C$.

A 53°
B 64°
C 74°
D 127°

22. Four 1's are written in the square so that no two 1's are on the same row, column or diagonal. Where must the '1' go in the third column?

		D	
		C	
1		B	
		A	

23. How many wine glasses of capacity 30 ml can be filled from a barrel containing 240 litres?

A 3
B 125
C 800
D 8000

24. A car travels half a mile in a minute. What is its speed?

A $\frac{1}{2}$ mph
B 30 mph
C 60 mph
D 120 mph

25. Without a calculator, work out
3.72×0.23

A 0·0856
B 0·7956
C 0·8556
D 8·556

Test 3

1. *Car Hire*

> £13 per day plus
> 14p per km

Mr. Hasam hired a car for 6 days and travelled 550 km. How much did it cost?

A £177
B £155
C £77·13
D £771·30

2. Find n if
$72 \div n = 9$

A $n = 4$
B $n = 36$
C $n = 8$
D $n = 9$

3. Anna has £4·80. She spends $\frac{1}{3}$ on presents, $\frac{1}{4}$ on a magazine and $\frac{1}{5}$ on sweets. How much is left?

A 84p
B 94p
C £1·04
D £1·14

4. 1 kg = 2·2 pounds. Which is closest to 7 pounds?

A 3 kg
B 4 kg
C 14 kg
D 15 kg

5. Which is the odd one out?

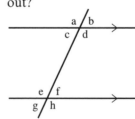

A b
B d
C f
D g

6. Paul's car averages 35 miles to 1 gallon of petrol. Petrol costs £2·40 a gallon. If Paul drives 28 770 miles in one year, how much does his petrol cost?

A £342·50
B £4195·62
C £822
D £1972·80

7. How many $\frac{1}{8}$'s are there in $\frac{3}{4}$?

   A 2
   B 5
   C 6
   D 7

8. I left the cinema at 22 25. The film lasted 2 hours and 35 minutes. At what time did it begin?

   A 19.50
   B 20.10
   C 19.10
   D 19.35

9. Which list is arranged in ascending order?
   A 0·14, 0·05, 0·062, 0·09
   B 0·14, 0·09, 0·062, 0·05
   C 0·050, 0·062, 0·09, 0·14
   D 0·050, 0·090, 0·14, 0·062

10. A greengrocer sells 9 kg of potatoes for £2·52. How many kg can be bought for £1·47?

   A 4·11
   B 5
   C $4\frac{1}{2}$
   D $5\frac{1}{4}$

11. How many lines of symmetry does the rectangle below have?

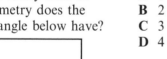

   A 1
   B 2
   C 3
   D 4

12. A window frame in a church measures 24·3 cm by 35·7 cm. 80% of the window is filled with stained glass. What is the area of stained glass in the window?

   A 868 cm^2
   B 174 cm^2
   C 1080 cm^2
   D 694 cm^2

13. One litre of water weighs 1 kg. One litre of ice weighs 870 g. What is the difference in weight between 5 litres of water and 4 litres of ice?

   A 220 g
   B 780 g
   C 1100 g
   D 320 g

14. There were 4 candidates in a class election. Mary got $\frac{1}{3}$ of the votes, George got $\frac{1}{4}$, Henry got $\frac{1}{6}$. What fraction did Sheena, the 4th candidate get?

   A $\frac{1}{5}$
   B $\frac{1}{4}$
   C $\frac{1}{3}$
   D $\frac{1}{2}$

15. What fraction of the shape below is shaded?

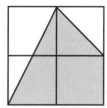

   A $\frac{3}{8}$
   B $\frac{1}{2}$
   C $\frac{5}{8}$
   D $\frac{3}{4}$

16. Which pair of angles is equal?

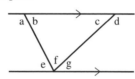

   A a and g
   B b and d
   C c and f
   D b and e

17. A box has a mass of 230 g when empty. When it is full of sugar the total mass is 650 g. What is its mass when it is half full?

   A 210 g
   B 860 g
   C 440 g
   D 420 g

18. Work out on a calculator, correct to 1 d.p.
$$\frac{1\cdot4}{1\cdot7}+\frac{1\cdot9}{2\cdot1}$$

   A 0·8
   B 0·9
   C 1·7
   D 1·8

19. One kilogram is increased by 200 g. The percentage increase is:

   A 20%
   B 0·2%
   C 2%
   D 120%

20. 999 mm is equal to

   A 99 m
   B 9·9 m
   C 0·99 m
   D 0·999 m

7.2 Mixed exercises

Revision exercise 1

In the diagram three vertices of a rectangle are given.
Find the coordinates of the fourth vertex and write down the equations of any lines of symmetry.

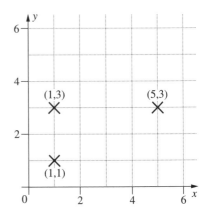

Put the answers in a table:

Shape	Vertices given	Other vertex	Lines of symmetry
Rectangle	(1, 1), (1, 3), (5, 3)	(5, 1)	$x = 3, y = 2$

Draw axes with values of x and y from -10 to $+10$.

Draw the shapes given and hence copy and complete the table.

	Shape	Vertices given	Other vertex	Lines of symmetry
1.	Rectangle	(1, 6), (1, 10), (3, 6)	?	? , ?
2.	Rectangle	(4, 3), (4, −1), (10, 3)	?	? , ?
3.	Rectangle	(5, −2), (10, −2), (5, −3)	?	? , ?
4.	Isosceles triangle	(5, −10), (10, −8)	?	$y = -8$ only
5.	Isosceles triangle	(2, −4), (0, −8)	?	$x = 2$ only
6.	Rhombus	(−6, 4), (−8, 7), (−6, 10)	?	? , ?
7.	Square	(3, 3), (3, −3), (−3, −3)	?	Give four lines.
8.	Trapezium	(−8, −2), (−7, 1), (−5, 1)	?	$x = -6$ only
9.	Parallelogram	(−8, −5), (−4, −5), (−5, −8)	Give three possibilities	none
10.	Parallelogram	(−3, 4), (−2, 6), (−1, 6)	Give three possibilities	none
11.	Square	(6, 6), (6, 9)	Give two points	$y = x$ is one line Find three more.

Revision exercise 2

1. A cake recipe calls for 500 g of flour to mix with 200 g of sugar. How much sugar should be used if you have only 300 g of flour?

2. Find the total cost:
    5 bags of cement at £3·95 per bag
    13 m of wire at 40p per m.
    8 sockets at 65p each.
    Add V.A.T. at $17\frac{1}{2}\%$.

3. In a History test Joe got 27 out of 40.
What was his mark as a percentage?

4. Work out to the nearest penny
    (a) 6% of £85·15   (b) 11·5% of £33·40

5. Here is a list of numbers
        5, 8, 9, 11, 12, 13, 17, 18, 20.
    Write down the numbers which are
    (a) factors of 40
    (b) multiples of 4
    (c) prime numbers.

6. Use a calculator to work out the following. Give your answers correct to 1 decimal place.
    (a) $18\cdot3 - (1\cdot91 \times 2\cdot62)$ (b) $\dfrac{5\cdot23}{9\cdot2 - 7\cdot63}$

    (c) $\dfrac{8\cdot91}{1\cdot6} + \dfrac{1\cdot54}{0\cdot97}$ (d) $\left(\dfrac{1\cdot4 + 0\cdot761}{1\cdot76}\right)^2$

7. Write down the next term in each sequence.
    (a) 75, 69, 63, 57
    (b) 1, 4, 10, 22
    (c) 8, 9, 11, 14

8. Calculate the shaded area

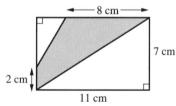

9. Solve the equations
    (a) $3x - 1 = 17$ (b) $3x - 8 = 13$
    (c) $22 = 5x + 7$.

10. Draw an accurate copy of each triangle and find the length x and the angle y.
    (a)

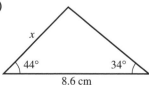

(b)

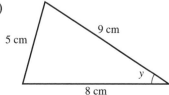

11. What fraction of each shape is shaded?

(a)   (b) 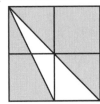   (c)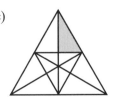

Revision exercise 3

1. (a) Draw a pair of axes with values from
     −5 to 5.
   (b) Draw and label the following lines
     line A: $x = 4$
     line B: $y = -2$
     line C: $y = x$
   (c) Write down the coordinates of the point
     where
     (i)   line A meets line B
     (ii) line A meets line C
     (iii) line B meets line C
     (iv) line B cuts the y axis.

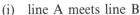

2. Work out the following, *without* using a calculator, giving your
   answer as a decimal.
   (a) $\frac{3}{5}$ of 17   (b) 22% of 30   (c) $\frac{17}{25}$ of 40

3. (a) The diagram shows a trapezium.
     Calculate the area of triangle ABD and
     the area of triangle DCB. Hence write
     down the area of the trapezium ABCD.

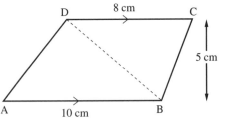

   (b) Calculate the area of each trapezium below.
     (i)   (ii)

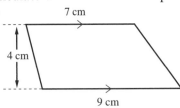

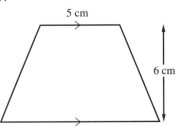

4. Copy and fill in the missing numbers
   (a) $2\cdot3\,\text{m} = \quad$ cm   (b) $45\,\text{g} = \quad$ kg   (c) 2 feet $= \quad$ inches
   (d) $260\,\text{m} = \quad$ km   (e) 3 litres $= \quad$ ml   (f) 1 pound $= \quad$ ounces
   (g) $25\,\text{mm} = \quad$ cm   (h) 1 yard $= \quad$ feet   (i) $2\cdot6\,\text{kg} = \quad$ g

5. A bag contains 6 coloured balls. One ball is selected at random and then replaced in the bag. This procedure is repeated until 50 selections have been made. Here are the results:

[B = Blue, G = Green, Y = Yellow]

```
B Y  B  Y  B  Y  B  Y  B  G  B  Y  B
 G  B  B  B  B  Y  G  B  Y  B  G  B  Y
 Y  B  Y  Y  B  B  B  G  B  B  Y  B
 B  Y  B  Y  G  B  Y  B  Y  B  G  B
```

What do you think were the colours of the balls in the bag? Justify your answer.

6. If 5 melons can be bought for £7, how many can be bought for £12·60?

7. If 7 bags of flour cost £6·44, find the cost of 3 bags.

8. Find the angles marked with letters

(a) 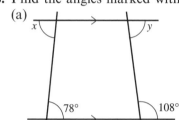 (b) 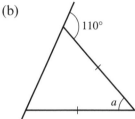 (c)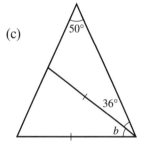

9. An opinion poll was conducted to find out which party people intended to vote for at the next election. The results were.

Conservative   768
Labour   840
Lib Dem   612
Don't know   180

Work out the angles on a pie chart and draw the chart to display the results of the poll.

10. A worker takes 8 minutes to make 12 items. How long would it take to make 15 items?

11. Draw a pair of axes with values from 0 to 8.
Plot two corners of a square at (2, 4) and (6, 4).
Find the coordinates of the six possible positions for the other corners of the square.

12. The diagram shows a rectangle.
The perimeter of the rectangle is 28 cm.
Work out x.

Revision exercise 4

1. Work out the total cost, including V.A.T.

   13 kg of sand at 57p per kg.
   2 tape measures at £4·20 each
   2000 screws at 80p per hundred
   250 g of varnish at £6·60 per kg

   V.A.T. at $17\frac{1}{2}\%$ is added to the total.

2. Use a calculator to work out the following and give your answers correct to 1 decimal place.

   (a) $8 \cdot 62 - \dfrac{1 \cdot 71}{0 \cdot 55}$ (b) $\dfrac{8 \cdot 02 - 6 \cdot 3}{1 \cdot 3^2 + 4 \cdot 6}$ (c) $\dfrac{5 \cdot 6}{1 \cdot 71} - \dfrac{9 \cdot 7}{11 \cdot 3}$

3. A normal pack of 52 playing cards (without jokers) is divided into two piles

   Pile A has all the picture cards (Kings, Queens, Jacks) 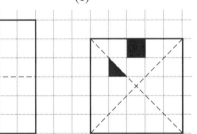 Pile B has the rest of the pack.

   Find the probability of selecting
   (a) any 'three' from pile B
   (b) the King of hearts from pile A
   (c) any red seven from pile B.

4. In each of the following diagrams, lines of symmetry are shown by broken lines. Copy and complete each diagram.

   (a)   (b)   (c)

5. Draw the two patterns on the right and shade in more squares so that the final patterns have rotational symmetry of order 2.

6. Write down five consecutive numbers whose mean value is 42.

7. There were ten children on a coach journey. The mean age of the children was 11 and the range of their ages was 4. Write each statement below and then write next to it whether it is *True, Possible* or *False*.
   (a) The youngest child was 9 years old.
   (b) Every child was 11 years old.
   (c) All the children were at least 10 years old

8. In number walls each brick is made by adding the two bricks underneath it.

   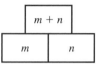

   Fill in the missing expressions on these walls

   (a)
   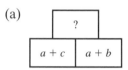
   (b)
   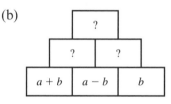
   (c)
   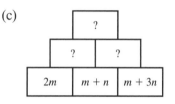

9. These nets form cubical dice. Opposite faces of a dice always add up to 7. Write down the value of a, b, c, d, e, and f so that opposite faces add up to 7.

   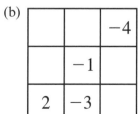

10. Work out the areas of A, B, C,..., I in the shapes below. The dots are 1 cm apart.

    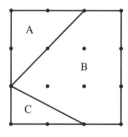
    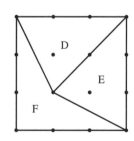
    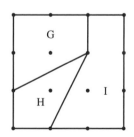

11. Copy and complete the magic squares

    (a)

3		
−4	1	6

    (b)

		−4
	−1	
2	−3	

Review exercise 5

1. Sketch a cuboid with dimensions 3 cm by 4 cm by 5 cm.
   Calculate the total surface area of the cuboid.

2. The same operations are in each chain of number machines

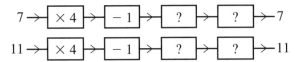

   Find the missing operations.

3. (a) Suppose the '5' button on your calculator does not work.
       Show how you can make your calculator show the number
       345.
   (b) Suppose none of the numbers 1, 3, 5, 7, 9 work. Show how
       you can make your calculator show the number 115.

4. (a) Copy the diagram.
   (b) Rotate triangle 1 90° clockwise around
       the point (0, 0). Label the image △2.
   (c) Rotate triangle 1 90° anti-clockwise around
       the point (4, 3). Label the image △3.

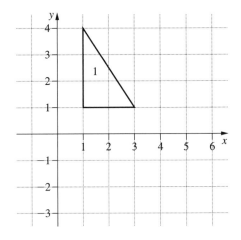

5. Which fraction is closer to one: $\frac{7}{8}$ or $\frac{8}{7}$?
   Show your working.

6. The price of a dress costing £45 was decreased by 10%.
   Six months later the price was increased by 10%.
   Calculate the final price of the dress.

7. Three friends share a prize of £5000 in the ratio 2:3:5.
   How much was the smallest share?

8. Draw a net for a cuboid 2 cm × 3 cm × 4 cm.

9. Copy and complete by filling in the boxes. You can use any of the numbers 1, 2, 3, 4, 5 but you cannot use a number more than once.

(a) ☐ + ☐ − ☐ = 7

(b) (☐ + ☐) ÷ ☐ = 3

(c) (☐ + ☐) ÷ (☐ − ☐) = 1½

(d) (☐ + ☐ + ☐) × ☐ = 33

10. Look at the diagram.
(a) Write down the ratio shaded length : unshaded length.

(b) As a percentage, what proportion of the diagram is shaded?

11. The star shape is made from four triangles like the one shown.
(a) Calculate the area of the star shape.
(b) Calculate the perimeter of the star shape.

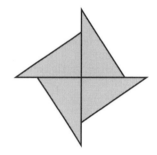

12. On a coordinate grid, plot the points A(1, 4) B(2, 1) C(5, 2)
What are the coordinates of D if ABCD is a square?

13. Two books cost £13·50 in total. One book is one-and-a-half times the price of the other. How much does each book cost?

14. In the box is a formula for working out heights.
Lindsey's mother is 162 cm tall and her father is 180 cm tall. What is the greatest height to which Lindsey is likely to grow?

> Add the height of each parent.
> Divide by 2
> Add 6 cm to the result.
>
> A girl is likely to be this height plus or minus 7 cm.

15. A map has a scale of 1 cm to 5 km.
A lake appears 3·2 cm long on the map. How long is the actual lake in km?

16. There are eight balls in a bag. The probability of taking a white ball from the bag is 0·5.
A white ball is taken from the bag and put on one side.
What is the probability of taking a white ball from the bag now?

INDEX

Algebra	58
Angles	128
Area	36
Averages	185
Balance puzzles	64
Bar charts	111
Calculator	96
Checking results	35
Codes	198
Compass directions	172
Constructing triangles	142
Coordinates	51
Counter examples	197
Cross number puzzles	78, 195
Cube numbers	86
Curves from straight lines	240
Decimals	27, 146, 208
Decimal places	33
Division	147
Equations	152
Equivalent fractions	46
Estimating	35
Expressions	60
Factors	83
Fractions	46, 208
Formulas	212
Frequency diagram	114
Games	238
Graphs	158, 221
Handling data	107
Happy numbers	91
H.C.F.	85
Hidden words	150
Imperial units	101
Improper fractions	47
Inverse operations	8, 19
Investigations	18, 43, 63, 145, 218
Isosceles triangle	130
L.C.M.	85
Line symmetry	175
Logo	170
Long multiplication, division	182
Mathematical reasoning	196

Mental arithmetic	72
Metric units	101
Mixed problems	16, 163, 230
Multiples	84
Multiple choice papers	241
n^{th} term	215
Negative numbers	189
Nets	25
Number machines	6
Operator squares	126
Ordinary decimals	28
Order of operations	62, 92
Parallel lines	132
Percentages	67, 208
Perimeter	41
Pie charts	107
Place value	12, 27
Prime numbers	83, 88
Prisms	21
Probability	199
Proportion	135
Protractor	139
Puzzles	80
Quadrilaterals	133
Range	185
Ratio	137
Reflection	175
Remainders	14
Rotation	168
Rounding	32
Satisfied numbers	90
Scale reading	30
Sequences	1, 215
Square numbers	86
Statistics problems	118
Symmetry	174, 175
Terms	61
Three dimensional object	21
Time	96
Translation	181
Travel graphs	221
Triangles	37, 130
Visualising shapes	23